State and Trade

BRITAIN
AND
THE NETHERLANDS

Volume X

*PAPERS DELIVERED TO THE
TENTH ANGLO-DUTCH HISTORICAL CONFERENCE,
NIJMEGEN, 1988*

STATE AND TRADE

GOVERNMENT AND THE ECONOMY
IN BRITAIN AND THE NETHERLANDS
SINCE THE MIDDLE AGES

EDITED BY
SIMON GROENVELD AND MICHAEL WINTLE

WALBURG PERS / ZUTPHEN

CIP-GEGEVENS KONINKLIJKE BIBLIOTHEEK, DEN HAAG

State

State and Trade: government and the economy in Britain and the Nederlands since the
Middle Ages / ed. by Simon Groenveld and Michael Wintle. — Zutphen: Walburg Pers.
— Ill. — (Britain and the Nederlands; vol. 10)
Papers delivered to the tenth Anglo-Dutch historical conference. — Met index.
ISBN 90-6011-794.8
NUGI 641
Trefw.: economie ; Nederland ; geschiedenis / economie ; Groot-Brittannië ; geschiedenis.

Cover illustration:
Artus Quellinus, The God of trade, Mercury, carrying a money-bag and
accompanied by the emblematic cock and goat, portrayed as sentinel at the
entrance to the Amsterdam Exchange Bank. In the Burgers' Hall in the former
Town Hall in Amsterdam, now Royal Palace (Photo: Royal Palace, Amsterdam)

Published with the support of grants from:
Directie der Oostersche Handel en Reederijen, Amsterdam
J.E. Jurriaanse Stichting, Rotterdam
Stichting Unger-van Brero Fonds, Wageningen

Contents

Acknowledgements

The Tenth Anglo-Dutch Historical Conference took place in Nijmegen in 1988, and the editors are more than pleased to take this opportunity of thanking, on behalf of the participants, both the town and the Catholic University of Nijmegen for their hospitality. In particular we are very grateful to Hardy Beekelaar and Peter Rietbergen for their skill and resourcefulness as local organizers of the conference, which was highly congenial in all its arrangements. Our thanks are also due to Hans Blom and Jonathan Israel, who are the moving forces behind both the conference and the published series *Britain and the Netherlands*: their continuing efforts and support are indispensable.

We are also happy to record our gratitude to those who made the conference and the publication possible by contributing financial support: the Directie der Oostersche Handel en Reederijen, Amsterdam, the J.E. Jurriaanse Stichting, Rotterdam, and the Stichting Unger-van Brero Fonds, Wageningen. Their generosity has greatly encouraged the Anglo-Dutch connection, and has helped to bring the work of Dutch historians more to the attention of the English-speaking world.

S. Groenveld
M. J. Wintle

Introduction: Government and the Economy in Britain and the Netherlands

Michael Wintle

This volume is the tenth in the series called *Britain and the Netherlands,* which began more than thirty years ago with the proceedings of the Oxford-Dutch Historical Conference held in 1959. Over the years the series has gained respectability, partly that due simply to age, but also because of the generally high quality of the papers delivered to the conferences. The volumes of *Britain and Netherlands* have become well-thumbed reference works in most of our university libraries, used by researchers and students interested in Britain, the Low Countries, or in the relations between those nations. Most of the volumes have been built around a theme which runs through the collected papers: mythology, war, church and state, historiography, or most recently, in Volume IX, the press and media. The present volume maintains that tradition, and has taken the theme of *State and Trade,* examining the role of government in the economic development of Britain and the Netherlands since the Middle Ages, and particularly its role in their commercial fortunes.

The period covered reaches from the Middle Ages up to 1950, and over the course of the centuries the degree of state intervention in economic matters altered considerably. The apparatus which states could command to execute policies grew in size and effectiveness, nation-states themselves grew up and matured, while economic theory took shape and developed, and governments began to attach increasing importance to economic policy. However, throughout the long period, the emphasis in this collection tends to be on the varying effectiveness of policy, and the unpredictability and very mixed success of governments' attempts to influence the course of economic events.

Leo Noordegraaf's article deals with the role of government in internal trade in the province of Holland in the later Middle Ages and the Republic. He unearths a great deal of empirical data to do with the commercial conflicts between towns and villages, and between the towns themselves, but his purpose is didactic, and certainly more than exploratory. He rightly asserts than economists have neglected internal trade as an area of study: the sources are complicated and the local amounts modest, but on a regional scale it must have been one of the largest and most significant kinds of economic activity. Noordegraaf also insists that economic historians have played down political factors in trying to explain economic circumstances, and maintains that the evolution of the trading situation is in large part a manifestation of a local balance of power in continual flux. The matrix of power-relations between the sovereign, the nobility, the towns and the villages was often fought out through internal trade regulation − both by legitimate means and by brute force. Up to 1750 the influence of the towns tended generally to increase at the expense of both the villages and the centre, but their victory was never comprehensive, and gradually the central state began to take over, finally triumphing with the Municipality Act in 1851. Noordegraaf argues convincingly that the state and trade, at the local level at least, were thoroughly intermingled, and indeed that the study of local power relations is itself in many cases the study of commercial relations.

Peter Ramsey, with his extensive knowledge of the economic and social aspects of the Tudor state, is primarily concerned with a methodological problem: what (if any) is the relationship between what we consider economic policy today, and what the Tudors concerned themselves with? Are we not guilty of an almost hopeless anachronism in trying to evaluate economic policies and their success in a world which had virtually no concept of or interest in our present-day macro-economic desiderata? The English governments of the fifteenth and sixteenth centuries were concerned with defending the realm, law and order, some degree of justice, and raising adequate revenues to support the court and government. Purely economic problems had a very low priority, and the means of enforcement were in any case highly questionable. Ramsey runs through an inventory of interested parties and policy areas which might conceivably be associated with economics, and concludes that it didn't amount to very much. This, however, is all in twentieth-century terms: the Tudors would, on the contrary, have been quite pleased with their record, pointing to the absence of invasion, successful insurrection, mass starvation or total government bankruptcy. And if the Tudor state had been more successful in carrying out 'economic' policy, then it surely would have wanted to suppress almost every innovative form of economic initiative, and so once again would have failed in the eyes of modern economists?

The contribution by Peter Klein (which has since been published in a Dutch version in the *Tijdschrift voor Geschiedenis*, CII (1989), 189-212) joins forces in the debate about the nature of mercantilism, using the Dutch Republic and its trade as a case-study to strip away the confusion surrounding the concept. He reverts to an old-fashioned definition: a system developed for the benefit of the mercantile interest. But in looking at his case-study of the Dutch Republic, Klein demonstrates that mercantilism was highly selective about the merchants it favoured: only the large-scale international traders in the carrying trades and the entrepôt were the long-term beneficiaries, with their activities more or less unregulated and very undertaxed, considering the increasing amount of defence resources these sectors demanded. Footing the bill were the smaller-scale domestic merchant interests and industries, who were heavily taxed and highly regulated. What Klein calls 'this dualism of the Dutch institutional economic system' played a significant role in the long-term development of the economy as a whole: whereas such polices promoting the interests of big commercial business were probably right for the early seventeenth century, when trading profits were high, after 1650 when Dutch relative profits were eroded it is by no means certain that the economy as a whole benefited from this favouritism towards one international sector. The article is intentionally provocative, and Klein readily admits that the archive research to prove the conclusions is yet to be done. In some ways there are more questions than answers provided here, and in time empirical research will help to show more of the truth of the matter.

Jonathan Israel also touches on the nature of seventeenth-century mercantilism, concentrating on the English reactions of the 1650s and 1660s to the reassertion of Dutch commercial supremacy after the conclusion of the peace between Spain and the Republic at the end of the 1640s. In the works of Benjamin Worsley, Thomas Violet, Henry Robinson and Josiah Child, Israel perceives what he calls the classical English articulation of mercantilism, calling in the main for a radical increase of the state's interference in defence of the the nation's economic interests, in particular those of its merchants. It was this campaign which led to the Navigation Act of 1651, and to a series of anti-Dutch regulations and measures which led into the three Anglo-Dutch Wars fought in the third quarter of the seventeenth century. This is a genuinely Anglo-Dutch historical study, excavating the depths of the rivalry and mutual perceptions of these two maritime nations. In the end, the English were unable to sustain their challenge to the Dutch, and, despite superior naval firepower, they lost the peace settlements and by the mid-1670s were forced to succumb to the strength of Dutch resources and market control the world over: state intervention and support proved not to be enough to turn the tide for the English. On the other hand, the Dutch were generally successful in mobilizing resources, regulating shipping and trade, devising naval strategies, and forging alliances which made the most of the Dutch situation.

Dwyryd Jones' contribution concerns the source of the truly massive sums which were required by Britain to finance the European wars of the 1690s and the first decade of the eighteenth century. The main theatres of war, in Spain and Flanders, were filled with English troops, and those of her partners in the Grand Alliance to a large extent financed by English subsidies. The armies needed paying, subsidizing and provisioning by means of huge cash payments from England, while almost none of the purchases for which the payments were used in the theatres of war benefited English industrial or agricultural production. The 1690s was, as a result, a disastrous decade which Britain was only able to survive by wholesale coin-clipping, thus sowing the seeds of hyper-inflation and other such destabilizing influences. The decade of 1700-10 ought to have been much worse (and much of Jones' account is counterfactual, telling us how awful it might have been), but instead England emerged financially resplendent, and thus able to carry the day in battle. The factors involved were a steady stream of bullion from India after 1701, an export boom to Brazil because of the expanding gold production there, and most importantly the disabling of Britain's competitors in supplying the warring armies of Europe with textiles and grain, as the campaigns of Charles XII, Peter the Great and Marlborough scythed down the production facilities of the Baltic regions, Silesia, Saxony and the Low Countries themselves. Coincidence, then: the state had almost nothing to do with it. Government economic and financial policy was almost completely ineffective in supplying these resources, and it was good fortune rather than sound management or policy which won the wars of the Spanish Succession.

The contribution by Paul Overmeer covers the Dutch state's attempts, in the period straddling the Napoleonic era (1780-1850), to direct the national economy, to improve it, and to give it some coherence and leadership. As Peter Ramsey is concerned about the intellectual honesty and indeed the usefulness of applying twentieth-century concepts to the Tudor state, Overmeer is at pains to point out that our expectations of the the economic performance of governments are quite unrealistic for the late eighteenth and early nineteenth centuries. In the late Republic, in the French-dominated regimes between 1795 and 1814, and under the rule of King Willem I, there was plenty of enthusiasm from Patriots, devotees of the Enlightenment and proponents of the young — mainly English — science of classical political economy, all of whom saw an important role for the state. Indeed, King Willem himself was a leader from the front, with strong policy initiatives and a vision of how the national economy should develop. But despite their ability (and some were very able indeed), the politicians all failed to impose their vision on the Dutch economy. Economic theory was inconsistent and incomplete, the bureaucratic apparatus was hopelessly inadequate and far too small, while political opposition and foreign domination made for radical swings in political climate which obviated continuity.

9

In this period at least, the conclusion is that the state was unable significantly to influence the course of events.

There follows a pair of essays on the interaction of the state and the economy in the colonial empires of Britain and the Netherlands. First Peter Cain undertakes a reassessment of the views of J.A. Hobson, who, writing at the turn of the century in what might be called a proto-Leninist vein, thought the New Imperialism of 1870-1914 to be City-driven, that is to say, motivated by a need to find new markets for Western European industry, and in particular for its capital, outside the saturated economies of Europe. These Eurocentric, economics-driven explanations were largely discredited in the sixties and seventies by a generation of scholars led by R.E. Robinson and J. Gallagher, who looked far more to excentric or non-European causes of imperialism, to strategic rather than to financial motives, and to what became known as the influence of 'the official mind'. Cain examines a number of British 'imperial situations', in Egypt, South Africa, China, Turkey, Canada, Australasia and South America, and concludes that, after all, Hobson lives. With certain exceptions (tropical Africa, China, the Ottoman Empire), Hobson's contemporary analysis still has much to recommend it, and is coming back into favour.

Maarten Kuitenbrouwer takes up the debate in regard to the Dutch experience with its overseas possessions between about 1870 and the First World War. Although reluctant to be sidetracked into a discussion on the meaning of imperialism, Kuitenbrouwer clearly believes that it differed from colonialism in being specifically expansionist, and (crucially for the purposes of this volume) insofar as that expansion was actively supported by the Dutch state and the Dutch economy. Imperialism occurred, then, when the state exerted political influence and both gave and encouraged economic assistance on behalf of expansion in the colonies, old and new. The Dutch, however, were very selective in their imperialism, confining it almost exclusively to the East Indies, and within that to Sumatra. Elsewhere, with a very few sabre-rattling exceptions, they were prepared to cede territory (on the Gold Coast and on Borneo), to stifle powerful nationalist sentiments (over the Dutch-related Boers) and generally to remain interestedly neutral, as long as Dutch interests in the Archipelago were intact, and were guaranteed by support from the domineering ally Britain. This, then, was limited imperialism, and so, according to Kuitenbrouwer's implied definition, limited state intervention.

The interwar peiod is the focus for Roger Middleton's study of the economic role of British state. By the time of the twentieth century, it has become no longer a question of whether the state should intervene in the economy, but to what extent it should, and how. Middleton guides us through the very extensive literature on these issues, and charts the expansion of the state's control of the economy in terms of the size of the public sector, and the volume of taxation. However, echoing parts of the studies of earlier periods in this volume, he also points to the regular failures of state intervention, for instance in budget management in conditions of cyclical fluctuation.

The final contribution to the volume, by Richard Griffiths, concerns the efforts of the Dutch government to direct trade policy in the thirties and forties of this century. It would be difficult to find two more catastrophic decades in the country's history, especially in an economic sense, and so perhaps it is hardly surprising that the state had only limited success. The government seemed hounded from pillar to post by the onslaught of disaster after disaster, first in the Depression of the 1930s, when Dutch exports collapsed, and then after the Second World War, with the dollar crises, the loss of major trading partners (Indonesia and Germany), devastation, and painful recovery. Griffiths explores the attempts and limitations of the Dutch state in improving trade with its principal partners in Europe, and it is anything but a happy tale, at least until the very end of the 1940s. At that point the 'strangling bilateralism' began to be broken down, first by American insistence that Marshall Aid involve some degree of European integration. Buffetted by two decades of disater, the Dutch were obliged to relinquish their cherished principle of general free trade on a global basis, and settle instead for a limited goal of customs union within the much more modest framework of the Six — which was of course to lead in time to the European Community.

Despite the range of centuries covered by the collection, these essays unite around their theme of *State and Trade*. This series of investigations into the Dutch, the English, and the Anglo-Dutch situation confirms emphatically that 'state' and 'trade' are inextricably intermingled, but that assumptions about the effectiveness of government in influencing the economy are not always justified, especially before the twentieth century. In the reverse direction, however, it is clearly demonstrated that economic affairs, and in particular trade, can and do have a decisive effect upon government. As Dwyryd Jones remarks in his essay: 'Historians have had perhaps rather more to say about what states have done to promote trade than about what trade has done to promote states.' In focusing on the cases of Britain and the Netherlands, this collection has enhanced our understanding of the relationship between the two.

1

Internal Trade and Internal Trade Conflicts in the Northern Netherlands: Autonomy, Centralism, and State Formation in the Pre-industrial Era

Leo Noordegraaf

The history of internal trade in the Netherlands during the pre-industrial era is filled with countless tensions, problems, and conflicts, in which the political institutions of the Middle Ages and early modern period played a prominent role. For example, there was the continuously recurring bickering between the Amsterdam city government and shippers' guilds, and the governments and guilds of other towns, concerning such things as the regular barge service: dozens of such disputes have been recorded for the period 1520-1668.[1] Another example, at the provincial level, was the opposition of the States of Holland to the quarantine measures taken by the States of Zeeland during the plague epidemic of 1664. This was not an isolated case, for there were similar conflicts between the provincial states and the States General.[2] There were also intense conflicts regarding transit past the staple markets, in which certain towns even threatened armed violence, and the highest governmental authority was forced to intervene. The reputations of Dordrecht, Venlo, and Groningen were especially notorious in this respect.[3] Equally infamous were the problems and legal proceedings concerning annual fairs, in which neighbouring towns came into conflict with each other. For example, in 1546 Gouda obtained a ruling from the *Grote Raad van Mechelen* (the highest judicial institution in the Low Countries) in which the right granted to Schoonhoven by Charles V to hold an annual fair was revoked.[4]

Two prominent types of conflicts can be distinguished, which continued to stir up ill-feeling right up to the nineteenth century. Firstly, there were the tensions between towns and the countryside which arose from the question of whether or not trade was permitted outside the towns. Secondly, there were problems which arose between the towns themselves as a result of these tensions. Both types are central in this paper. The study of these conflicts not only provides insight into the nature of domestic trade, its organizational forms, trade flows, and trade routes, but also into the institutional relations of that period. On the other hand, the nature of these conflicts can to a large degree be understood in the light of political relations at that time. There is also, of course, a direct relationship between the origin of the conflicts and certain economic developments; however, I have by and large excluded these from consideration. This decision does not rest on the conviction that politics is more important than economics in explaining historical processes, but on the consideration that the importance of political power-relations in understanding economic processes has not been sufficiently recognized in current Dutch economic historiography.

Because the problem seems to have been the most pronounced in the province of Holland, I have based my argument primarily on examples from that region. An explanation for this concentration possibly lies in the fact that the province had been highly urbanized since the fourteenth century, and that it had developed into the economic centre of the north. The likelihood of conflict seems to have been promoted through this demographic and economic 'density'. Nonetheless, I have also found the same problems and conflicts in the other provinces, between town and countryside, and between the towns themselves.

Town and countryside

With the rise and growth of towns, numerous problems developed with the surrounding countryside, which were either economic in nature or had an economic background. From the late Middle Ages onwards, the idea became widespread among urban governments that the towns ought to be the centres of trade and industry, and that the countryside should almost exclusively engage in agricultural production and supply these goods to the urban markets.[5] They were only willing to make an exception for activities outside the agricultural sector which were strictly limited to the village.[6] This division of labour may have seemed reasonable to the townsmen, but all kinds of objections arose in the countryside. While the villagers could see advantages in the concentration of buying and selling, they were not necessarily convinced that taking goods to and from the urban markets yielded them the greatest economic advantages, to say nothing of other non-trading activities.[7] The towns, which gave up their agricultural base, saw an assault on their continued existence in the aspirations of the countryside, and they did not fail to have their urban and market rights interpreted in such a way that trade was permitted to be an exclusively urban activity. This was not just the case with towns of only, or primarily, regional importance. This point of view was also endorsed by towns which developed trade beyond their immediate region or even derived their importance primarily from international trade. An economic tie with their region remained essential for these places especially with respect to the supply of food, and certainly for the growth of the permanent staple markets.

In short, according to the townsmen, trade was to be primarily an urban activity. This viewpoint is vividly expressed by the attempts to monopolize concrete markets.[8] When the privileges and charters permitting urban markets were understood as meaning that markets were not permitted and could be forbidden in places where these rights had not been granted by the sovereign, conflicts arose. Many villages left the trade within their boundaries unhampered or even played an active role in organizing markets. Thus, they rejected the urban interpretation of municipal privileges. A number of villages could also consider themselves to be completely justified in doing so; they had received market rights, of the same legal status as those of the towns, from the sovereign or an official appointed by him.[9]

This can be illustrated with several examples. First, however, something must be said about the rights of the towns. In the urban privileges which were granted by the Count to the towns of Holland in the thirteenth century, trade was not usually mentioned until the end of the century. Markets are mentioned only in the charters of Geertruidenberg (1213) and Delft (1246).[10] The explicit conferring of market rights did not usually take place. This of course does not mean that trade did not take place in the towns or that markets were not held there. Rather, a number of specific rights and guarantees were absent in the areas of jurisprudence and law enforcement which could be granted by the sovereign.[11] With the growth of towns in the late Middle Ages, and as a result of the related complexity in legal and economic affairs, the desire arose for market rights that had been explicitly granted, with which buyers and sellers could be given all kinds of legal guarantees. Financial considerations

– such as the collection of market tolls – will also have played a role in the legal regulation of the markets. The granting of these rights to towns became relatively normal after the end of the thirteenth century, and usually involved annual fairs, sometimes weekly markets, and on occasion daily markets.[12] This is hardly surprising. The economic relations and legal issues became increasingly complicated in the annual fairs, with their large-scale and relatively expensive transactions in the sale and purchase of goods by visitors from outside the town and its jurisdiction. In addition to the desire for 'free' markets (that is to say, officially regulated markets) as a result of economic growth, the rulers granted such rights in order to be able to ensure for themselves the political support of the towns.[13] The towns, of course, saw the possibility of stimulating their economy by obtaining these rights, through, for example, preventing competition from outside or, conversely, through granting favorable conditions to foreigners. It remains debatable whether or not annual fairs did indeed attract more foreign visitors. Just as the urban privileges granted to a number of places did not lead them to become real cities, so the development of annual fairs could lag behind expectations. Although 's-Gravenzande received urban privileges in 1246, it was never able to develop into a 'city'.[14] This holds true to an even stronger degree for a number of West-Frisian villages in the fifteenth century, which received urban rights from the Count in return for political support, but always remained typical rural communities.[15] Insofar as markets are concerned, Alkmaar received the privilege to hold an annual fair in 1339, in which the level of the tolls that were to be paid by the merchants from Flanders, Brabant, and Denmark were determined, but it is questionable whether merchants from these areas ever visited the city.[16]

Towns, then, tended to interpret urban and market privileges in their own favour. Some, however, went a step further and were able to obtain regional staple rights from the sovereign. This not only implied that the rural inhabitants were not allowed to have their own markets, but also that they could only visit the markets of the town which had the staple right, thus excluding them from the other towns. This not only created problems for a town with the residents in its region, but also with the surrounding towns, which wanted these villagers to attend their markets. The claims made by Dordrecht and Groningen with respect to this point are especially well known.[17] Others (like Brielle, Naarden, Utrecht, and Woudrichem), however, did not lag behind.[18]

Moving to the rights of the countryside, centres of trade also developed in numerous places in the countryside which never achieved urban status. In a number of cases official permission for this was obtained from the sovereign. Both annual fairs and weekly markets were involved. It is possible that Vlaardingen, Voorschoten, and Valkenburg had official annual fairs before the rise of the towns in Holland.[19] But the sovereign also granted market rights to rural communities in the late Middle Ages. In Rijsoord a weekly market and annual fair were allowed to be held after 1339. One year later Heerjansdam received market rights. Brouwershaven, which was not then a town, received the right to hold a herring market in 1344. Akersloot had a market from as early as the end of the fourteenth century. Schoorl was granted the right to hold an annual fair in 1446; Oude Tonge a weekly market in 1473. Niedorp's right to hold weekly markets and two annual fairs was confirmed in 1557. The States of Holland also granted permission to organize markets to several villages after it assumed the rights of the sovereign.[20]

For that matter, market rights were granted not only by the count. Certain *ambachtsheren*, or lords of the manor, also appear to have been entitled to do this.[21]

Examples are the weekly market granted to Dreischor in 1356, the market granted to Westenrijk (Blinkvliet or Zuidland) in 1439, and the weekly market and annual fair granted to Breskens in about 1550. Thus, the possession of market privileges, whether or not granted by the sovereign, was not exceptional in the countryside.[22]

Finally, in this context, there were certain places which had been granted urban rights, but which never became genuine towns. Formally these villages were indeed towns, but they were actually never recognized as such. In many cases market privileges were granted, whether or not at the same time as the urban privileges. These places formed, as it were, a category between town and countryside. This did not help to clarify matters and was a potential source of conflict. Examples of such places have already been given: 's-Gravenzande, Beverwijk, and a dozen West-Frisian villages.[23] Again in the case of these 'towns', it was not always the sovereign who granted the market rights. In 1383 Guy van Castillon granted Texel an annual fair. In 1469 Heenvliet received a town charter from its lord with the right to hold an annual fair and a weekly market.[24]

In summary, it must be concluded that towns did not necessarily possess formally conferred market rights.[25] That, however, does not mean that markets were not held there. This is also the case for the countryside: where market rights were absent, markets could nonetheless be organized.

It is clear that the town and the market were not exclusively and inextricably intertwined. This fact is of fundamental importance in understanding the development of trade conflicts. With the demographic and economic development of the towns, and in connection with a growing self-awareness and an active economic policy, the idea matured that the right to markets must be reserved for the towns.[26] Whether or not they had been granted market privileges, the urban governments increasingly became convinced that they had the right to a monopoly of trade because of their economic, fiscal, and political interests and their exceptional legal status. The pressure on the countryside to acknowledge this increased, but the villages did not submit to this without a struggle. Numerous tensions, of which only a few examples can be given in what follows, were the consequence of this.

Towns versus villages

The nature and scale of the trade conflicts could vary enormously. Major and long-lasting problems developed as a result of the regional staple rights of Dordrecht and Groningen.[27] In particular after the St. Elizabeth's Day Flood of 1421, by which Dordrecht was partially robbed of its hinterland, the situation was ripe for this city to monopolize the regional market functions. Numerous conflicts with the countryside were a consequence of this, in which — not least because of the central government's inconsistent policy — first one party achieved success, and then the other. Throughout virtually the entire fifteenth and sixteenth centuries, the villages (and other towns, as will be seen below) resisted Dordrecht's claims with all kinds of protest actions.[28]

A small case-study gives a good insight into the strained relations. From an inquiry made in 1553 by the highest judicial authority in the province, it quickly becomes clear how disadvantageous Dordrecht's market rights were for the surrounding countryside. The villagers who were questioned testified that they were often detained by Dordrecht's inspectors on their way to other markets. Their goods were then confiscated, even when only small quantities were involved; such as a bushel of two hundred pears, a basket of poultry, a pound of butter, or a bunch of hennep. A woman from IJsselmonde declared that four years earlier when she was on her way to Rotterdam with butter, cheese, eggs, and fowl, eight or ten inspectors from Dordrecht had come aboard her boat and had declared all her goods confiscated. She was even refused a pound of butter 'with which to feed her poor children that evening'. During inspections attempts were made to keep butter and eggs hidden underneath clothing, but the officials were not lenient. The lock-keeper of Nieuw-Lekkerland complained that the inspectors had destroyed his boat and compelled him to bring the fish which he caught in the locks to market in Dordrecht, even though the lock-keeper had been exempted from this as long as anyone could remember. The 'offenders' were even maltreated by the inspectors.

There were innumerable protests against the requirement to attend the market in Dordrecht. The country people complained in particular that they could not get the 'just value' for their goods. They were required to sell their goods at the market in Dordrecht, by which means a lower price came about than would have been the case with a free market. The possibility of attending markets in other towns would have driven the process of price formation in the market in Dordrecht in an advantageous direction for the villages. In addition to financial drawbacks, other complaints were also brought forward. The residents of the further outlying villages, who lived closer to other markets, felt that they were disadvantaged through the loss of time which the forced attendance at the market in Dordrecht entailed − particularly during the winter when the city was difficult to reach. The residents of Lekkerkerk, for example, declared that they preferred to attend the market in Schoonhoven, because they could row there within an hour. They could reach Rotterdam within two or three hours, but the trip to Dordrecht was very inconvenient because they first had to travel down the Lek with the ebb and then wait for the flood before they could sail to Dordrecht. For the return trip they also needed two tides. Neither could they reach Dordrecht by wagon, which was possible in travelling to other towns.[29] Similar problems and conflicts occurred between Groningen and the Ommelanden.

Towns which did not possess explicit staple rights also attempted to compel the use of their markets. In a number of cases they appealed to declarations in which the sovereign prohibited village markets. An early example dates from 1347. On 25 September of that year, Willem de Verbeider ordered the bailiff of Kennemerland to see to it that weekly markets were not held in the villages there and that the villagers attended the weekly market in Alkmaar. In the privileges granted to Sneek in 1517 by Karel van Gelder, it was specified that annual fairs and weekly markets were not permitted in the countryside. After the end of the sixteenth century, various requests made by villages to the States of Holland to establish markets were turned down or kept under deliberation. In 1740 the States of Holland ordered the village elders of Oost-Zaandam to ensure that the illegal village market held there would be stopped.[30]

The opposition of the towns to the village markets was one aspect of their policy. It was part of a policy which in fact attempted to attract to the towns all trade which was more than strictly local in nature.[31] That is also why the trade which appeared not to be bound to concrete markets became the explicit target of legal action. In 1516, for example, an ordinance was proclaimed in Holland and Zeeland prohibiting the purchase or sale of casks of butter (that is to say in bulk) in the countryside and requiring the farmers to attend the market in the town in the area in which they resided. The measure was taken because it had become apparent that many country people secretly sold butter in casks in their homes. Eleven years later the sale of turf was prohibited in Rijnland, Schieland, and Delfland. On 20 December 1602, the States of Holland prohibited the trade in foreign grain in the villages. In the beginning of January of the following year, the bailiff and judiciary of Zaandam and other villages in the area, and the bailiff of Kennemerland, were in particular directed to put a stop to the grain trade upon the request of Amsterdam, which saw itself possibly put at a strong disadvantage. Less than two months later, a protest had been submitted to the States by a large part of the countryside in Holland north of the IJ. Especially the Zaanstreek and the surrounding area, with its growing industry, continued to give the towns problems. In 1613 the towns and the villages clashed once again. A meeting was organized to protest the measures taken by the States, *casu quo* the towns. The meeting was however forbidden, even though the trade in the countryside did not stop after this. The towns continued to be watchful and enacted regulations. In 1641 a large number of villages north of the IJ once again protested. In 1668 the towns once again co-operated with each other to curb trade (and industry) in the countryside.[32]

The towns were willing to tolerate retail trade in the villages, that is to say purchase for personal use, as long as it was run by and for the villagers. As soon as urban residents went to the villages to buy items, the town councils took action. This often happened when the sale and purchase of alcoholic beverages was concerned. The relatively cheap public houses in the countryside were a continuous irritant to urban tavern keepers and the municipal treasury, which lost tax revenue. Numerous measures against this form of retail trade were taken, ranging from forbidding village beers to raising the taxes on them, and from increasing the area under the town's jurisdiction to making agreements with the manorial lords (*ambachtsheren*). Nonetheless, 'drinking in the countryside' appeared to be ineradicable. One example is the squabble between the city of Haarlem and the lord of Heemstede in the sixteenth century about the inns in the villages, which in addition to being drinking establishments, were also in part brothels and gambling dens. According to a knowledgeable 'source' of the local scene, the owners consorted with thieves and fugitives. Murder was alleged to be the order of the day there. It is clear that the towns used every argument available to them.[33]

One form of trade which presented many problems for the towns, especially in periods of price increases and food shortages, was the so-called forward sale.[34] It involved the trade in grain which had not yet been harvested, or in products which were en route to the market.[35] Measures against this kind of trade arose from the fear of a decline in municipal tax revenues, and from the inflationary effects which were ascribed to these practices, which restricted the supply of goods to the market. For the measures to be effective, the co-operation of government officials in the countryside was necessary, and this frequently led to friction. The sale of goods by pedlars, or from boats by vendors, who did not come from the village or region, led to all sorts of clamour by the towns, which yet again saw their markets, shops, and tax yields adversely affected.[36]

Finally, the fraught relations between the town and the countryside can be seen in the light of the problems regarding the right to have a weigh-house. Just as with the village market, the village weigh-house was a potential source of conflicts. The right to have a weigh-house could be granted either by the sovereign or by the *ambachtsheren*.[37] Furthermore, there were villages with weigh-houses which had not been officially sanctioned.[38] When the towns undertook action against the weigh-houses, the village officials resorted to any number of arguments in their defence; legal, historical, or even simply opportunistic ones.

Just as in the case of the village markets and other forms of trade, the towns saw their financial and commercial interests threatened by the rural weigh-houses. Where weighing was done outside the town gates, the town lost revenue from its weigh-house and the total volume of trade could also be reduced as a result. Moreover, it always remained questionable whether the goods were just being weighed. There was a good chance that buying and selling also took place in goods which therefore would no longer be offered for sale on the urban market. It was for this reason that the towns put pressure on the sovereign not to permit weigh-houses in the villages. At the beginning of the sixteenth century, for example, Sneek and Leeuwarden were able to have the weigh-houses in the surrounding area forbidden.[39] In the last decades of the century, the village weigh-houses were more than once the target of action taken by the States of Holland, in which the towns took the lead. It is possible that a power vacuum developed as a result of the political unrest at the beginning of the Revolt, which allowed many villages to seize the opportunity to establish their own weigh-house. Restrictive measures and prohibitions followed. The weigh-house continued to be a subject of enduring concern in the seventeenth century.[40]

The measures discussed so far which were taken against trade in the countryside, such as official prohibitions, legal actions and lawsuits, contracts and agreements with *ambachtsheren*, the expansion of municipal jurisdiction, and attempts at uniform taxation, can all be described as more or less legitimate. However, the towns also undertook activities which had more to do with the sheer exercise of power than the concept of law or right. The history of the *waterstaat* (administration, construction, and maintenance of roads, bridges, and waterways) gives eloquent examples of this. A good example is the action taken by Haarlem against the village of Jisp in 1665. The village had presented a request to the States for permission to widen certain ditches. The request was granted, but Haarlem was able to see to it that, nonetheless, the ditches could not be used for shipping. Furthermore, the city was free to have the ditches filled in at any time, and this was to be paid for by Jisp![41] Through a sophisticated policy in the construction and maintenance of waterways, the town governments attempted to prevent the farmers bypassing the cities. To stop them from visiting other markets, not only were existing waterways improved or new ones constructed, but 'escape routes' were filled with rubbish, bridges were purposefully kept low, waterways were poorly maintained, and the water level in certain waterways was lowered, so that the barges did not draw enough water.

The towns, for that matter, also clashed with each other in this policy. Amsterdam and Haarlem, for example, complained in 1638 that Alkmaar had not kept an agreement made in 1629 to make the Jan Booijes portage navigable. Maintaining the portage, where the ships were hauled over with the help of a windlass, fitted in with the 'delaying tactics' of Alkmaar. The trip to other towns took so long, that the countryfolk decided simply to attend the market in Alkmaar.[42]

In 1654 Schagen, Barsingerhorn, Oude and Nieuwe Niedorp, Winkel, Opmeer, Spanbroek, Obdam, and Hensbroek presented a petition to the States of Holland requesting that they be permitted to sail unhindered past Alkmaar *via* the new circular canal of Heerhugowaard. What actually transpired? The villages notified the States that they found it remarkable that the waterway had come to have so little water in it in the course of time that they had difficulty in sailing, even with ships which were not heavily laden. Sometimes waterways became shallower because of drift-sand or duckweed, but in this case there was something else afoot: 'this drying up was not simply caused by this ordinary drift-sand or duckweed, but by the city's workers who dumped entire barges full of sand and refuse along the side'. It was Alkmaar's intention that only small barges, for which the trip to Amsterdam was not profitable, could make use of this waterway. At this point Amsterdam also began to get involved in the dispute.[43]

Town versus town

These last examples show that tensions were not restricted to those between town and countryside, but that pressure by a town on the surrounding villages could also lead to conflicts with other towns.[44] The extent to which compulsory municipal market rights could be extended without resulting in conflicts with neighbouring towns was, in the case of the highly urbanized province of Holland, clearly very limited.

The tensions which stemmed from the conflicts are part of a general characteristic of the Middle Ages and the early modern period, namely, that of the changing balance of power between the towns. Nurtured by a large degree of local autonomy and marked self-awareness, and in relation to the powerful feelings of mutual rivalry, the towns often waged confrontations with each other. Political, economic, and cultural aspirations struggled for priority in the competition. As a result of this struggle, hierarchical relations developed between the towns which were not stable, but in which the centres of power, in part because of changing problems in working together, regularly shifted.

In economic history the delineation of spheres of influence, in this case of market and service areas, has been a constant source of numerous inter-municipal tensions and conflicts. The problems associated with the staple rights of Groningen and Dordrecht once again are illustrative. Groningen clashed with Appingedam, the only other place in the northernmost region which had been able to obtain full market functions;[45] meanwhile Dordrecht clashed with nearby towns such as Schoonhoven, Gorinchem, and Rotterdam. Numerous legal proceedings were waged as consequence of problems involving staple rights, especially during the sixteenth century. Difficulties could also arise with towns which were located further afield. For example, in the sixteenth century Delft opposed Dordrecht, because Delft's breweries – which had to rely on the countryside of South Holland for both raw materials and markets – experienced great disadvantages because of Dordrecht's staple right.[46] In the case of Dordrecht, the problems ran parallel to those which the staple right caused with the transit trade.[47] The intensity of the clashes is probably also due to the combination of conflicts stemming from both types of staple rights. Indeed, the legal and conceptual distinction between the two, which was repeatedly made in these cases, often referred in practice to the same goods; it was only their place in the flow of trade that differed.

Disagreements about the market area were not limited to the towns with staple rights and their neighbours. Even when 'rights' were not involved,[48] disagreements regularly arose between the towns about the question of where the rural residents were to go to market. At the end of the fifteenth century Leeuwarden did everything it could to prevent farmers from attending the market in Sneek.[49]

The Revolt did not bring an end to these disputes. On the contrary, the towns continued to battle with each other deep into the seventeenth century, sometimes with remarkable ferocity. While the significance of the staple rights was eroded in the course of the sixteenth century through developments which are not here at issue, the struggle to consolidate or expand their market area remained a constant in the policy of all towns. This protectionism of markets is clearly illustrated in the tensions between Alkmaar and Hoorn. In the conflicts, which sometimes dragged on for more than several decades, there were not only endless wranglings and legal proceedings, but direct action was also taken, and there were even threats of armed violence. Two examples will suffice: the two towns clashed over their market policy around Avenhorn and Rustenburg. In 1577 Hoorn conceived a plan to build two *verlaten* (small locks for barges) with the intention of attracting the farmers from the area north of Alkmaar to the market in Hoorn. Alkmaar viewed this as subversive to its own market function. Before the construction work started, the burgomasters, bailiff, and aldermen of Alkmaar marched out on 14 September, armed and with their flag flying. The building materials which were already at the site were burned. Hoorn felt deeply insulted, but before the situation deteriorated even further, William of Orange was able to pour oil on troubled waters.[50] The second example: in 1634 Hoorn was once again active near Avenhorn with the intention of constructing a lock. Diggers, bricklayers, carriers, and carpenters were busy and their work was guarded by a sergeant with twenty-five armed men. Extra weapons had been taken along, so that the workers could be armed in case the militia from Alkmaar should appear. The conflict continued to flare up and a decision was finally made in favour of Alkmaar in 1684. When examining these and other incidents in detail, it is clear that the surrounding villages and towns did not always side with the same party. The composition of the alliances was in constant flux, showing that the internal power relations were continuously under pressure.[51]

Protection and expansion

The tensions and problems which arose in this manner initially appear to be independent phenomena, but on further investigation it transpires that they were the result of a long-lasting and consistently maintained principle in the domestic policy of the towns in the Netherlands, which I am inclined to describe from an economic point of view as a form of protectionism, and as a form of expansionism from a political point of view.[52] When the trade conflicts are placed in this context, they acquire a significance beyond that of incidents only of local or regional importance. Without an interpretation of this kind, the writing of history is reduced to a compilation of unconnected *petites histoires*, which may excite interest as curiosities, but which do not sufficiently address the question of causation.

In contrast to international trade, in which the authorities did not intervene, internal trade and transportation were subjected to extensive governmental interference.[53] The resulting laws and regulations were to an important degree designed to protect the urban market, in the broadest sense of the term. Within this policy, the consolidation and expansion of a market area, as exclusive as possible, played a role of the utmost importance for the towns. It is clear from the material presented above that there was, in this respect, an attempt to create monopolies at the regional level, in which no active role was allotted to the countryside, other than agriculture. The towns were unanimous in this policy, even though their solidarity quickly showed ruptures when it came to the delineation of the spheres of influence.

In their attempts to bring the countryside under their control, the towns encountered impediments and resistance which were to a considerable degree political and institutional in nature. The communities which became towns, and thus obtained a large measure of autonomy with municipal privileges as a foundation,[54] could not depend upon immediately acquiring a status above that of the rural communities in the area of regional trade. The conferment of market rights was not guaranteed to towns. The sovereign, or local lord (whether or not he held such rights), also granted market rights to villages, while the towns which did not enjoy the sovereign's support lacked the legal means to forbid trade which was not officially regulated outside the towns and centres of trade.[55]

From the late Middle Ages onwards, the towns, which continued to grow stronger, increasingly exercised pressure on the sovereign to limit the economic opportunities of the countryside. In cases where the sovereign needed the financial or political support of certain towns, he was often prepared to grant their wishes. The prohibition of weekly markets in the villages of Kennemerland by Willem de Verbeider in 1347 was certainly done in order to ensure the political support of Alkmaar.[56] On the other hand, the sovereign granted similar rights to certain villages for the same reasons. In the charter to establish a weigh-house granted by Philip of Burgundy to Sloten and Osdorp in 1465, the resulting increases in the Count's income are explicitly mentioned.[57]

This implies that insight into the political balance of power is of major importance in understanding the trade conflicts. In the triangle of sovereign, town and countryside, it always centres on the question of power, a question which is further complicated by the fact that other political problems, such as conflicts between the towns and the nobility (also in continual flux),[58] were related to economic policy.

The tension between sovereign centralism and municipal autonomy is also reflected in economic policy and in economic relations. In August 1477, Maria of Burgundy granted Brielle a regional staple right. It is tempting to see this a consequence of the *Groot Privilege* which had been granted to Holland and Zeeland less than six months previously, in which she had to make a number of concessions which blocked the centralizing policies of the Burgundians in order to guarantee her position as the successor of her father, Charles the Bold.[59] The ordinances against trade in the countryside enacted in 1516 and 1517, shortly after the succession of Charles V, were also attempts to gain the support of the towns.[60]

As a consequence of changes in political power relations, privileges which had been granted by one sovereign could be revoked by a later ruler. The history of Dordrecht's staple right in the fifteenth and sixteenth centuries is an example of this. Philip of Burgundy turned against this city in the 1440s, while his son Charles patronized it. Although Maximilian of Austria recognized Dordrecht's rights in 1494, Charles V opposed its staple rights in 1515. Five years later, Dordrecht was able to persuade the same ruler to recognize them again.[61]

The pressure exercised by the towns was thus not always successful. The sovereign could pursue a policy which thwarted municipal interests. Moreover, the countryside was not a placid victim, but offered resistance, both actively through protests, legal proceedings, and appeals privileges, and passively by inventing excuses and not carrying out the ordinances. Often it was able to gain support from the nobility who owned land locally and controlled the manorial rights (*ambachtsheerlijkheden*), and thus much of the local legal and administrative power. The sovereign certainly had to take the higher nobility into consideration, while even *ambachtsheren* had seats on the highest legal body in Holland.[62] Conflicts between nobility, supporting their villages, and the towns, were by no means an exception.[63]

It is certain that the pressure of the towns steadily increased, but it remains difficult to determine the outcome of the struggle. It is possible that the towns obtained the best concessions from the Habsburgs. Support for centralizing policies, including the accompanying financial obligations, was the price which had to be paid.

The increase in the pressure, for that matter, must partly be ascribed to more co-operative action on the part of the towns. On the other hand, the villages generally also succeeded in maintaining their rights to markets, weigh-houses, and free trade, and in obtaining new rights. In a lawsuit against Leiden, fought out around 1500 before the highest court in the Netherlands, the *Grote Raad van Mechelen*, the villages of Valkenburg and Voorschoten succeeded in preserving their annual fairs.[64]

The Habsburgs, like their predecessors, will have understood that they could not take the risk of supporting only the towns. Charles V made concessions to the towns in 1516, 1517, 1524, 1527, and 1531, but at the same time, *ambachtsheren* in the vicinity of Alkmaar appear to have received permission to hold horse markets in the early 1520s.[65] The prohibition of forward sales in 1524 allowed certain exceptions and a number of villages in the Zaan region promptly took advantage of this.[66]

In short, the towns achieved progress in their commercial policy regarding the countryside through the concessions which they received from the rulers, but their dominance was never complete, precisely because of the difficulties involved in implementing policies in a pre-industrial society, with its deficient means of communication and power. Although the towns more or less controlled financial matters, the role of the countryside was certainly not completely finished.[67]

The towns achieved their greatest successes during the Republic. It is likely that political and institutional circumstances were responsible for this. After 1588, sovereign authority came into the hands of the provincial estates, in which (with Holland once again as the pre-eminent example) the towns dominated. Furthermore, the position of the nobility was weakened. In the province of Holland where the noble estate, or *Ridderschap*, held one vote in the States against the eighteen held by the cities, the nobles were meant to represent the countryside. The villages continued to count on the support of the noble *ambachtsheren*, but the latter seem to have developed few initiatives to the benefit of the countryside.[68] At the same time, the towns were able to expand their influence through increasing their administrative powers. One of the ways in which town governments achieved this was through purchasing manorial rights or *ambachtsheerlijkheden*, and thus assuming administrative posts in the local councils or *waterschappen*. This policy was certainly not unknown in the Middle Ages, but during the Republic the objective of exercising direct control in the administration of the countryside became quite common.[69] In this way, from the fifteenth century onwards, Rotterdam slowly but surely gained control of the administrative power in the surrounding region.[70]

Although trade in the countryside was made increasingly difficult in this way, the towns appear never to have succeeded in expanding their influence to the extent of gaining a monopoly. Inter-urban conflicts did not promote the effectiveness of their actions against the countryside. The conflicts related to the regional staple rights were certainly a thing of the past by the beginning of the seventeenth century, but other kinds of conflicts reached their high-point precisely at that time.

Moreover, while it is true that the villages received only a few new rights, and that existing rights were eroded, illegal commercial activities remained the order of the day, through the laxity and obstinacy of numerous villages. Forward sales, especially of grain, and peddling, were issues which continued to keep the towns and the States occupied. For example, in 1751 the wine trade was once again explicitly forbidden in the villages.[71] Tensions and conflicts were still continuing in the eighteenth century, though they had lost some of their intensity by then.

These enduring conflicts were partly a result of economic changes,[72] but were also due to changes in economic and political thinking regarding the friction between municipal autonomy, provincial particularism, and state centralism, especially after 1750. Centralism came to the fore after the fall of the Republic in 1795, by means of which town and countryside came to develop a more equal relationship.[73] This process, however, did not proceed quickly or smoothly. For example, Alkmaar was still making it difficult for farmers in the Schermer to bring their cattle to market in Amsterdam at the beginning of the nineteenth century. In the same period Alkmaar complained about the market-gardeners from Langedijk who thought that the changed political situation allowed them to bypass the market in Alkmaar and sail directly to Amsterdam.[74] It was only with the Municipality Act of 1851 that the formal subordination of the villages ended and the process of legal and political emancipation was completed.

In reviewing the entire period treated here, it is difficult (given the current state of the research) to give an exact chronology of the problem. From the time of the late Middle Ages, the pressure of the towns grew steadily, and the countryside appeared officially (that is to say purely legally and institutionally) to be the weaker party, especially after 1588. The number and extent of the conflicts certainly appears to have decreased after the end of the seventeenth century, but the struggle was clearly not over even by 1800, in part because of the stance of the villages concerning illegal commercial practices.

An important reason why relatively little is known about the trade conflicts in the context of relations between town and countryside, with the exception of the conflicts involving Dordrecht's staple rights, is the fact that the history of internal trade and commercial policy is a neglected area in Dutch historiography.[75] The intention of this article is then primarily programmatic. It is an invitation for further research into these matters, and an invitation to concentrate, without neglecting the primary economic interpretation, on the political and institutional aspects which have been presented here.[76]

Notes

1. *Bronnen tot de geschiedenis van het bedrijfsleven en gildewezen van Amsterdam* (ed. J.G. van Dillen, 3 vol., The Hague, 1929-1974), Rijks Geschiedkundige Publicatiën: Grote Serie, 69, 78, 144.
2. A.A. Fokker, *Onderzoek naar den aard van de epidemische en contagieuse ziekten die vroeger in Zeeland geheerscht hebben* (Middelburg, 1860), pp.90-1; Leo Noordegraaf and Gerrit Valk, *De gave Gods. De pest in Holland vanaf de late middeleeuwen* (Bergen, 1988), p.152ff.
3. See successively Z.W. Sneller, 'Handel en verkeer in het Beneden-Maasgebied tot het eind der zestiende eeuw', *Nederlandsche Historiebladen*, II (1939), 341-72; T.L.M. Thurlings, *De Maashandel van Venlo en Roermond in de 16e eeuw, 1473-1572* (Amsterdam, 1949); P.G. Bos, *Het Groningsche gild- en stapelrecht tot de Reductie in 1594* (Groningen, 1904); and *idem*, 'Het Groningsche gild- en stapelrecht na de Reductie in 1594', in *Historische Avonden* (Groningen, 1907).
4. Gemeentearchief [GA] Schoonhoven, Stadsarchief no. 909 (2), cf. 948-951; GA Gouda, OA no. 2349.
5. See for example the extensive argument made against village markets by Alkmaar and Purmerend in 1739 (GA Alkmaar, Stadsarchief vóór 1815, no. 1911).
6. See T.S. Theissen, *Centraal gezag en Friese vrijheid* (Groningen, 1907), pp.318-19.
7. An article similar to this could have been written about the conflicts and discussions between the towns and villages over rural industry. The struggle against rural industry has received more attention in modern Dutch historiography than the opposition to trade in

the countryside (with the exception of retail trade in beer, wine, and distilled spirits). It is possible that an early monograph on the subject set the tone: E.C.G. Brünner, *De order op de buitennering van 1531* (Utrecht, 1918). Also see T.S. Jansma, 'Het economisch overwicht van de laat-middeleeuwse stad t.a.v. haar agrarisch ommeland, in het bijzonder toegelicht met de verhouding tussen Leiden en Rijnland', in T.S. Jansma, *Tekst en uitleg* (The Hague, 1974), pp.35-53.

8. For an extensive and annotated bibliography on concrete markets, see Leo Noordegraaf, *Atlas van de Nederlandse marktsteden* (Utrecht/Antwerpen/Amsterdam, 1985), pp.214-19.

9. I have not included the complicated legal problems here (cf. J.L. van der Gouw, 'Schieland als koloniaal gebied van Rotterdam', *Rotterdams Jaarboekje*, V (1977), 235-9; P. Leupen, *Philip of Leyden: A Fourteenth Century Jurist. A Study of his Life and Treatise 'De cura reipublicae et sorte principantis'* (The Hague/Zwolle, 1981), 89N-90N; and J. Fox, 'De ontwikkeling van Gorinchem's stedelijke autonomie in de middeleeuwen', *Holland*, I (1969), 166.

10. G. van Herwijnen, 'Stad en land in het graafschap Holland en Zeeland in de dertiende eeuw', in *De Hollandse stad in de dertiende eeuw* (ed.. J.M. Baart, et. al., Muiderberg, 1988) p.19; Dick E.H. de Boer, '"Op weg naar volwassenheid". De ontwikkeling van produktie en consumptie in de Hollandse en Zeeuwse steden in de dertiende eeuw', *ibid.*, p.36.

11. In the towns in Holland a *stadsheer* was sometimes empowered to grant rights in the areas of trade and markets (see P.H.D. Leupen, 'Heer en stad, stad en heer in de dertiende eeuw', in *De Hollandse stad, op. cit*, pp.14-15). For the specific situation in Friesland, where initially there was no sovereign, see M.P. van Buytenen, *Frieslands middeleeuwsche marktrechten* (Leeuwarden, 1965), p.6.

12. In 1298 Beverwijk received with its town charter the right to hold two free annual fairs. The village is alleged to have received the right to hold a weekly market from the Count in 1276. (N.J.J. Scholtens, *Uit het verleden van Midden-Kennemerland* (The Hague, 1947), pp.111-12.). In 1270 Schiedam obtained the right to a free annual fair (H. Brugmans and C.H. Peters, *Oud-Nederlandsche steden in haar ontstaan, groei en ontwikkeling* (Leiden, n.d.), pp.170-1.

13. For the different meanings of the concept 'free', see Noordegraaf, *Atlas*, pp.43-4. On annual fairs, see Robert Feenstra, 'Les foires aux Pays-Bas septentrionaux', in *La Foire* (Brussels, 1953), pp.209-39.

14. Van Herwijnen, 'Stad en land', p.24.

15. M. S. Pols, *Westfriesche stadrechten* (The Hague, 1888), I, p.22ff.

16. GA Alkmaar, Stadsarchief vóór 1815, no. 1902. See no. 22, fol. 174v. For an interpretation which is to the point, see W.A. Fasel, *Alkmaar in het drijfzand* (Alkmaar, 1979), p.55.

17. The staple rights of these towns not only involved transit trade, but also required the surrounding countryside to use their market. See note 3 and note 26. For the distinction between the two, see O. van Rees, *Geschiedenis der staathuishoudkunde in Nederland tot het einde der achttiende eeuw* (Utrecht, 1865), p.62ff. I have borrowed the term 'regional staple rights' from J.F. Niermeyer, *De wording van onze volkshuishouding. Hoofdlijnen uit de economische geschiedenis der Noordelijke Nederlanden in de Middeleeuwen* (The Hague, 1946), p.97.

18. W.S. Unger, *De levensmiddelenvoorziening der Hollandsche steden in de middeleeuwen* (Amsterdam, 1916), pp.22-3.

19. J.L. van der Gouw, 'Het ambacht Voorschoten', *Zuid-Hollandse Studiën*, V (1956), 47. Cf. De Boer, 'Op weg naar volwassenheid', p.35.

20. H.M. Brokken, *Het ontstaan van de Hoekse en Kabeljauwse twisten* (Zutphen, 1982), p.21; D.E.H. de Boer, *Graaf en grafiek. Sociale en economische ontwikkelingen in het middeleeuwse 'Noordholland' tussen ± 1345 en ± 1415* (Leiden, 1978), p.320; Frans van Mieris, *Groot Charterboek der Graaven van Holland, van Zeeland en Heeren van Vriesland* (Leiden, 1754), II, p.688; R.P. Goetsch, *Schoorl. Een mooi en rustig dorp met een rijk verleden* (Alkmaar, n.d.), p.43; J. van de Waal and F.O. Vervoorn, *Beschrijving van het eiland Goedereede en Overflakkee, zijn wording en zijn voortbestaan tot op heden* (Sommelsdijk, 1895), p.412; L. Noordegraaf, 'Het platteland van Holland in de zestiende eeuw. Anachronismen, modelgebruik en traditionele bronnenkritiek', *Economisch- en Sociaal-Historisch Jaarboek*, XXXXVIII (1985), 13; Resoluties Staten van Holland 27-2-1603; 15-3-1605; 4-11-1606; 19-2-1609; 16-7-1617.

21. See note 9; cf. note 11.

22. E. Wiersum and B.M. de Jonge van Ellemeet, 'Rechten van Schouwen en Duiveland', *Verslagen en Mededeelingen van de Vereeniging tot uitgave der bronnen van het oude vaderlandsche recht*, V (1909), 499; *Boergoensche charters 1428-1482* (ed. P.A.S. van Limburg Brouwer, Amsterdam/The Hague, 1869), p.50; R. Fruin, 'Ordonnantie van Willem V, hertog van Kleef, voor de heerlijkheid Breskens', *Verslagen en Mededeelingen*, V (1909), 22-3.
23. See notes 14 and 15; J. Bergman, *Schagen door de eeuwen heen* (Den Helder, 1965), p.18.
24. *Privilegien en handvesten der Stede en des Eilands van Texel* (Amsterdam, 1745), p.8; the town privileges are of a later date (pp.21-5); G. 't Hart, *Historische beschrijving der vrije en hoge heerlijkheid van Heenvliet* (n.p., 1949), p.450 (the privilege was confirmed two months later by the sovereign).
25. To make it even more complicated, rights were often only granted for a certain kind of market. In the sixteenth century, for example, a considerable number of annual fairs were granted by the sovereign for the leather trade (see for example, GA Alkmaar, Stadsarchief vóór 1815, no. 1908). This does not mean that other kinds of products were not sold there or that other kinds of markets were not held in those places.
26. Cf. De Boer, 'Op weg naar volwassenheid', p.34-5. For the origin and the growth of towns and the role of urban privileges in this, see Jaap Kruisheer, 'Stadsrechtbeoorkondiging en stedelijke ontwikkeling' in *De Hollandse stad in de dertiende eeuw*, pp.44-5, 51.
27. See note 17.
28. Unger, *De levensmiddelenvoorziening*, p.175ff.; T.S. Jansma, 'De betekenis van Dordrecht en Rotterdam omstreeks het midden der zestiende eeuw', in *Tekst en uitleg*, p.147. In 1377 Dordrecht had received the right to a mandatory turf staple for the countryside (see note 61 for the politics involved).
29. Unger, *De levensmiddelenvoorziening*, p.180ff.
30. Brokken, *Het ontstaan van de Hoekse en Kabeljauwse twisten*, p.50; Theissen, *Centraal gezag en Friese vrijheid*, p.307; GA Alkmaar, Stadsarchief vóór 1815, no. 1911; Resoluties Staten van Holland 2-1-1581; 9-7-1588; 27-10-1601.
31. The *Order op de buitennering* (see note 7) is also explained in such a way that it includes a prohibition against trade in the countryside. For actions by Amsterdam against the unloading of ships in Durgerdam, see T.S. Jansma, 'Scheepvaartpolitiek in de tweede helft der vijftiende eeuw', *Jaarboek Amstelodamum*, XXXXVII (1955), 13-14.
32. *Groot Placaet-boeck* (ed. Cau, et. al., The Hague, 1658-1770), II, p.2053; Aert van der Goes, *Register van alle die dachvaerden* .... (n.p., n.d.), I, p.125; Resoluties Staten van Holland 20-12-1602, 10-1-1603, and 3-3-1603; *Besondere privilegien ende handvesten, verleent aen d'inwoonders van Westzaanden en Crommenie* (Zaandam, 1661), pp.169-73, 225-41; Resoluties Staten van Holland 1613 (43); 4/20-3-1614 (58/9); 2-2-1641; 6-12-1668; 5-4-1669.
33. T.S. Theissen, *De regeering van Karel V in de Noordelijke Nederlanden* (Amsterdam, 1912), pp.151-2. During the Republic rural drinking continued to be a point of concern for the towns: see for example, J.L. van Dalen, *Geschiedenis van Dordrecht* (Dordrecht, 1931-3), I, pp.267-8.
34. Leo Noordegraaf, *Hollands welvaren? Levensstandaard in Holland 1450-1650* (Bergen, 1985), p.48; Theissen, *Centraal gezag en Friese vrijheid*, p.307ff.
35. This could also occur within the town.
36. Jacob Honig Jzn. Jr., 'Een langdurige strijd', *Zaanlandsch Jaarboek* (1932), 74; Van Rees, *Geschiedenis der staathuishoudkunde*, p.169. This so-called peddling also took place in the towns on a large scale and also led to many regulations, often at the instigation of the shopkeepers and retailers (cf. C. Wiskerke, *De afschaffing der gilden in Nederland* (Amsterdam, 1938), pp.135, 216).
37. Several examples: Sloten and Osdorp in 1465 (*Generale Privilegien ende hantvesten van Kennemer-landt ende Kennemer-gevolgh* (The Hague, 1652), pp.176-7); cf. Van Mieris, *Groot Charterboek* (Leiden, 1756), IV, p.849; Schoorl in 1565 (Oudarchief, no. 13, fol. 75); Assendelft at least since 1441 (*Hantvesten ende privilegien, mitsgaders keuren en ordonnantien van Assendelft* (Amsterdam, 1768), pp.35-6, cf. pp.150-1); Warmenhuizen in 1584 (Oudarchief, no. 83, 21 July 1584); Resolutie Staten van Holland 7-3-1597 (here it is specified for a large part of Holland, village by village, whether there was a weigh-house; and if so, from when it dated and by whom it was granted).
38. See for example 'Placcaet, beroerende Wagen van Vrieslandt, Kennemerlant, Aemstellandt, Waterlandt, Zeevanck ende Goylandt', in *Generale Privilegien*, pp.92-4.
39. J.J. Spahr van der Hoek and O. Postma, *Geschiedenis van de Friese landbouw* (Leeuwarden, 1952), pp.379-80.

40. Resoluties Staten van Holland 26-9-1570; 13-3-1585; 7-5-1585; 7-3-1597; 22-1-1642; 19-3-1653; 28-11-1668; 22-2-1669; 20-3-1681. See also Eduard van Zurck, *Codex Batavus* (Leiden, 1764), pp.465-6. These actions in part run parallel with those mentioned in note 32. See L. Noordegraaf, 'De waag: schakel in de pre-industriële economie', in *Het waagstuk: de geschiedenis van waaggebouwen en wegen in Nederland* (ed. C.H. Slechte and N. Herweijer, Amsterdam, 1990), pp.11-25.
41. *Handvesten, Privilegien, Octroyen, Vry- en Gerechtigheden, aan de stad Haerlem en haare burgers verleend* (Haarlem, 1751), pp.549-50.
42. GA Alkmaar, Stadsarchief vóór 1815, no. 2268; Collectie Aanwinsten, no. 86, fol. 714.
43. GA Alkmaar, Collectie Aanwinsten, no. 19, fol. 721-33.
44. In addition to these inter-urban conflicts motivated by the struggle to control the countryside, there were extensive economy-related problems between the towns concerning the infrastructure of waterways, bridges and roads, which are not discussed here. See for example J.L. van der Gouw, *De landscheidingen tussen Delfland, Rijnland en Schieland* (Hilversum, 1987), pp.43-4; J. Tersteeg, 'Een bijdrage tot de geschiedenis der binnenlandsche vaart', *Bijdragen voor Vaderlandsche Geschiedenis en Oudheidkunde*, 4, III (1903), 148-215; H.C. Hazewinkel, 'De heerlijkheid Hogenban en de commerciële rivaliteit tusschen Delft en Rotterdam', *Bijdragen voor Vaderlandsche Geschiedenis en Oudheidkunde*, IV (1934), 217-25, 227.
45. See note 3 and R.P. Cleveringa Pzn., *Ontwikkelingslijnen van het rechtsbestel der stad Appingedam in het bijzonder vóór de 18e eeuw* (Groningen, 1927), pp.12-14.
46. Unger, *De levensmiddelenvoorziening*, pp.177-8.
47. The problems involving transit probably led to larger conflicts, which could be explained on the basis of the greater economic importance of this trade and, in a number of cases, the related political problems. See H.C.H. Moquette, 'De strijd op economisch gebied tusschen Rotterdam en Dordrecht', *Tijdschrift voor Geschiedenis*, XXXXI (1926), 40-63; J.F. Niermeyer, 'Een vijftiende-eeuwse handelsoorlog: Dordrecht contra de bovenlandse steden, 1442-1445', *Bijdragen en Mededelingen van het Historisch Genootschap*, LXIIII (1948), 1-59.
48. The legal status of the regional staple rights was disputed in particular. Groningen had appropriated the staple right itself (Bos, *Het Groningsche gild- en stapelrecht na de Reductie*, p.233).
49. *Hedendaagsche Historie of tegenwoordige staat van alle volkeren* (Amsterdam, 1788), vol. XXV-3, p.268.
50. C. van der Woude, *Kronijcke van Alcmaer met sijn dorpen* (Alkmaar, 1645), p.80; Gysbert Boomkamp, *Alkmaar en deszelfs geschiedenissen* (Rotterdam, 1747), p.376; GA Alkmaar, Stadsarchief vóór 1815, no. 1921.
51. GA Alkmaar, Stadsarchief vóór 1815, no. 2277, 2278; Collectie Aanwinsten, no. 14, fol. 220 ff. The history of the conflict in 1634 dates from 1618.
52. The concept of urban mercantilism is also used. In 1865 Van Rees typified the treatment of the countryside by the cities 'as the colonies were treated by the motherland in the colonial system' (*Geschiedenis der staathuishoudkunde*). For the following see *Stedelijke naijver: de betekenis van interstedelijke conflicten in de geschiedenis* (ed. P.B.M. Blaas and J. van Herwaarden, The Hague, 1986); and W.P. Blockmans, 'Voracious States and Obstructing Cities', *Theory and Society*, XVIII (1989), 133-55.
53. P.W. Klein, 'De Nederlandse handelspolitiek in de tijd van het mercantilisme: Een nieuwe kijk op een oude kwestie?', in *Tijdschrift voor Geschiedenis*, CII (1989), 205; or his article in this volume. For exceptions to the free trade policy in international trade, see Leo Noordegraaf, 'Dearth, Plague and Trade. Economy and Politics in the Northern Netherlands, 15th-19th centuries', *Economic and Social History in the Netherlands*, I (1989), 49-66.
54. C. van der Kieft, 'De stedelijke autonomie in het graafschap Holland gedurende de middeleeuwen', *Holland*, I (1969), 100-3.
55. Of course there were provincial variations, caused in particular by the different position of the sovereign, which cannot be treated here.
56. See note 30.
57. See note 37.
58. Certain towns could also ally themselves with the countryside against other towns and the sovereign. Cf. J.W. Marsilje, 'Het Haarlemse klerkambt in de 15e eeuw', and J. Scheurkogel, 'Opstand in Holland', in *De Nederlanden in de late middeleeuwen* (ed. D.E.H. de Boer and J.W. Marsilje, Utrecht, 1987), pp.192, 364-5, 369.
59. Kornelis van Alkemade and P. van der Schelling, *Beschryving van de stad Brielle, en den*

Lande van Voorn (Rotterdam, 1729), pp.39-40; H.P.J. Jansen, 'Holland-Zeeland 1433-1482', in *Algemene Geschiedenis der Nederlanden*, IV (Haarlem, 1980), p.290.
60. See note 32.
61. Moquette, 'De strijd op economisch gebied', p.41; Unger, *De levensmiddelenvoorziening*, pp.176-7. Also see the revocation of the right to a weekly market in Amsterdam in 1304 by William III (J. Wagenaar, *Amsterdam in zyne opkomst, aanwas, geschiedenissen* (Amsterdam, 1759), II, p.107.
62. Theissen, *De regeering van Karel V*, p.153. H.F.K. van Nierop, *Van Ridders tot regenten. De Hollandse adel in de zestiende en de eerste helft van de zeventiende eeuw* (Diemen, 1984), p.156.
63. For an example see note 33. In my opinion, the *Order op de buitennering* (see note 7) must also be interpreted from a political point of view.
64. Van der Gouw, 'Schieland als koloniaal gebied', p.240.
65. See note 36; GA Alkmaar, Stadsarchief vóór 1815, no. 1924.
66. *Besondere privilegien*, pp.86-8.
67. Cf. W. van Ravesteyn jr., *Onderzoekingen over de economische en sociale ontwikkeling van Amsterdam gedurende de 16de en het eerste kwart der 17de eeuw* (Amsterdam, 1906), p.28.
68. *Besondere privilegien*, p.225. With respect to the relation between the town, nobility, and countryside, it must be taken into account that the relation could be somewhat different outside Holland; see for example, S.W. Verstegen, *Gegoede ingezetenen. Jonkers en geërfden op de Veluwe tijdens Ancien Regime, Revolutie en Restauratie (1650-1830)* (Amsterdam, 1989), pp.47, 101, 103.
69. Helga Danner, *Van Schermeer-water tot Schermeer-land. Perikelen bij een 17de eeuwse bedijking* (n.p., 1983), p.14; Van Nierop, *Van ridders tot regenten*, p.161.
70. Van der Gouw, 'Schieland als koloniaal gebied', p.241.
71. Van Zurck, *Codex Batavus*, pp.228-9, 486; *Nederlandsche Jaarboeken* (1751), 645-6 (ordinance 16-8-1751, renewal of ordinance 11-8-1656); Resoluties Staten van Holland 27-4, 20-12-1765.
72. The pull of Amsterdam, and the related declining economic activity in many other towns, with all of its consequences for the mutual balance of power, played a major role in this change (for this 'contraction' see Johan de Vries, *De economische achteruitgang der Republiek in de achttiende eeuw* (Leiden, 1968)).
73. The final word has not been said regarding the extent to which municipal autonomy already had begun to dissolve before 1795, and the nation state to grow. This is also the case for state centralism and the emancipation of the countryside; see H. Wansink, 'Holland and Six Allies: the Republic of the Seven United Provinces', in *Metropolis, Dominion and Province* (ed. J.S. Bromley and E.H. Kossmann, 1971), Britain and the Netherlands, vol. IV, pp.133-55; Jojada Verrips and Ton Zwaan, 'De mannen van het groene laken. Burokraten, boeren en staatsvormingsprocessen in Nederland (1795-1815) en de E(E)G (1945-1979)', *Symposion*, I (1979), 28-36).
74. GA Alkmaar, Stadsarchief vóór 1815, no. 337.
75. This is also the case for international trade at the moment, but before 1965 this was at least a topic which received much attention (see Klein, 'De Nederlandse handelspolitiek', pp.189-90).
76. The intellectual history of the relation between town and countryside, which has not been considered here, is also of interest, and was already a subject of discussion in the fourteenth century (see Leupen, *Philip of Leyden*, p.232).

2

The Tudor State and Economic Problems

Peter Ramsey

Numerous scholars have addressed the problem of whether successive Tudor monarchs and their ministers had an 'economic policy' and if so, how far it was successful. A broad consensus can probably be said to exist now among sixteenth-century specialists, and this seems unlikely to be upset dramatically in the immediate future.[1] It is not likely that a great new deposit of central records will suddenly be discovered, allowing new shafts of light into the minds of the central characters, so discussion of 'policy' is likely to go on revolving round the same long-familiar and well-studied documents in the PRO, the British Library and a few great private collections. On the question of implementation it is equally unlikely that some undreamed-of statistical material on Tudor trade and industry will suddenly appear to answer our questions and permit us to set up our counter-factual models of the Tudor economy. The only likely hope is that more detailed studies of particular geographical areas or particular trades and industries will gradually modify our present picture.

What was the 'state' in sixteenth-century England? Most historians working in the period would probably wish to avoid the word – just as we avoid 'policy' - and substitute 'government'. For many purposes government means first and foremost the monarch, but not perhaps for ours. It is not clear that any Tudor monarch, with the possible exception of Henry VII, took any great personal interest in trade or industry, and Henry VII's reputation in this respect seems to rest rather heavily on an over-worked phrase of Francis Bacon written a century later. Henry VIII has been partly rescued by Scarisbrick from his former reputation as a generally idle king, but his energy was admittedly fitful and selective and his interest concentrated heavily on foreign relations, religion and patronage.[2] Concern for more mundane matters was left to his councillors, and this pattern seems to be broadly true of his successors.

Under the monarch the Council or Privy Council was the main executive organ of government. It played a significant role in the formulation of policy, and was the main but not the sole initiator of legislation. It was necessarily concerned with economic matters when these presented themselves as urgent problems, particularly problems of law and order. However, it would not seem that very many Tudor Councillors had a strong and continuing interest in such matters – with the conspicuous exceptions of Wolsey and Cromwell under Henry VIII, Thomas Smith under Edward VI, and William Cecil under both Edward VI and Elizabeth I.[3]

Parliament was not properly part of government, of course, having no executive function and meeting only intermittently. But it could on occasion thwart or modify significantly the legislation initiated by monarch and council, as it did with Cromwell's grandiose Poor Law scheme of 1536 or the Statute of Apprentices in 1563.[4] It could have a similar but less publicized impact when especially vocal and energetic MPs secured the inclusion of exemption clauses for particular areas or bodies of people, sometimes with the effect of emasculating an Act to near futility.

Recently we have been taught by David Starkey to look to another influence in policy-making, namely the Court, or more particularly the personal attendants on the king, who could whisper in his ear at intimate moments (including some very intimate moments), and perhaps more importantly could allow or deny access to the king for those seeking an audience.[5] Starkey has highlighted a hitherto neglected subject, and has made out a persuasive if not conclusive case for the importance of Henry VIII's personal entourage in political and religious issues. Clearly Wolsey and Cromwell thought it important to control its membership in order to preserve their own positions and secure continuing support for their policies. But whether the influence of courtiers was at all significant in economic matters (apart, obviously, from patronage) is not at all clear, since affiliations cannot easily be traced. Women attendants of Elizabeth I were unlikely to play as informed and positive a political role as their male predecessors under Henry. But both they and the Court more widely defined could no doubt play a role in directing the flow of royal patronage, and this may have been important in the latter years of Elizabeth, after about 1585, when the granting of patents and monopolies seems to have got increasingly out of hand.[6] Beyond this rather tentative speculation one has to say that Starkey has raised provocative doubts and anxieties without, as yet, the means to resolve them.

Outside the Court and the royal administration there were other informal advisers and lobbyists, who may have influenced ministers in economic matters. These could be relatively disinterested advisers like Starkey and Morrison under Cromwell or John Hales and others – for a long time mistakenly thought to constitute a 'Commonwealth Party' - under Protector Somerset. Or they could be highly interested parties promoting a very particular policy or seeking a lucrative job or monopoly for themselves. In a few cases the origins of statutes or proclamations can be clearly attributed to such special pressures – for example in successive statutes for the leather industry.[7] What is disturbing is that the language of the relevant act or proclamation gives the impression of a high-minded general enactment for the common weal. How many other, less well documented measures, which we are tempted to see as the lofty 'policy' of a William Cecil, are in fact likewise the result of intrigue? Was the measure truly Cecil's own brainchild, or had he been lobbied?

With these perhaps unhelpful reservations, we have necessarily to concentrate our main attention on the Privy Council. At least formally they were the main initiators of economic measures, and it is unlikely that any measure would succeed against a firm majority of the membership and of the dominant ministers of the day. Did the Tudor Privy Council have for any length of time anything that could fairly be called an economic policy or a set of such policies?

There was undoubtedly a massive increase of government intervention in the sixteenth century compared with earlier periods. About half the statutes and proclamations of the century could be broadly defined as 'economic' in our terminology.[8] But the 'our' is important. The words 'economic' and 'economy' were not, of course, used at this time. It also seems doubtful whether the concepts existed, certainly as we understand them. It seems reasonably clear that there is no concept of 'an economy', whether national or regional, and therefore no possibility even of planning it. It is doubtful whether men of the sixteenth century could or would categorize any form of activity as 'economic' and separable from other multifarious human activities, even if governments could draw a rough and ready distinction between high matters of state and religion and lowly ones of earning a livelihood by farming, trade or handicraft. The Acts of the Privy Council certainly do not suggest any such differentiation, or indeed *any* very clear differentiation at all between items on its agenda. What we choose to separate out as economic activities were for the Councillors simply some among many of the doings of the king's or queen's subjects, which might or might not require regulating for the peace and good order of the community. Conversely subjects do not appear to have distinguished any category of economic affairs that ought to be free from interference – though of course they might protest vehemently against specific and particular interferences. It was assumed on both sides that the crown had the right to regulate all kinds of activity whenever the good health of the commonwealth demanded it. Any dispute would be on the merits of the particular case.

Since it is difficult to avoid using the word 'economic', we must continue to do so, but its use does have an unavoidable distorting effect, and to some extent imposes on the sixteenth century a twentieth-century vocabulary and pattern of thought. It is fairly obvious that within the sixteenth-century pattern of thought no 'economic policy' in the sense of a grand strategy for managing a national economy was likely or even possible. Probably most historians of the period would fairly readily agree to this proposition, and would also agree that sixteenth-century governments were not pursuing a doctrine known as 'Mercantilism'. It can still be asked, however, whether sixteenth-century governments showed enough consistency in their handling of what we call economic problems to justify our talking of policies with a small 'p'. Here perhaps a case may be argued, but with the reservation that the apparent consistency may in reality be a consistency in handling other non-economic problems and priorities, which happen to have economic implications and consequences.

What were the overriding priorities for Tudor monarchs and their ministers? Defence of the realm was obviously at the top of the list. For most of the period defence meant just that, if you allow the idea of a pre-emptive strike or expedition. (With Henry VIII one would have to stretch the word further to include the warlike pursuit of 'just claims' - whether to 'lost lands' in France or suzerainty over Scotland.) Effective defence required a degree of self-sufficiency in war materials, the encouragement of domestic arms and gunpowder manufacture, and correspondingly bans on the export of war materials such as arms and horses, and specie which might fund foreign mercenaries. The Wealden iron industry almost certainly profited from and expanded with the war demands of the 1540s, and the mainly abortive copper-prospecting of the 1560s was probably inspired at least in part by military needs.[9]

The maintenance of law and order came second only to national defence, and the suppression or prevention of even minor riots and disorders was vital in the absence of a police force and standing army. Minor affrays could easily escalate into major rebellions, as happened twice in 1549. Food shortages were a dangerous potential cause of riot, especially when perhaps half the population of a major town or city was living on the very edge of subsistence, and when riot was seen by the poor as a semi-legitimate form of protest at hunger brought about by profiteering middlemen; hence the Privy Council's recurrent urgent concern for grain supplies in bad harvest years. 'Order' also implied the maintenance of a deferential hierarchic society. One minor aspect of this was Elizabeth's and Cecil's obsessive concern with the dress of their subjects, ideally to be graded in twelve categories according to a statute of 1531, corresponding to social status. This concern produced nine proclamations in Elizabeth's reign alone, and an intriguing attempt under Mary to combine sumptuary regulation with the establishment of a national militia.[10] More generally the government showed a consistent preference for social and economic organizations that assigned men to masters and tied them to a particular occupation and place. It was far better to have a work force tidily organized under qualified masters in town guilds than straggling in the countryside where they were notoriously prone to disorder and provided especially poor-quality recruits to the militia.

Protection of the poor from exploitation was not only a way to anticipate violence, but also derived from the crown's traditional duty to do justice to all its subjects. This was easier as long as monarchs and ministers shared the assumptions and prejudices of subjects on such issues as the 'just price' and their suspicions of all kinds of dealers and middlemen.

The raising of revenue to support these various duties – and to maintain a proper display of royal magnificence – was an obvious preoccupation of government, and financial problems feature particularly prominently in the Acts of the Privy Council, partly because such discussions ended with specific warrants for payment that were formally minuted. A concern for revenue implied some concern for the general economic health of the community, or at least the more easily taxable sectors of it. This meant especially overseas trade, taxed quite efficiently through a long-established customs service, and providing revenue that was effectively free from parliamentary control. The efficiency of tax-collection was reinforced if a particular trade was conducted by a monopoly company, like the Merchant Adventurers, whose organized cloth-shipments had the effect of policing the trade and making smuggling and tax evasion more difficult.[11] An organized group of merchants could also be more easily approached for loans. In general, merchant companies could expect a degree of favour for fiscal reasons. The favour, however, also brought risks. A trade could be killed by over-taxation, as happened to the wool merchants of the Staple of Calais in the later Middle Ages, when the tax rate rose to 30 per cent on raw wool. This mistake was not repeated for other trades in the sixteenth century, but merchants could still suffer from government fiscalism through the erratic issue of licences and monopolies, while in 1558 the Merchant Adventurers found themselves called upon to settle the crown's debts in Antwerp at considerable cost to themselves – all the more irritatingly in that this manoeuvre had been contrived by Thomas Gresham, one of their own leading members.

The various preoccupations and priorities of government could both overlap and conflict. In case of conflict the demands of defence and law and order would probably be the overriding ones, as when justice and order required the assured supply of grain to a local population, but the needs of an expeditionary force came first. What we could perceive as purely economic problems would have low priority, and would in any case rarely present themselves as such. They would be seen rather as some among many overlapping and competing social and policing problems requiring *ad hoc* solutions, and as such part of the Council's day-to-day job of maintaining a peaceful and well ordered common wealth.

When the government did decide on specific measures, its means of enforcement were meagre and dubious. As in other contemporary monarchies there was only a thin scattering of paid local officers, and these were mainly concerned with the customs system or the administration of the crown lands. The Tudors were overwhelmingly dependent in the localities on the unpaid services of the Justices of the Peace. In spite of a constantly increasing workload there was no shortage of volunteers, and since the office carried some local prestige the crown did have some disciplinary control over them. In extreme cases they could be dismissed outright, with great loss of face in their county, or alternatively placed below their expectations on the annual list of precedence, a somewhat less severe blow to their pride. However, some JPs were too prestigious to be active members of the commission (for example, Privy Councillors who might nominally serve in every county where they had lands or an interest), others were simply idle, and yet others were found by occasional inquiries to be blatantly unsuitable and unsatisfactory. Hence the real work fell on a hard core of conscientious JPs who might comprise as little as half the commission.

Scepticism about the JPs' performance has in the past emphasized mainly the factor of self-interest: how could it be expected that they would implement anti-enclosure laws or assess wages fairly when this went against their own interests as landowners and employers? There is obviously something in this, but it is possible to feel that much more weight should be put on the sheer size of their workload and on the choices that they were forced to make between competing claims. Through the whole century there was a progressive and massive increase in their duties, with every second statute adding something new. It was probably not physically possible to attend meticulously and continuously to all these, especially in the last decades of the century. This would be especially true of economic legislation, the enforcement of which demanded painstaking and sustained effort over long periods of time. To enforce the apprenticeship regulations or the statutory standards in the woollen cloth industry meant much more work than the occasional hunt for suspect Catholics or a round-up of the local vagabonds. In a general way, moreover, the JPs had much the same problem of competing priorities as did the Privy Councillors at a higher level. Their first concern was to keep the peace in their locality, at a time when violence was more common than today, and when unlicensed ale-houses seemed to give growing and especial cause for concern. They also had to put down crime, which likewise was probably more common than today, though not dramatically so. Economic hardship in the last years of the century would tend to aggravate both sets of problems. Some JPs would set their priorities differently from one another. In Norfolk under Elizabeth there seems to have been a discernible division between those who saw it was their first duty to serve the Queen in such matters as mustering troops and collecting taxes, and others who championed local interests and amenities, if need be against the instructions coming from the Council.[12] And even within the secondary field of social and economic legislation there might be conflicts of interest: was a JP to enforce strictly the wage and settlement provisions of the 1563 Act if this produced a labour shortage in his own county? As a result we cannot expect that every law was meticulously enforced, and although the JPs' shortcomings are documented fully only for recusancy and the apprenticeship regulations,[13] we must suspect that their shortcomings in those areas were typical rather than exceptional.

The efforts of the JPs were supplemented erratically by those of informers. In the penal acts of the period, informers were increasingly encouraged to prosecute offenders, by rewarding them with a share of the consequent fine or forfeited goods. Some made a living from pursuing miscellaneous offences, while others acquired monopoly rights by patent for the pursuit of specific ones. A growing body of complaint in and out of parliament, as well as numerous actions in the law courts, attest their activity. A well documented case-history of the 1530s suggests that it was not easy to make a living in this way.[14] But the story can take account only of formal actions and official forfeitures, and not of unofficial blackmail and compounding. It is likely that informers could acquire an income by threatening action against their victims rather than taking it, a potent threat if the action was to be pursued in a distant court at considerable trouble and expense to the defendant. This particular abuse was curtailed by statutes of 1576 and 1589 insisting that actions be brought in a local court, and with a twelve-months limitation. But the volume of complaint does suggest that informers did make an impact, and exerted a real pressure, even if the complaints in part arose from the sordid nature of their trade rather than the weight of its effects.

In spite of continuing doubts about JPs, informers and patentees, current opinion is probably less sceptical than it once was of their efficacy. Their combined activities, even if sporadic or half-hearted, did raise the risks and possible expenses of those who contravened statutes and proclamations. Sixteenth-century governments cannot realistically have expected 95 per cent compliance rates, such as we might today consider normal. Although they could hardly be expected to say so, and indeed vehemently protested the contrary, those governments may well have felt that 50 per cent or less was well worth having, and much better than nothing at all.

A few suggestions may be offered about certain specific areas of activity where there existed some form of government action, and some even more tentative ones about its effects. We may start with overseas trade, and more especially the export trade in woollen cloth and the industry that supplied it. From the beginning Henry VII's government gave diplomatic backing to the London cloth-exporters, as indeed he did to those trading with Spain and Italy, though his diplomacy was probably more concerned with the securing and recognition of his new dynasty than with the promotion of trade for its own sake. The security of the English merchants trading in the Netherlands was formally established by the Magnus Intercursus of 1496, though an aggressive attempt to improve on its terms ten years later proved unsuccessful. The favourable terms extracted in 1496 were certainly a useful basis for the Adventurers, but it is arguable that these were due as much to the merchants' strong bargaining position at that date as to royal influence. For another twenty years the Adventurers were able to extort ever-increasing advantages from the municipality of Antwerp, using as a lever the threat of removing themselves and their cloths *en bloc*. They finished up as the most privileged of the foreign merchant groups in Antwerp, having a position there comparable to that held by the Hansards in the London Steelyard – more favoured than native merchants. After about 1520, however, the threat of mass departure became increasingly unrealistic and by 1542 was ineffective as a threat. Nor could Henry VIII, anxious above all for the political and military support of Charles V for his French and Scottish campaigns, extort any better terms by high-level diplomacy. Henry VII's reign had also seen the formal recognition of the Adventurers as a monopoly company with exclusive rights in the Netherlands market. They had, however, also been compelled to moderate their demands for a prohibitive entrance fee, effectively excluding provincial merchants from the trade, and this had been fixed at the moderate level of ten marks, later lowered to five pounds. For the first half of the century this remained the situation. In practice the richer London merchants enjoyed a near-monopoly, but it was not total.[15]

The crisis in the cloth trade of 1550-51 allowed the London oligarchs to strengthen their position with government support. The dominance of a small inner ring of very rich merchants had in any case steadily grown since 1496, both in their share of the cloths handled and in their political control of the company. Their preferred explanation of what had gone wrong in 1550 was that the market had been spoiled by a multitude of inexperienced merchants and by the poor quality of too much of the cloth – the 'naughtiness of the making'.[16] (There is some evidence to support the latter contention, but the former is implausible.) Shortly after these allegations the Adventurers were able to raise the entrance fee to the prohibitive level of one hundred marks, thus squeezing out all but the richest provincial merchants. The Cloth Act of 1552 also seems to have been a response to their views. Although it was only one in a series of such acts to maintain standards in the cloth industry, this was by far the most detailed and specific of the century, cataloguing twenty-two distinct makes, and for the first time specifying a minimum weight for each, in addition to a minimum length and breadth.[17] The link between merchant opinion and government legislation seems in this case fairly clear; one is left to wonder how many other similar acts were so inspired, rather than being due to spontaneous government concern for high manufacturing standards in England's principal industry. At the same time there occurred a temporary suspension of the special privileges of the Hansard merchants in England – long a source of grievance. The English merchants do not seem to have been able to take immediate advantage of this. The slump in cloth exports after 1551 almost exactly matches that in the Hanse's normal export, and recovery occurred with the restoration of their privileges under Mary.

It would not be fair to suggest that the Council always favoured the merchants against the clothiers. It was prepared on occasion to insist – with uncertain success – that the merchants continue to buy cloths in time of slump so as to ensure continued employment in the industry. It was likewise not in the merchants' interest that statutorily they were bound to export one fully finished cloth in every ten, in a period when English cloth-finishing techniques were so inferior to Netherlands ones that the finished articles actually fetched lower prices than the unfinished on the Antwerp market. The statute was, however, commonly mitigated by licences exempting individual merchants from it. Similarly the Council's willing acceptance of substantial numbers of immigrant Flemish weavers in the 1560s may have been due to a genuine desire to improve quality and diversity in the industry, which it achieved in the form of the New Draperies. But even this was a policy more likely to appeal immediately to the merchants than the clothiers and cloth-workers, with whom the immigrants were in obvious competition.

In the latter half of the century the Council continued to show its preference for trades organized and handled by monopoly companies, this being no doubt also the preference of the merchants and perhaps unavoidable in sixteenth-century conditions. A reasonable defence of this policy could perhaps be made in the case of new enterprises to develop new markets – in Russia, Morocco, the Levant or the East Indies, just as a case could be made for monopolies where a genuinely new invention or process was given temporary protection to establish itself. It is not so clear why the established and powerful Merchant Adventurers should continue to need such protection, at least after they were safely resettled at Hamburg, especially when their own attitude was manifestly exclusive *vis-à-vis* provincial merchants and cautiously restrictive among their own members. It is not surprising that they met increasing criticism and faced increasing (technically illegal) trading competition from interlopers.

The overall impression is that – at least after Henry VII's reign – the government followed and supported merchant initiatives (when political circumstances permitted), rather than creating or directing them, consistently supporting monopoly companies and giving them diplomatic backing where possible. It did not attempt to use the tariff system to encourage or discourage particular imports or exports. (The high duty on exports of raw wool and imports of French wines was probably a historical accident rather than a calculation.) Specifically it did not do anything through the

34

customs tariff to check the import of foreign luxuries and trifles, however economically and morally undesirable these were, though a few undesirables were banned in 1563. In 1600 the export trade was more diversified in its outlets and in its products, though the market in north-western Europe still heavily predominated, and even with the growth of the New Draperies it was still woollen cloth of various kinds that made up the bulk of the goods sent overseas. As contrasted with the situation in 1500, the trade was now overwhelmingly in the hands of English merchants, and the obnoxious Hanse privileges had been finally abolished, though this probably reflected the weakness of traditional competitors rather than the strength of the English government and merchants. Compared with the recent performance of a new rival, the emergent Dutch Republic, the achievement was fairly modest.

The trade, albeit a mainly inland trade, that the government most strenuously sought to control from time to time, was the grain trade.[18] The motives here were fairly clearly the alleviation of hardship and the maintenance of law and order, rather than the direction of trade as such. Although farming efficiency improved through the century with the development of new techniques, overall production was barely keeping pace with rising population. More particularly the growth of some towns and cities, and most spectacularly of London (with a four- or five-fold rise during the century), meant more people were divorced from the land and unable to grow even a proportion of their own food. Added to this was the problem of rising unemployment and underemployment, so that an increasing number of people were very dangerously vulnerable to a bad harvest, and especially to a series of bad harvests such as that of 1595-97. The worst potential trouble-spot was clearly London, and not surprisingly the Privy Council had a special concern for the population of the capital, the most at risk and the most dangerous for law and order. This led N.S.B. Gras to put forward a thesis that the government's whole grain policy was directed in the interests of London and to the disadvantage of all other sectors of the population.[19] This thesis does not really stand up to scrutiny, however, and V. Ponko demonstrated ably in 1968 that the Council strove to safeguard the interests of all its subjects at risk, and to that end wrestled continuously with a complicated and changing set of problems. A stream of proclamations in Elizabeth's later years sought to prevent the export of grain at times of high prices, to prevent the hoarding of it, and to ensure as far as possible its free circulation and its availability at reasonable prices to the most needy. Particularly detailed and forceful instructions were issued to the JPs in the Book of Orders or Book of Dearth in 1586. A vigorous drive was launched against some Norfolk merchants in the Star Chamber in October 1597. Scattered local evidence, where available (for Southampton and York, for instance), suggests that these instructions were vigorously acted upon by the JPs. Whether this vigour was universal is impossible to say, but *a priori* we would expect it to be. They would have shared the Council's concern for law and order and would have been acutely conscious of the visible hardship in their own counties, while the proclamations demanded a series of relatively brief enforcement drives rather than extended effort. Co-operation would have been readily forthcoming from the great majority of local people, while the immediate targets were allegedly greedy, profiteering middlemen, for whom there would have been little sympathy.

There is no way of accurately measuring the success of the policy, or of concomitant national and local efforts to relieve poverty and unemployment. In the crude sense that actual starvation on any scale was averted in London and the towns, and that there was no major riot or insurrection even in the worst hunger years, it was a success. Only in Cumbria, in the far north-west, was there apparently actual starvation in the 1590s, and in that area there was a peculiarly disastrous combination of harvest failure, too many marginal farms, and the collapse of the modest low-quality cloth industry.[20] The government reasonably deserves credit for helping to avert major disaster, though not severe hardship. Even more credit should perhaps go to the farmers of England for expanding production to make this possible, an expansion which has not always had proper recognition from historians in the past, but has now been clearly established through the work of Kerridge and others.[21]

An expansion of the fishing industry and of shipbuilding was a government concern for most of the period. In both cases a prime concern was once again national defence, since the fishing industry could supply a pool of trained seamen in time of war, and an enlarged merchant marine, more especially of large ocean-going vessels (rather than the small cross-Channel boats that dominated the Antwerp trade), likewise supplemented the navy's purpose-built warships in time of need. To stimulate fishing, the celebrated 'political Lent' was enforced in principle for the latter half of the century. Good Protestant Englishmen were required to abstain from meat on Wednesday, Friday and Saturday every week, as well as during Lent itself. In theory they were eating fish about half the days of the year, but the Acts and supporting proclamations were notoriously difficult to enforce and the real boost to the industry was no doubt somewhat less than was ideally envisaged. However, no government could realistically expect total obedience, and in practice successive Councils may have contented themselves with the thought that, again, some measure of compliance was better than none.

Efforts to encourage the building of larger ships likewise achieved only limited success. Bounties were offered for the construction of larger vessels, and the favour shown to the new monopoly trading companies was partly due to their claims that their longer-range trades would require the larger tonnages that the government desired. The government also showed increasing concern for the disafforestation of the Weald, where allegedly timber was cut down wholesale to supply charcoal for the ironworks of that area, to the detriment of shipbuilding. Insofar as the proclamations had any success they necessarily discouraged one growing industry for the supposed benefit of another. The policy was in any case probably mistaken and irrelevant, since the wood burnt for charcoal was unlikely to be prime shipbuilding timber, and the calculations of George Hammersley suggest that in any case a sensible policy of forest management − notably the practice of 'coppicing' - could comfortably have maintained fuel supplies for iron-making over an indefinite period.[22] The end-results of government attempts to boost shipbuilding were mixed. High-quality fighting vessels were indeed built in fluctuating numbers and at considerable expense in the royal dockyards. Otherwise the main expenditure seems to have been in the building of heavy vessels to carry coal from Newcastle to London (the coastal trade was legally reserved to English ships). This was a useful development, but it is hard to imagine that such ships added much to England's war potential. In neither the fishing nor the shipbuilding industry did the English performance remotely match the Dutch, and this in spite of the fact that England was much less heavily committed to war throughout the second half of the century. The disparity was to become painfully obvious once the war ended.

It is very difficult to draw up any balance sheet to assess the overall success of Tudor government measures in the economic field. This is partly because we lack the statistics to make accurate measurements of anything, partly because it is virtually impossible to isolate the government's contribution from other factors, and most of all because our definitions, categories and priorities are different from theirs and the criteria of success very different indeed. We are naturally tempted to look to such indicators as expansion of production, diversification of products, the establishment of new overseas markets, or comparative advance as measured against England's main competitors. By these criteria we could claim that modest progress had been achieved by 1600, and that specific government measures plausibly contributed to those results. We would complain, on the other hand, that the measures were not single-minded or whole-hearted, that they were sometimes based on a false diagnosis and at other times conflicted with one another, or with other policies, and that implementation of measures was often half-hearted and ineffectual. In 1600 England was clearly out-classed in every relevant field by the Dutch Republic, and her 'victories' had been won over relatively moribund rivals like the Hansards and Venetians.

On the government's own scale of priorities the success rate was rather better. The realm had been adequately defended against foreign invasion, albeit rather precariously. There had been no major rebellion since 1569 and no serious general disorder since 1549. Law and order were better maintained in 1600 than in 1500, especially in the trouble areas like the Welsh Marches and the Northern Borders, although there were still many 'lewd individuals' and criminals abounding. The crown remained more or less solvent, certainly in comparison with other European monarchies, even if there had been a run-down of its capital and some resort to unhealthy expedients like monopolies. The poor and vulnerable had been cushioned against the worst consequences of famine, unemployment and exploitation, and this had helped to keep them quiet and obedient. The results of some initiatives in trade and industry had been a little disappointing, but these were relatively unimportant areas, and without the successes in the more important ones things would have been much worse. There were limits to what a government could do in the face of the disobedience and notorious idleness of its lesser subjects, nor could it strain too far the loyal support of its more substantial ones.

Finally one might indulge in an unprofessional flight of imagination. What if the government had been much more successful in its measures, and by this is meant all its measures, insofar as they were compatible, rather than simply the ones we might prefer. One might list the same successes, according to the Privy Council's thinking, as before, with a few major additions: the complete pacification of Ireland, the elimination of both Catholics and Puritans, and the abolition of crime and idleness. How, putting on our own spectacles, would the English economy and society have looked — the England of Elizabeth as William Cecil and his mistress would have wished it? It would certainly have been a very orderly and tidy place, with the population firmly corralled in their places of birth and pursuing their traditional vocations, preferably tilling the soil rather than engaged in disorderly industries. They would be working hard, attending only Anglican church services every Sunday, properly dressed according to their status and profession, deferential to their social superiors, eating a great deal of fish but shunning the ale-house. Mobility of labour would be low, both geographically and occupationally, which would have the welcome effect of curbing the inordinate growth of London's unruly population. Some changes in agricultural organization and techniques would be cautiously permitted as the century went on, but with continued hostility to necessary middlemen like corn merchants and wool-broggers. Industry would be well disciplined within the confines of the guild system, and restricted as far as practicable to the towns rather than straggling untidily over the countryside. The woods and forests would be secure from the ravages of the iron-masters. Overseas trade would be modestly expanding, but carefully confined to old and new monopoly companies, whose charters and privileges would be strictly observed. Money-lending, exchange-dealing and insurance would be hesitantly permitted but viewed with qualified suspicion.

This is the image of a society that is not merely stable and traditional but nearly static if not stagnant, and at best it could probably have achieved only a brief existence. It is not a picture of innovation, change and economic vitality. So perhaps we should be glad, from our anachronistic standpoint, that the Tudor state was not so very efficient. The gains that we may like to imagine arising from more ruthless discipline and commitment might have been outweighed by losses we choose not to imagine.

Notes

1. Recent general surveys include C.G.A. Clay, *Economic and Social Change. England 1500-1700* (2 vol., Cambridge, 1984); D.C. Coleman, *The Economy of England, 1450-1750* (Oxford, 1977); B.A. Holderness, *Pre-industrial England. Economy and Society (1500-1750)* (London, 1976); P. Williams, *The Tudor Regime* (Oxford, 1979), pp.139-215 for government intervention in the economic sphere; and the earlier more specialized study by V. Ponko, *The Privy Council and the Spirit of Elizabethan Economic Management* (Philadelphia, 1968).
2. J.J. Scarisbrick, *Henry VIII* (London, 1968), pp.45-6.
3. For Wolsey, see J.J. Scarisbrick, 'Cardinal Wolsey and the Common Weal', in *Wealth and Power in Tudor England* (ed. E.W. Ives, R.J. Knecht and J.J. Scarisbrick, London, 1978); for Thomas Cromwell see G.R. Elton, *Reform and Renewal. Thomas Cromwell and the Common Weal* (Cambridge, 1973); for Thomas Smith see Mary Dewar, *Sir Thomas Smith. A Tudor Intellectual in Office* (London, 1964); for Cecil see V. Ponko, *The Privy Council*.
4. G.R. Elton, *Reform and Renewal*, pp.122-6.
5. D. Starkey, *The Reign of Henry VIII. Personalities and Politics* (London, 1985).
6. G.D. Duncan, 'Monopolies under Elizabeth I, 1558-85' (unpublished PhD thesis, University of Cambridge, 1977).
7. L.A. Clarkson, 'The Organisation of the English Leather Industry in the Late Sixteenth and Seventeenth Centuries', *Economic History Review*, 2nd ser., XIII (1960), no. 2.
8. For detailed discussion of Tudor proclamations, the indispensable studies are: R.W. Heinze, *The Proclamations of the Tudor Kings* (Cambridge, 1976); and F.A. Youngs, *The Proclamations of the Tudor Queens* (Cambridge, 1976).
9. See articles by G. Hammersley, 'The Charcoal Iron Industry and its Fuel, 1540-1750', in *Economic History Review*, 2nd ser., XXVI (1973), no. 4; *idem*, 'Technique or Economy? The Rise and Decline of the Early English Copper Industry', *Business History*, XV, Part I (1973); *idem*, 'The State and the English Iron Industry in the Sixteenth and Seventeenth Centuries', in *Trade, Government and the Economy in Pre-Industrial England* (ed. D.C. Coleman and A.H. John, London, 1976).
10. 4 & 5 Ph. & Mary c.2.
11. The private merchant accounts of Thomas Kitson (1519-39) and Thomas Gresham (1546-52) show clearly that both merchants duly paid customs duties on both their exports and imports. The use of outdated Books of Rates, however, meant that they paid significantly less on their imports than the theoretical 5 per cent due.
12. A. Hassel Smith, *County and Court. Government and Politics in Norfolk, 1558-1603* (Oxford, 1974).
13. M.G. Davies, *The Enforcement of English Apprenticeship* (Cambridge Mass., 1956).
14. G.R. Elton, 'Informing for Profit: a Sidelight on Tudor Methods of Law Enforcement', *Cambridge Historical Journal*, XI (1954), no. 2.
15. In 1547-8, 41 merchants exporting 500 cloths or more handled 53 per cent of the total cloth exports from London in the year (PRO Exch. K.R. Customs Accounts, 167/1).
16. *Tudor Economic Documents* (ed. R.H. Tawney and E. Power, 3 vol., London, 1924), I, pp.184-5.
17. 5 & 6 Edward VI c.6.
18. For this see especially Ponko, *The Privy Council*, pp.8-18.
19. N.S.B. Gras, *The Evolution of the English Corn Market* (Cambridge Mass., 1915).
20. A.B. Appleby, *Famine in Tudor and Stuart England* (Liverpool, 1978).
21. E. Kerridge, *The Agricultural Revolution* (London, 1967).
22. G. Hammersley, 'The Charcoal Iron Industry'.

3

A New Look at an Old Subject:
Dutch Trade Policies in the Age of Mercantilism

P. W. Klein

It would be straining the truth somewhat to say that the discussions about Dutch trade policy during the age of mercantilism have been very lively of late. At first sight this neglect of the subject may appear understandable, because economic historians presently prefer studying more recent times; the few who still take an interest in early modern times tend to keep away from commercial history. They go to agrarian and demographic history instead, obviously believing that trade and commerce were of lesser importance to the economics of pre-industrial societies. Whether this was really the case as far as the United Provinces were concerned remains to be seen, however: the general opinion expressed in early modern times certainly reads quite differently.

When still fashionable topics of study, up to the mid-1960s, the economic and the commercial history of the Dutch Republic were understood to be virtually one and the same thing. Many historians have had their say on it; nevertheless, there are some problems left to be solved. For example, the precise character of Dutch trade policy was never established unambiguously,[1] and the extent to which it actually conformed to the prevailing pattern of European mercantilism has remained a moot point.

But it seems hardly justified to expect a unanimous opinion on the matter. Economic history and the history of economics have been making such a hash of the concept of mercantilism itself that it is no longer possible to know with which precise ingredients the dish was actually prepared.[2] As a consequence, mercantilism has lost much of its attraction as an object of study. The great and inspiring debate about mercantilism which began in the 1930s evaporated sometime during the 1960s. What is left is the hazy notion that mercantilism had somehow to do with 'the deliberate pursuit of the economic interest of the state'.[3] Since then, little new information has come to light. The exception is perhaps the 'polinomic' study of mercantilism as a rent-seeking system, published by Ekelund and Tollison in 1981.[4] They conceived of mercantilism as a system of regulation for providing both government revenues as well as economic rents for holders of state-sanctioned monopoly rights. As the authors remarked themselves, however, their explorations are quite compatible with a number of classic analyses.

By combining some of their ideas with a few notions from the modern theory of international trade about uncertainty and risk aversion, I hope to be able to draw a line of approach that may shed some new light on the nature of the Dutch trade policy in early modern times. My contention will be that the Dutch case was no exception. It rather conformed to the normal conditons of the early modern economy. I will try to show that these conditions were conducive to a mix-up of increasingly inconsistent economic policies. By their very inconsistency they could be developing checks which impeded economic institutions from adapting smoothly to any occurring change. In these circumstances an economy might be adversely affected by a trade policy that had been quite adequate in former times.

I will first relate some of the main views on early modern Dutch trade and trade policy, and its relation to the changing concepts of mercantilism. By referring to international trade theory I will then try to evaluate the function of international commerce in the development path of the early modern Dutch economy. I will conclude by considering the public choice between two possible sources of early modern government revenue: customs duty, and internal revenue. Although I have not substantiated my argumentation through any original research in primary sources, I hope that my thesis will be sufficiently provocative to induce the research required for putting it really to the test.

Anyone taking stock of the historiography on the Dutch Republic's trade policy after the end of the sixteenth century will be struck by its rather surprising inconclusiveness. To be sure: in accordance with Ricardo's prevailing classic theory of international trade, few had any doubts that commerce and trade lay at the heart of the nation's economic welfare.[5] There appears many a quotation to prove it, invoking all sorts of observers: pamphleteers, politicians, statesmen, officials, foreigners, Dutchmen, aristocratic regents and bourgeois merchants. The verbosity of the time itself seems to have carried the case unanimously. Later generations found little room for developing any doubt in the matter, although some conflicts of interest were taken into account, like that between commercial Holland and grain-growing Zeeland.[6] Yet few historians asked themselves whether the remarkable unison in praise of trade was not struck up by a single ruling group of interested parties. Doubts only arose at the moment when the true nature of Dutch trade policies was put up for discussion. Was it a case of mercantilism? Was it not? Recently the general opinion seems to favour the idea that it was something in-between. 'The view that this policy aimed at "free trade" is no longer upheld, but it would be equally wrong to classify it as a variety of "mercantilisme" adapted to the specific needs and circumstances of the Republic', concluded Hovy in his standard work on Dutch trade policy in the eighteenth century.[7] According to Johan de Vries there was no particular guideline for Dutch trade policy during the seventeenth century, but during the eighteenth century the importance of entrepôt trade became its leading principle.[8] It was not much of a principle really, however, for De Vries himself conceded that trade policy retained its mainly expedient nature. Pragmatism still prevailed over principle. Although various tariff reforms were introduced, they were too modest to change the picture substantially. The most important one was the reform of 1725, but its consequences remained of small account.

But historians have failed to explain *why* opportunism prevailed. Nor have they investigated what it essentially consisted of. Instead they have contented themselves with a predominantly factual description of the proceedings. Once historians agreed that the international commodity trade was the nation's main economic interest, they tended to take it for granted that the state's trade policy was to promote it. It was understood that economic policy in general and trade policy in particular accorded first priority to trade. If any exceptions were made, they were not taken as a reaction to an overall change of circumstances, but rather were implemented for special cases of particular interest, such as paper manufacturing or herring fishery. It is also generally maintained that trade policies were successful, at least until about the middle of the seventeenth century. But as time proceeded the policy seems to have lost its initial drive. Some historians have laid the blame for its shortcomings at the doorstep of the ruling class. They suddenly opened their eyes to the notion of group interest. It was decided that the regent class had released its ties of interest with trade and commerce. As a consequence there was no sufficient impetus to the vigorous reforms the situation required. But how to improve on a trade policy that was considered already to be of maximum benefit to trade? Other historians therefore took what seemed to be a more realistic point of view. They tried to maintain that an irreversible change of external economic and political conditions brought a more or less irretrievable deterioration, particularly in Dutch entrepôt trade. Trade may not have declined in absolute terms, but its growth certainly stopped. Here the matter seems to have rested.

There remains a rather interesting problem to be solved, however. The puzzling thing is the way the Dutch economy actually adapted itself to this worsening of circumstances. The normal procedure would of course have been to turn to the exploitation of next-best opportunities, as soon as the international economy began to affect things adversely. But according to general opinion no such switch occurred, at least not to the degree which the situation obviously required. This is to be deduced from the increase of poverty and unemployment during the eighteenth century, at a time when capital exports were rising. Evidently natural resources were also left underdeveloped or insufficiently exploited, even though the expansion of agriculture may have retrieved some of the loss. This obvious rigidity implies that the early modern Dutch economy had been unable to get any nearer to the full use of its factor endowments. In fact it was even moving away from an optimal equilibrium, for it did not even succeed in maintaining the previously high levels. The increasing inflexiblity of the Dutch economy is remarkable, considering the then current trade policy of keeping to extraordinarily low customs duties. This policy should have ensured a smooth, perhaps somewhat painful, adaptation to the requirements of the emerging new international economic order. If Dutch production factors could no longer find sufficient employment in the international economy, they should have been used in the domestic economy in order to avoid their underutilization. There would have been ample time for this adaptation, as historians agree that the change occurred so slowly that it went practically unnoticed. The Dutch, moreover, disposed of ample resources for a flexible response. Capital had been accumulating, technologies had certainly not been lagging behind, the potential labour force was relatively well developed, and so were natural resources. As the future was going to show, raw materials could be imported anyway. What is it then that kept the Dutch economy from responding positively to the challenge?

This enigma of the Dutch economic rigidity can only be solved by going right back to the start.[9] A new look is required at the matter of Dutch international commodity trade, its relations to institutional economic policies, and its function in the development of the domestic economy. Can it be true that the nation's economic interest was not always served best by trade and commerce? Is it even possible that the implementation of trade-promoting economic policies contained impediments which at some time actually prevented the economy from following its optimal development path? There are no definite or even obvious answers to questions like these. Any answers would have to be constructed in a changing context of variable conditions and relations.

Most essential is a proper understanding of how early modern state-building generally proceeded in giving shape to its economic policies. Ever since the days of Adam Smith it has been usual to conceive of these policies as mercantilism, although the idea of mercantilism was soon to dissolve in a flood of differing and quite often contradictory opinions. What remained, nonetheless, was the conviction that mercantilism was a real system. And reality was to be defined by very particular ends and no less specifically applied means. At the same time early modern state-building was similarly conceived of as a specific historical stage in a well defined process. Thus it is usual to speak of the age of absolutism, and after it that of the modern nation-state, with its unpersonal central government extending its indiscriminate care to all who might live within its geographically fixed borders. However, the closer one looked at the reality of history, the less attractive it became to lace up early modern state-building into any straitjacket of conceptual abstraction such as absolutism. There were simply too many deviations, diversifications and differences about. It moreover appeared that the public order in even the mightiest absolutist state consisted of a changing variety of complicated and obscure layers of rights and duties. The absolutist state was made up of an astonishing mixture of old and new, of tradition and innovation. Amidst so much complexity of institutional relations no central authority was able to establish a fixed course for pursuing the common good. There could be no question of instituting any deliberate, long-run economic policy. Any measure that actually came to be implemented tended to be the shaky outcome of compromise between changing power-groups and their confusing diversity of interests. Actual economic policy was therefore of necessity a hotch-potch of short-run policies, and so was mercantilism.

As soon as historians came to realize all this, the whole national character of early modern state-building fell prey to doubt. There seemed to be little sense left in considering *ancien régime* policies merely as a prelude to the modern nation state. As a policy goal the national common good actually ranked far behind a dark muddle of discriminating and powerful group interests. This is how Adam Smith conceived of the matter when he came to speak of mercantilism. According to him the practice of mercantilism was due to the compelling drive of the mercantile class. It is a concept which fits very well with Charles Wilson's view of economic policy in the Dutch Republic. According to him it was 'predominantly a conception of business welfare working upwards from the merchant community towards a government with minimum powers'.[10] It is difficult to see why the business community would have pressed for government regulation under any circumstances: one may rather take it for granted that men of business generally prefer non-intervention.

As I will try to show, this applied to the case of early modern Dutch trade. There is no reason for denying Dutch economic policy its mercantilistic nature just because of its expediency, its haphazardness, or because of the government's reluctance to interfere with trade. As long as policy gave priority to the interest of trade — and nobody disputes that it did in the case of the Dutch — it ought to be called mercantilistic by definition.

From this point of view it is difficult to understand why some have considered mercantilism as a pre-eminently absolutist policy. It is far more likely that a mercantile republic such as the United Provinces was in a better condition to promote the mercantile interest than any absolute monarchy which might try to do so. If there was any difference on this point between the two state systems, it was a difference in practice, not in essence or principle.

What therefore remains to be seen is by what precise means and measures the mercantile interests were served best in practice. Ever since the days of Adam Smith it has been maintained that mercantilism was actually comprised of a more or less fixed set of standard rules. At first it seemed natural, for instance, to identify mercantilism as bullionism. In this case the main object of foreign trade policies was to increase treasure by means of securing a positive surplus in the balance of trade. From this point of view the Dutch Republic certainly did not comply with the concept, if only by its failure to put an effective ban on the exports of precious metals.

Exports were actually promoted. It has been estimated that about ten per cent of Dutch mint production between 1690 and 1750 was carried to Asian markets, and a similar proportion may have gone to other foreign markets.[11] It was a policy greatly to the advantage of Dutch business. Some of the standard rules were applied, however. Historians have discovered quite a few cases making it easy to understand why the notion of mercantile opportunism − *'gelegenheidsmercantilisme'* − was evolved and why Van Dillen spoke of *'Mercantilisme in het klein'* (micro-mercantilism).[12]

But Dutch economic policy does not seem to have corresponded with another and rather important feature of Adam Smith's model of mercantilism. According to Smith, mercantilism must necessarily develop as a governmental system of growing restraint and control. The narrow-minded selfishness of mercantile business interests was to be held responsible. They were constantly on the alert for establishing legally protected monopolies, for this was their way to ensure profits, however much monopolies acted against common welfare. The more monopolies were instituted, the more they would need protection against their encroachment, and the more restraint and control would be required. Although there were some very important legal monopolies in Dutch trade (like the Dutch East India Company), it is going too far to maintain that it amounted to a straightforward system of state intervention. As a matter of fact the Dutch entrepôt trade flourished under the seal of singularly free competition, as governmental authorities seemed to strive for as little interference as was possible.

It should be realized in the first place that there was no *laissez-faire* ideology whatsoever to this type of non-interference. *Laissez-faire* would have implied the conviction that non-intervention was for the common good. In this case, however, the benign neglect was probably considered to be primarily for the good of big business. The rulers of the absolutist monarchies of the time were selling strings of legal monopolies mainly because it served them as a most welcome source of public revenue. The private entrepreneur probably only bought them because there was no better way of earning a monopoly profit. But Dutch entrepôt trade in particular offered the merchant no such scarcity of chances. 'Free competition' refers only to the absence of government intervention, and does not in this instance mean perfectly unrestrained competition. On the contrary, as I have tried to maintain in earlier publications, Dutch entrepôt trade actually conformed to a very large extent to theoretical models, not of perfect, but of monopolistic competition.[13] It is therefore very likely that Dutch entrepreneurs had only limited need of legal monopoly protection. Its advantages or similar ones could no doubt be obtained in cheaper ways. As soon as it appeared that this was no longer the case Dutch merchants were certainly not slow in clamouring for government support.

In the second place it should be realized that non-interference was dominant only in two particular wholesale branches of the Dutch international commodity trade, namely the carrying trade, and its appendix, the entrepôt trade. Things were rather different for the rest. Dutch business as a whole therefore bore the stamp of institutional duality. At the top the big international wholesale traders were largely left to their own devices, but the lower industries and labour-intensive servicing trades were very much the object of regulating and restraining government intervention.[14] It established amongst other things severe wage and price controls, that most certainly were contrary to the benign neglect of big business. It may very well have helped in enforcing the monopoly profits which the great merchants were looking for. It may have contributed to the cost advantage the Dutch international commodity trade was looking for. Promoting the mercantile interest in this rather poorly organized and therefore inconspicuous way, instead of implementing direct trade tariffs, was perhaps rather efficient. It certainly was the only way available to the decentralized and scarcely integrated state system the Dutch had adopted. It allowed all sorts of public authorities to intervene where it suited big business best. The dualism of the Dutch institutional economic system was the dualism of regulated domestic activities alongside unregulated international trade.

It was big business, though, which reaped the benefits. It did not generate the profits, however great its success in practising its monopolistic competition, and however much it was helped in this by government restraint and control. The gains from trade came rather from the prevailing structure of the international economy, which allowed Dutch enterprise to achieve its position of dominance. As has been remarked very often before, the Dutch dominated only as long as others were kept from competing. It may be assumed that this was a temporary condition to begin with. It may further be assumed that it was less due to deliberately organized government policies than to rather fortuitous differences in comparative costs as considered in Ricardo's classic theory of international trade. In accordance with this theory, any Dutch domination in the international economy would depend on the efficiency of the Dutch economy as a whole, including its domestic sector. One may even argue that the development of Dutch international commodity trade actually depended on domestic activities, and not vice versa. It is a construction which fits the specialization model as applied by Jan de Vries in his analysis of Dutch agriculture in the Golden Age.[15] It may be deduced from this model that the relatively strong position of Dutch enterprise in the international economy was indeed an offshoot of the specialization, differentiation and professionalization of the domestic economy's rural sector.

But Ricardian classics may not quite have applied to the Dutch case. The comparative cost theory assumes that an economy's resources are given and fully employed *before* it enters into the business of international trade. It is only *after* having been opened to trade that the economy faces a new set of relative international prices, and accordingly reallocates its given resources in a more efficient way.[16] Obviously the Dutch case did not meet these assumptions. A cruder form of classical trade theory may therefore be in order. It is to be found in Adam Smith's 'vent for surplus theory'. According to Smith, economies enter into international trade with surplus productive capacity over domestic consumption requirements. In this way the international trade provides an effective demand for absorbing the output of surplus resources, which would otherwise remain unutilized. The expansion of the international economy is therefore not only the way of increasing exports and imports but also the means to the expansion of domestic activities.

But Ricardo and Smith are quite in agreement as soon as it comes to the matter of the gains from trade. In fact all classical and neo-classical theory looks optimistically at the contribution of international trade to economic development. From this point of view there is no need to worry about any negative effects of free competition. And it is true of course that the Dutch entrepôt would automatically have passed on its gains from trade to the domestic economy, had only the great traders kept to the idea of perfect competition. What was good for Dutch shipping and trade would be good for the Dutch domestic economy as well. The benign neglect of big business was therefore quite justified, and the great majority of historians agreed. They saw no cause for reconsideration, even when it was realized that other economies were not to be kept from competition indefinitely. Yet no revolutionary economic change was required to compel Dutch enterprise to relinquish its virtual control of the international economy. As a matter of fact quite a few other pre-industrial economies were busily and continuously engaged with the reorganization of their production function in order to catch up with the Dutch.[17] After the middle of the seventeenth century their success gradually increased: there had been no particular secret to the Dutch miracle after all. But no foreign success story could change the opinion of most observers that the Dutch had little cause for changing their trade-promotion policies. Thanks to these policies the Dutch economy had already been perfected as much as had been possible under the given circumstances. The fact that in history, circumstances are never given, was of small account. It seemed that if the best was not good enough in the case of the Dutch, they would simply have to wait for better times. In the meantime their economy would have to adapt itself to the exploitation of the opportunities which circumstances had left to them.

Such a view implies many things, for instance the reduction of costs in order to maintain economic activity at its former levels, and it is especially the cost of labour − the wage level − that is to be reduced. Adaptation in this sense implies loss of income and lower levels of welfare, though employment would not suffer. However, while the Dutch kept biding their time for generation after generation, things did not proceed in precisely this way. It was not the wage level that fell, but employment. In actual fact, adaptation proceeded by shifting income to the idling propertied class, rather than by reconquering the income loss of the labouring poor.

The reason is not to be found in classical trade theory, if only because of its failure to account for structural unemployment. Classical theory hardly applied: as I have indicated before, the Dutch economy failed to meet the fundamental classical assumption of free and perfect comptetition. Modern trade theory may be of greater help in explaining why the original flexibility of the Dutch economy had so obviously diminished by the time of the eighteenth century. Modern trade theory has lost the unqualified optimism of the classical view. Like the mercantilism of former times, it recognizes that trade may have its disadvantages. It is therefore no longer taken for granted that a country realizing its comparative advantage is automatically following its optimal development path. It is included in the modern perspective that a country may do better to relinquish gains from trade in order to secure a higher domestic growth. Economists do not agree any more that international trade is a pure 'engine of growth'.

Some authors indicate that the gains from trade tend to fluctuate according to a country's relative level of economic development. While the world's most advanced economy tends to profit most, the least developed country may even stand to lose from trade. The theoretical analysis to that effect is so poor that it cannot be taken very seriously, however. What should be taken seriously is the possibility that any economy's gains from trade may fluctuate in a dynamic way as conditions change. Accordingly it may be advisable to change trade policies as time proceeds. Trade-promoting policies may not be best at all times. Serving the mercantile interest by desisting from state intervention is perhaps best when the gains from trade are relatively high. Considering the matter from this angle, the implementation of trade-promoting low customs duties at the Union of Utrecht in 1579 may have been quite the right thing to do; but as soon as the Dutch comparative cost advantage was eroded, the matter was ripe for reconsideration. Indeed, some Dutch Patriots of the eighteenth century did actually attempt to reconsider, though to little effect.

As a small open economy the Netherlands moreover presented a special case to trade theories. The small domestic market carried quite a few diseconomies of scale, and the Dutch had to struggle continuously to overcome them in order to keep to their comparative cost advantage. Modern trade theory acknowledges that the dynamic change in the conditions which secured this advantage to begin with would require an extra effort. Continuing to promote trade as if nothing had happened would in this case not be the best course for policy makers: it would impede the structural economic transformation which the change of situation was requiring. The rising cost of trade promotion would in these circumstances exceed transformation costs sooner than would be the case in economies with a large domestic market. Modern trade theory therefore allows that small open economies may have especially good reasons for expecting better results from import-substitution policies than from any roundabout promotion of their foreign trade.

Modern trade theory finally indicates that the changing uncertainties of trade should be taken into account too.[18] It is maintained that foreign trade generally carries more risks than domestic trade, owing to the greater uncertainties in foreign supply and demand. A greater effort of risk aversion is therefore required. Consequently the cost of risk avoidance will be higher too. There are a great number of ways and means of risk avoidance. One of them is of course switching from foreign trade to a domestic activity. Private decision-makers may choose from a host of other opportunities, however. They may vary and increase their mix of activities, they may resort to insurance, they may avail themselves of government support, and so on. Government assistance is, however, not warranted in all cases and circumstances. It is likely that the taxpayers will be left with an unduly high burden of risk-taking, which probably was not the case when the United Provinces came into being. At that time foreign trade was still limited to relatively well known nearby markets such as the Baltic. Consequently, risk aversion was cheap. Under these conditions there was probably more good than harm in the implementation of low customs duties. They actually helped the Dutch entrepôt towards its monopolistic hegemony. It seems likely, however, that the cost of commercial risk aversion was rising during the first half of the seventeenth century, as Dutch foreign trade was very much expanding into new, far-flung and unfamiliar markets. Risk and uncertainty must have risen accordingly. The average cost of trade increased, following the rise of marginal cost, which in its turn was induced by the greater effort of risk aversion. After the middle of the seventeenth century, rising foreign competition probably began to reduce the returns of trade as well. But the Dutch international wholesale trade would nevertheless remain in a position to hold its own as long as it could collect an economic rent, or a payment higher than the amount mercantile resources could command in their next-best alternative use. The prevailing system of trade-promoting policies may have helped considerably.

A full understanding of this matter requires another look at the idea of mercantilism as a system of political economy. According to Adam Smith this system not only serves the purpose of providing the people with the means to a plentiful subsistence, but must also supply the state with a revenue for public services. When the Dutch Republic came into being, the task of procuring the state's revenue was basically left to its rather autonomous components, the Provinces. The exception was customs duties. Economic considerations had probably little or nothing to do with their implementation. In the earliest beginnings they were simply conceived of as a contribution covering the cost of maritime defence.[19] The States General realized only after some time that they now disposed of the means to execute an economic policy as well. But as a source of public revenue customs duties were of course quite insufficient. The Dutch policy makers of 1579 could, however, afford a measure of carelessness in this respect. As far as public finance was concerned they already had access to a much more efficient system of public borrowing than any other European state.[20] The financial requirements of the state were also perhaps more modest than elsewhere, for they were confined mainly to the single sector of defence. Defence was in fact the only reason why the United Provinces had been established at all, and there was little discussion of more integrated state systems. As time proceeded, the cost of defence rose, however, even in times of peace, and especially during the eighteenth century. Dutch foreign policy, then trying to avoid involvement in war, may have been rather successful, but army and navy budgets still failed to meet the standards considered to be appropriate.[21]

It seems reasonable to assume that mercantile interests had the greatest stake in maritime protection, but that was not the way the Dutch government was actually supporting overseas trade. As I have tried to indicate, support came by means of restraint and regulation in the domestic sector through a variety of public authorities, and by means of a suitable trade policy. In the meantime domestic tax-payers were left to foot the bill for defence costs. Public borrowing, however efficient, brought only a short reprieve, for the burden of debt-servicing increased. When Dutch international commodity trade was expanding into ever-wider markets, its need for maritime protection must have been rising disproportionately, but trade was never fully charged for this rise. Perhaps there was no need for it to be, but there must have been a crucial moment when the social optimum was left behind.

A reorganization of Dutch public revenue, shifting the tax burden from domestic sources towards the least rewarding branches of foreign trade, would have certainly reduced the monopolistic rent which merchants continued to enjoy, thanks to a policy that really can only be classified as mercantilism. A shift such as this would have reduced Dutch foreign trade, but it would also have contributed to bringing the Dutch economy nearer to its social optimum. It would have detracted from the inflexibility that was impeding the economy's output capacity from adapting more smoothly to the change in circumstances than was in fact the case. From an economist's point of view, one is tempted to speculate whether the Dutch wouldn't have performed even better if they had turned to state integration sooner. After all, this is what they did eventually.

But I am afraid that I have been speculating too much already. As I remarked before my views have certainly not been tested sufficiently, and I am fully aware of the existence of some convincing evidence to the contrary.[22] I have nevertheless felt justified in expounding them, if only to show that unfashionable subjects like commercial history should not be neglected just because of their supposed lack of interest. And whatever shortcomings my argument may have, it has at least the merit that it helps to solve the puzzling paradox which emerges from the writings of two contemporary observers of the early Dutch economy, who are both justly famous for their discerning acuteness. Josiah Child, writing in 1693, confessed to the belief that the Dutch had advanced their trade by 'the lowness of their Customs and the height of their Excise'. Writing three quarters of a century later, Adam Smith adhered of course to the contrary. He maintained that the Dutch were ruining their economy by their excessively high internal revenue.[23] Taking the change of historical conditions into account, I conclude that they were both right.

Notes

1. There is an extensive literature on the matter. Prominent examples are: J.L.F. Engelhard, *Het Generaal-Plakaat van 31 juli 1725 op de Convooien en Licenten en het lastgeld van de schepen*; J. Ratté, *De Nederlandse doorvoerpolitiek (tot 1850)* (Rotterdam, 1950); E. Verviers, *De nederlandsche handelspolitiek tot aan de toepassing der vrijhandelspolitiek* (Leiden, 1914); C. Wilson, *Profit and Power. A Study of England and the Dutch Wars* (second printing, The Hague, 1978); J.G. van Dillen, *Van rijkdom en regenten. Handboek tot de economische en sociale geschiedenis van Nederland tijdens de Republiek* (Assen, 1970). The following notes will refer to more literature.
2. P.W. Klein, 'Het Mercantilisme', in *Kernproblemen der economische geschiedenis* (ed. H. Baudet and H. van der Meulen, Groningen, 1978), pp.117-27.
3. J.I. Israel, *European Jewry in the Age of Mercantilism 1550-1750* (Oxford, 1985), p.3.
4. R.B. Ekelund Jr. and R.D. Tollison, *Mercantilism as a Rent-Seeking Society. Economic Regulation in Historical Perspective* (Austin Texas, 1981).
5. The Dutch state itself and its foreign policy have been subject to a similar, somewhat idyllic approach. Boogman maintained that the 'avancement van de neringe ende traffycke deser Landen' had been the object of Dutch foreign policy as early as 1588. Accordingly the peace-loving 'republican' Dutch notion of the 'raison d'état' stood opposite to the prevailing opinion in aggressive absolutist monarchies with their militarism and power politics. Jan de Witt himself simply gave expression to what Boogman called 'de Hollandse traditie' when he actually justified the state by its social function for the 'welvaaren der ingeseetenen'. The reality of words is not always the reality of practice, however. It all depends on what is precisely understood by such words as 'bonum publicum', 'bien public', 'common good', 'gemeenebest'. It may be quite wrong to accord them the modern democratic meaning of general public welfare. J.C.Boogman, 'De raison d'état-politicus Johan de Witt', *Bijdragen en Mededelingen betreffende de Geschiedenis der Nederlanden*, XC (1975), 379-408.
6. J.G. van Dillen, 'Stukken betreffende den Amsterdamschen graanhandel omstreeks het jaar 1681, met Inleiding', *Economisch-Historisch Jaarboek*, III (1917).
7. J. Hovy, *Het Voorstel van 1751 tot instelling van een beperkt vrijhavenstelsel in de Republiek* (Groningen, 1966), p.654.
8. Johan de Vries, *De economische achteruitgang der Republiek in de achttiende eeuw* (Amsterdam, 1959) chapter II, section 2.
9. It is logically possible of course to attribute the failure to transform to a loss of enterprising spirit. It is, however, not clear how to find an appropriate standard for determining such a loss. Neither is it clear how to distinguish between cause and effect.
10. Wilson, *Profit and Power*, pp.153-4.
11. A. Pol, 'Tot gerieff van India. Geldexport door de VOC en de muntproduktie in Nederland, 1720-1740', *Jaarboek voor Munt- en Penningkunde*, LXXII (1985), 123; A. Attman, 'Dutch Enterprise in the World Bullion Trade 1550-1800', in *Acta Regiae Societatis Acientiarum et Literarum Gothoburgensis, Humaniora*, XXIII (1983).
12. W.D. Voorthuysen, *De Republiek der Verenigde Nederlanden en het mercantilisme* (The Hague, 1964), p.130. J.G. van Dillen, *Rijkdom*, chapter 22.
13. P.W. Klein, *De Trippen in de 17e eeuw. Een studie over het ondernemersgedrag op de Hollandse stapelmarkt* (Assen, 1965); idem, 'A 17th Century Monopoly Game: the Swedish-Dutch Trade in Tar and Pitch', in *Wirtschaftskräfte und Wirtschaftswege II. Wirtschaftskräfte in der europäischen Expansion* (ed. J. Schneider, *et al.*, Bamberg, 1978). J.W. Veluwenkamp, *Ondernemersgedrag op de Hollandse stapelmarkt in de tijd van de Republiek. De Amsterdamse handelsfirma Jan Isääc de Neufville & Comp., 1730-1764* (Zwolle, 1981), has disputed my views. I believe, however, that our differences are mainly ones of terminology.
14. T.P. van der Kooy, *Hollands stapelmarkt en haar verval* (Amsterdam, 1931); Violet Barbour, *Capitalism in Amsterdam in the 17th Century* (second printing, Ann Arbor, 1963), p.22, pointed to 'mercantilist restrictions at home'.
15. Jan de Vries, *The Dutch Rural Economy in the Golden Age, 1500-1700* (New Haven, 1974).
16. G.M. Meier, 'Theoretical issues concerning the history of international trade and economic development' (unpublished paper, 1988).
17. England was of course the most successful. Another example is Sweden: J.T. Lindblad, *Sweden's Trade with the Dutch Republic 1738-1795* (Assen, 1982).
18. W.M. Corden, *Trade Policy and Economic Welfare* (Oxford, 1980), pp.318-22.

19. Engelhard, *Het Generaal-Plakaat*.
20. J.D. Tracy, *A Financial Revolution in the Habsburg Netherlands. Renten and Renteniers in the County of Holland 1515-1565* (Berkeley, 1985).
21. J.R. Bruijn, *De Admiraliteit van Amsterdam in Rustige Jaren 1713-1751* (Amsterdam/Haarlem, 1970).
22. See by W. Fritschy, *De Patriotten en de financiën van de Bataafse Republiek. Hollands krediet en de smalle marges voor een nieuw beleid (1795-1801)* (The Hague, 1988).
23. Quoted by Akio Ishizaka, 'Die niederländische und englische Akzise im 17. Jahrhundert. Ein Beitrag zur vergleichenden Steuergeschichte der merkantilistische Periode', in *Wirtschaftkräfte, op. cit.*, p.510.

4

England's Mercantilist Response to Dutch World Trade Primacy, 1647-1674

Jonathan I. Israel

During the great period of the Dutch overseas trading system from 1590 down to about 1740, there were three major, sustained challenges to Dutch primacy in world trade.[1] First Spain with her embargoes and maritime raiding campaign down to 1647, then England from the Navigation Act (1651) until 1674, and finally France from Colbert's second tariff of 1667 down to the Peace of Utrecht (1713), all tried to mobilize every resource and expedient to break the Dutch system and siphon off the Republic's trade.

Of these three sustained challenges, that of England was the shortest in duration but was also the most dramatic and intensive. The Anglo-Dutch confrontation over commercial and colonial issues led to three bitter sea wars (1652-4; 1665-7; and 1672-4) which constitute the most direct and violent attack launched during the seventeenth century on Dutch trade and shipping. Yet it does not follow from this that England's challenge was actually the most serious or damaging of the three or, as we shall see, caused the kind of fundamental damage to the Dutch trading system that Spain and France were both able to inflict. For although England was a more successful trading and maritime power in her own right in this period than either Spain or France, and while the English navy posed a more formidable armed threat to the Dutch than the navies of either Spain or France, England nevertheless lacked the leverage over key markets which Spain and France both possessed and this, combined with the Dutch naval and privateering response, in the end largely frustrated England's efforts.

In this present study I shall endeavour to show why the English began to react so strongly to the Dutch overseas trading system in the years around 1650, and why they continued to do so for a quarter of a century; I shall then analyse English perceptions of Dutch commercial and maritime success, and finally set out the inherent limitations in England's position which effectively prevented her from seriously disrupting the Dutch overseas trade system.

To understand the background to the Anglo-Dutch Wars of the third quarter of the seventeenth century one must first of all grasp that this tremendous maritime conflict had relatively little, as Simon Groenveld has shown,[2] to do with the Anglo-Dutch quarrels about economic matters of the early part of the century. The clashes in the East Indies of the 1613-23 perod were still vividly remembered as was the wrangling of those years over the Cockayne Project and cloth dyeing and the Spitsbergen whale fishery.[3] But while, by the 1640s, Englishmen still spoke bitterly of real and alleged 'Amboina-like cruelties', all these encounters had long since faded into the background. By the time the new phase of Anglo-Dutch economic confrontation began in the late 1640s none of the specific quarrels of the 1613-23 period was any longer a live issue. It is true that English merchants had fresh cause for resentment after 1623 as they continued to lose ground to the Dutch in the furnishing of cloth to the Baltic and in northern European commerce generally — except the traffic to Flanders.[4] But England's failure in the north was more than offset, especially since the Anglo-Spanish peace of 1630, by the triumphant success of her trade with Spain, Portugal, and the entire Mediterranean region.[5] Here the English had matters all their own way. By the early 1640s England was by far the leading northern trading power in the Iberian Peninsula, Italy and the Levant. When in 1644 Amsterdam merchants declared that the Dutch Levant trade, which had once, during the Twelve Years' Truce period, been in a flourishing condition, was now in a state of virtual collapse and that the valuable traffic had now fallen completely into English hands, they were not exaggerating.[6] England reigned not just supreme but unchallenged in Mediterranean commerce; and her ascendancy in this sector, one of the largest markets for pepper, spices and other East India commodities, enabled the English East India Company to recover from its serious reverses at Dutch hands of the 1620s.

England then was immensely successful in the 1630s and early 1640s in the maritime trade of southern Europe. But her supremacy in this sphere was based less on inherent strengths than on essentially external and basically precarious factors, as was realised by some perceptive onlookers at the time. Sir Thomas Roe, for example, commenting on England's trade in 1641 in the aftermath of the Portuguese secession from Spain, at a time when the Dutch were returning to the Portugal trade, thus giving English merchants a foretaste of what was later to happen on a larger scale, declared in Parliament that 'we enjoy almost the trade of Christendom, but if a peace happen betwixt France, Spain and the United Provinces, all these will share what we now possess alone, and therefore we must provide for that day, for nothing stands secure but upon its own foundation.'[7]

The basic reason for England's supremacy in southern European trade between 1630 and 1647 was the prolonged impact of the Spanish embargo of 1621-47 against Dutch ships, goods, and Dutch-owned cargoes which was in force in all the territories of the Spanish crown, an embargo backed up by a vigorous maritime raiding campaign waged from the Flemish sea-ports. The latter, which accounted for hundreds of Dutch merchant vessels during the 1630s and early 1640s, forced up Dutch freight and maritime insurance charges on all routes not only for Mediterranean destinations.[8] But except in the case of carrying Baltic stores and southern goods to the Flemish sea-ports (from which the Dutch were excluded by their own navy as well as the Spaniards), in northern European markets the English lacked the additional prop of the Spanish embargoes. It was the combination of embargo and crippling freight charges which had so devastating an effect on Dutch commerce with southern Europe between 1621 and 1647, and which gave England her southern ascendancy, so to speak, on a plate.

The moment the maritime raiding campaign ceased, however, with the French capture of Dunkirk in 1646, and when the Spanish embargoes against the Dutch were finally lifted in the summer of 1647,[9] the precariousness of England's trade hegemony in southern European and Flemish waters was suddenly revealed. And how very fragile it was soon shown to be! Within a year or two much of the edifice of English commercial supremacy in the Mediterranean world came crashing down with grim consequences for much of the rest of English economic life. With the Spanish embargoes and the Flemish privateering menace lifted, Dutch freight and marine insurance rates began to fall precipitately, wiping out the advantage previously enjoyed by English merchants shipping in Mediterranean waters.[10] England's recently flourishing transit traffic between Spain and Flanders evaporated almost overnight. Dutch ships and goods, and also Dutch factors, returned to the ports of Spain, Flanders and Spanish Italy on highly favourable terms, more favourable in some respects than those enjoyed by the English.[11] The Republic of Genoa which down to 1647 had, under Spanish pressure, purchased its grain and naval stores for the granaries and arsenals of the state from the English and Hanseatics lost no time in switching back to the Dutch whose costs were now appreciably lower.[12]

The Dutch-Spanish peace and its many adverse effects on English overseas commerce was thus the main reason for the sudden sharp deterioration in English economic life at the end of the 1640s. To this we must add certain damaging consequences of the English Civil War, especially in the Caribbean area where the Royalists remained in control at Barbados, Surinam and elsewhere down to 1651, and where almost the whole trade of England's colonies in the region was re-channelled from around 1645 to 1651 into Dutch hands, with an appreciable slice of the Barbados sugar trade remaining in Dutch and Dutch-Jewish hands for long after that.[13] Taken together, the Dutch-Spanish peace and the English Civil War in the New World suddenly enabled the Dutch in the late 1640s to make very rapid progress at English expense in practically every important market – Spain, Italy, the Ottoman Levant, Flanders, the Baltic, Russia and the Caribbean. Of course, the English were not the only trading power adversely affected by the restructuring of the Dutch overseas trade system in the late 1640s. The Hanseatics, Danes and others lost ground also. But no other trading power lost ground so rapidly and in so many sectors at once as the English.

Clearly the restructuring of the Dutch trade system at the end of the 1640s was one of the most decisive factors in seventeenth-century English economic development. 'This sudden maritime crisis', as Ralph Davis expressed it, 'was the background to the first thoroughly worked out piece of English protective leglislation – the Navigation Act of 1651 – and of the first Anglo-Dutch War'.[14] But it was also the background to what I shall term the classic phase of English mercantilist economic writing, by which I mean that batch of tracts and proposals which appeared between 1647 and 1672, which were concerned as a matter of great urgency with the problem of Dutch economic superiority, and which sought England's economic salvation in a wide-ranging protectionist system. Among the key examples of this mercantilist literature are Benjamin Worsley's *The Advocate* (1651), Thomas Violet's *The Advancement of Merchandise* (1651), Henry Robinson's *Certain Proposals* (1652) and Sir Josiah Child's *A New Discourse of Trade*, which was originally drafted in the mid-1660s. These writings were part of a spectrum of thought and action which consciously sought to erect a protective shield not only around England's overseas trade and shipping but also around her industries: for the Dutch restructuring severely damaged English shipbuilding and her cloth exports to Spain,[15] and caused serious damage to the English whaling and fishing industries. English fish exports to Flanders, for example, collapsed almost totally. 'In 1645', as Roland Baetens has shown, 'the vast majority of the fish [imported into the Spanish Netherlands] came from Britain . . . whereas in 1648 virtually all of it came from the United Provinces'.[16] And like the other markets lost, this one was not subsequently regained.

English mercantilist deliberation, writing and action in the 1647-74 period sought to grapple with the specific problems posed by Dutch economic expansion during those years. Once the pre-1647 balance – almost a division of labour – between England and the Dutch in international commerce was overturned, a whole range of major economic challenges arose simultaneously. The most immediately pressing for English merchants trading with Spain and Italy, for the Levant Company, and also for the Caribbean merchants, was the sudden post-1647 influx of commodities from these distant markets into England indirectly, carried by the Dutch, via the Dutch entrepôt. Before 1647 there was no penetration of the English market by Italian silks, Canary wines or Zante currants shipped in via the Dutch enrepôt – at least not since 1621. Then all at once, from 1647, there was a massive and utterly disorientating influx. Benjamin Worsely was not exaggerating when he wrote in 1651 that 'at Spain, Canaries, Zante, with several other places in the Straits where they formerly rarely laded hither one ship of goods; they now lately laded hither more than we.'[17]

The obvious answer to this challenge was to seal off the English market, and also Scotland,[18] to merchandise shipped via the Dutch entrepôt. In 1645 the Greenland Company, confronting the massive expansion of the Dutch whale fishery of the 1640s, had obtained from Parliament an Act forbidding the importing of whale products into England in any but their own ships.[19] What was now required was to generalize this principle. In January 1648 the Levant Company in London petitioned Parliament 'against the importation of Turkey commodities from Holland and other places but directly from the places of their growth'.[20] Further pressure, including that of the Baltic merchants, built up rapidly from all sides. During 1650 the standing Council for Trade and the Council of State, assisted by Worsely who was the secretary of the former, and by Thomas Violet, laboured on a general measure designed to halt the flood of southern European and colonial commodities into England indirectly via Holland and Zeeland. After prolonged deliberation and several drafts all this endeavour finally gave birth to the Navigation Act of 1651, the most celebrated piece of English mercantilist legislation.

But the Navigation Act dealt only with one particular aspect of the English 'maritime crisis' precipitated by the post-1647 restructuring of the Dutch trading system. What the Navigation Act did not, and could not, do was tackle the alarming deterioration in England's trading position in overseas markets, except where, as in the case of the Canaries wine trade and Puglian olive oil, England herself was the principal consumer. For the rest, other methods of intervention by the English state would have to be found. The Caribbean colonies required more than just the establishment of Parliament's authority, in 1651, and the Navigation Act for its solution, for most of the sugar output of Barbados and elsewhere bought up by the Dutch was destined not for England but for the sugar refineries of Amsterdam. In any case, the root of the problem was that the settlers in the Caribbean possessions preferred to buy the linen, tools, brandy and black slaves that they needed from the Dutch and from Dutch Jews because they knew that from them they would get a better deal than they would trading with London. 'The islanders here', it was reported from Barbados in 1655, 'much desire commerce with strangers [i.e. with the Dutch and Jews], our English merchants traffiquing in those parts generally being great extortioners'.[21] Despite the success of the authorities in seizing a considerable number of Dutch ships, often from Zeeland, attempting to trade with the colonies during the 1650s, an illegal contraband traffic using Dutch vessels continued to flourish at least into the late 1650s.[22] After that the direct Dutch traffic does seem to have tailed off. But this still left the problem of how to close the loopholes through which a largely Dutch-Jewish indirect traffic continued to flourish.[23] An important step here was the Act of March 1664 forbidding English vessels to sail to the colonies other than direct from an English port, thereby stopping English ships from sailing first to a Dutch port to load their goods and then from Holland or Zeeland on to the Caribbean. The English ambassador at The Hague, Sir George Downing, commented on this occasion that this Act

> doth very much trouble them here; for that it breakes all the Jewes correspondency att Barbados and elsewhere, and hinders them of their sale of vast quantities of the manufactures of the country; for that it will not quitt cost to send them first to England, and pay customes there, and then to ship them againe for his Majesty's plantations; but instead thereof, the English manuufacturers are, and will be, new rented, which also will be felt in his Majesty's customes.[24]

But in the Caribbean and also North America, where the local Dutch loophole in the shape of New Netherland was suppressed by the simple expedient of sending out a military expedition in the autumn of 1664, England could rely on her superior political and military leverage to impose a framework advantageous to England no matter how disadvantageous to the local consumer. But the crux of England's difficulties was not the unco-operative attitude of her American colonists but her reduced competitiveness in European markets where she lacked the leverage to shut the Dutch out by political means or force. Until 1647 England had experienced no difficulty in selling great quantities of her manufactures, above all woollen products, in Spain, as there was no other way – with both Dutch and (since 1635) French goods excluded – that the merchants of Madrid and Seville could furnish Spain and Spanish America with an adequate range of textiles. In exchange for her cloth, fish and other products, England had bought up the bulk of Spain's wool and dyestuff exports and supplied much of the rest of Europe, including the Dutch entrepôt,[25] with these key commodities. But the trade revolution of the late 1640s had totally transformed the picture. 'That the commodities of Spaine are so inhanced', lamented one English onlooker,

> and bought up, and the cloathing of Holland within these few years so thriveth and increaseth that whereas we formerly brought home foure or five thousand baggs of cloth wooll and the Hollanders scarce a thousand, which they had then by re-shipping, theirs being prohibited, they now carry away five or six thousand and wee bring not past 12 or 1500 in the yeare at most.[26]

How was such a setback to be reversed? Some dreamed that England could somehow use her power and influence to pressure Spain into making special arrangements for English merchants, excluding the Dutch. One observer proposed that 'it can be done by the authority of the king of Spain' who should be persuaded 'by our state' to

> undertake for us the pre-emption of all the woolls of Segovia and Castile, which he will permit to be exported and that for a certain term of years, and at such a price as the owners of the wooll and the English contractor may both have reasonable content; and that the said king be obliged that no woolls shall be exported out of any of his ports but by the English contractor.[27]

But the only part of this reasoning which was at all realistic was that England did indeed need to prise the Spanish wool traffic out of Dutch hands if she was fully to restore her own previous position as an exporter of woollen textiles not only to Spain but also to other key markets such as the Baltic, Russia and Ottoman Turkey. This was not because England required Spanish wool as such; she had her own plentiful supplies of wool albeit of a cheaper and less fine type than Castilian merino wool. The reason was that Spanish wool was the basic raw material of the Dutch fine cloth industry and it was with their high-quality cloth, *lakens* (made from Castilian wool) and camlets (made from Turkish mohair yarn) that the Dutch were making their most spectacular gains as suppliers of textiles to European markets. As one English commentator expressed it, 'our getting all the Spanish cloth woolls into our hands will totally dissolve the clothing of Holland, which, by means of the woolls, hath of late years mightily increased, to the destruction of the vent of all fine cloths of English making, both in Holland, France, and the East lands [as well as Spain]'.[28]

The fall in English cloth exports to Spain since 1647 was rightly seen as inseparable from the post-1647 influx into Spain, and via Cadiz to Spanish America, of Dutch fine cloth and camlets. Clearly the most straightforward remedy for this state of affairs was to undermine the Dutch fine cloth industry by capturing the Spanish wool supply, through political influence or by force. But if such feverish plans were rife in the crisis atmosphere of the late 1640s and early 1650s, the frustrations of the indecisive Anglo-Spanish War of 1655-60 finally put paid to all such notions. This left no alternative but to concentrate on other, more practicable methods of restoring England's exports and competitiveness.

Dutch commercial superiority over England in the 1647-74 period had various aspects. There was the enviably low level of Dutch shipping costs, and their unrivalled shipping and shipbuilding capacity. There was the strength of Dutch financial institutions and their low interest rates. But no aspect of Dutch world primacy in these decades provoked greater anxiety in England than the universally admitted superior quality of Dutch manufactures: a most interesting strand of classic English mercantilist thought was concerned with improving the quality of English output by means of state intervention. Almost without exception English economic writers of the mid-seventeenth century were acutely conscious of, even obsessed with, the inferiority of English to Dutch processing and products.

In Worsley's view one of the principal strengths of the Dutch

> over us was the singular and prudent care they took in preserving the credit of those commodities which are their own proper manufactures, by which they keep up their repute and sale of them abroad, and by this means, likewise, very much daminifying and spoiling us.[29]

A Brief Narration drew attention to the somewhat tarnished reputation of English bays, serges, perpetuanes, says, fustians, and Norwich stuffs.[30] Henry Robinson pointed out how 'exceeding destructive' were the 'deceitfulnesse' and 'frauds' prevalent in English cloth manufacture.[31] Sir Josiah Child, struck by the difference in repute between English and Dutch fish products, affirmed that English fish exports 'often prove false and deceitfully made and our pilchards from the West-Country false packed.'[32] All these writers saw the source of Dutch qualitative superiority, probably rightly, in the close − the Dutch economic writer Pieter de la Court thought stifling[33] − supervision exercised by the Dutch provincial, municipal and guild authorities over every aspect both of manufacture and of weighing, measuring and packaging. It was this meticulous, unceasing official scrutiny of the Dutch manufacturing process, according to Worsley, which was the 'cause of the so great thriving of our neighbour's cloathing, and of the so great ruine and decaie (on the contrarie) of our own'. He contrasts the scrupulous care of the Dutch authorities in this respect with the 'carelessness of this nation, in keeping our manufactures to their due contents, weight and goodness'.[34]

All these writers are much more concerned to stress the need to regulate the quality of English output, and improve it, than to specify by what official mechanisms this should be done. Henry Robinson merely states that fraud and 'deceitfulnesse' in cloth production should 'be enquired after and prevented in future'.[35] *A Brief Narration* advocates that English textiles 'be so regulated for goodnesse, so faithfully viewed, searched and sealed, for length, breadth and weight than men how unskilful soever, may buy them upon the credit of seals and contents upon them, without feare or hazzard of being abused or deceived by the makers of them.'[36] No doubt there was much entrenched resistance to the idea of closer regulation and relatively little was achieved. Nevertheless tighter public regulation of the processes of manufacture was certainly one of the central priorities of English mercantilist thought in its classic phase and there is some reflection of this in the legislative activity of the government. One of the early achievements of the Council for Trade, set up in August 1650 to deal with the economic crisis facing the country, was the steering through of an Act 'for regulating the making of stuffs in Norfolk and Norwich' which sought to set up new checking arrangements at Norwich to supervise their manufacture.[37]

Another central concern was that of wanting to provide England with the financial facilities and, above all, the very low interest rates which the Dutch entrepôt enjoyed and which were rightly identified as one of the major strengths of the Dutch trading system. English mercantilist writers of the third quarter of the seventeenth century could not but be painfully aware of the gap between their country and the United Provinces in this respect. By 1670 Dutch interest rates stood as low as three per cent while English rates were at twice that level. Sir Josiah Child commented that 'Dutch low interest hath miserably lessened us in all trades of the world not secured us by laws, or by some natural advantage which over-ballanceth the disproportion of our interest of money'.[38] In the early 1650s Thomas Violet and Henry Robinson were both emphatic that the state must intervene to generate a better store of money and easier access to it, Robinson lamenting the ease with which in Holland money 'was available to one and all at four or five per cent interest'.[39] He is also quite clear that the state should provide England with a public bank.

Seventeenth-century European mercantilism was not just the advocacy of increased, and more systematic, state intervention in order to promote the economic interest of the state, but also deregulation in the sense of removing all economic privileges, concessions and charters which restrict or obstruct the activity of the whole.[40]

English mercantilist thought, writing and action during the 1647-74 period were in this, as in other respects, fully typical of the wider phenomenon. It is well known that the old chartered companies were by no means looked on with favour by many of the new men in positions of influence under the Commonwealth regime. When the Council for Trade was set up in August 1650 it was set, as one of its specific tasks, to deliberate 'whether it be necessary to give way to a more open and free trade than that of Companies and Societies, and in what manner it is fittest to be done'.[41] No doubt in some sectors of European trade, privilege and charter were weakened during these decades. But there could be no generalized attack on the chartered company as such, for the Dutch themselves relied on such organizations, or other forms of cartel, for a great part of their traffic to the Americas and Africa, as well as to the East Indies and for regulating their fisheries. If England was going to compete successfully in regions such as Asia, Africa and the Levant then chartered companies not only had to stay; they had to be strengthened or in the case of the Royal Africa Company set up by Charles II, increased.

An element of deregulation and liberalization was also present regarding the issues of foreign immigration and religious toleration. Several English mercantilist writers lamented Dutch success in drawing off skilled workers to Leiden and urged the English state to endeavour to attract skilled operatives from the continent to England.[42] Thomas Violet, whose writings frequently exemplify that mixture of advocacy of state intervention and deregulating tendencies so characteristic of English economic thought of the period, wanted Dover turned into a free port and England to be altogether more accommodating to 'merchants strangers', pointing out that Genoa, Livorno and Amsterdam had all achieved commercial greatness by granting foreigners 'equal privileges with their own natives'.[43] The pressure for the re-admission of the Jews into England, and subsequently the arguments for keeping them there, certainly emanated in part from mercantilist sources.[44] Sir Josiah Child judged that the commerce of the Jews, even if prejudicial to particular groups of established merchants in England, should be regarded as advantageous to England's trade as a whole.[45]

The central idea in the work of men such as Worsely, Violet, Robinson, Downing and Child, who shaped English mercantilist thought in its classic phase, was that

> for recovery of trade and commerce, the merchants need encouragement and protection from the state, at home and abroad, according to the practice of the lords of the United Provinces who are so vigilant over their traffic that, upon the least complaint of obstruction, they use all means, either by treaty or by force, to remove it.[46]

But how much of the state action inspired by this central idea proved effective? Certain strands of English mercantilist legislation, the Navigation Acts and the restrictions on shipping sailing to the colonies, undoubtedly had a considerable effect. Yet, all considered, the impact of England's mercantilist challenge to Dutch world trade primacy proved relatively weak. When it came to using the power of the state to manipulate markets and engineer shifts in international trade, it would seem that England could not really hope to match Spain or France. For there was nothing which the Dutch obtained from England which was essential for the functioning of their trade system, while England was never of the first importance as a market for Dutch products and re-exports.[47] Indeed, insofar as the Navigation Act reduced Dutch re-exports to England, and their carrying of goods from other markets to England, it served, paradoxically, to free the Dutch further from any reliance they may have had on England. How different was the position with regard to pre-1647 Spain or post-1667 France! Spanish and Spanish American commodities, in particular silver, dyestuffs and merino wool, were all vitally important to the functioning of Dutch overseas trade and Holland's industries, as were the commodities of France, especially wine, brandy, and salt. Similarly both Spain and France were many times more important than England as markets for Dutch products and re-exports.[48] In the case of Dutch exports of fine cloth and camlets and re-exports of spices, for example, France and Spain were the two largest markets whilst England was of almost negligible significance. Thus ultimately England had no other effective weapon against the Dutch overseas trading system during the classic period of English mercantilism than her formidable naval power.

Potentially, England's naval might did represent an overwhelming threat to Dutch world trade primacy, and there were many foreign diplomatic observers who were of the opinion that England's navy and privateers would indeed soon overthrow Dutch hegemony over maritime trade.[49] In England, in the midst of the 'maritime crisis' which began in the late 1640s, the temptation to use the country's naval might to bludgeon the nation's way out of its difficulties was almost overwhelming. It was not mercantilist legislation such as the Navigation Act of 1651 which made the First Anglo-Dutch War inevitable but, as Simon Groenveld has shown,[50] the escalating English harrassment of Dutch shipping in the Channel, North Sea, Irish Sea, and Caribbean. By 1651 English seizures of Dutch merchant vessels on the high seas on a variety of pretexts, such as that they were carrying arms to Ireland or Scotland, or trading with English colonies in the Caribbean — frequently well-grounded suspicions but not ones the Dutch authorities had any sympathy for — had reached intolerable levels. During 1651 no less than 140 Dutch merchant vessels were brought into English ports by the navy or privateers on one charge or another.[51] Another thirty Dutch ships were seized on the high seas in the month of January 1652 alone. For the Dutch, interference on such a scale was totally unacceptable. Either the Dutch state possessed the power to compel England to stop disrupting Dutch commerce, or it did not. If it did not then Dutch world trade primacy was at an end.

Nor is there any question that if it came to a fight, England's navy had the edge over that of the Dutch. Initially, the Dutch may have had more recent experience of naval warfare than the English, and it may be that their best commanders, Tromp and De Ruyter, had more flair than their counterparts. But England's navy had more and larger purpose-built warships and a decided superiority in terms of weight of guns.[52] By the time of the Second War, the Dutch navy had been greatly stengthened, but so had England's, so that the gap in firepower was never closed. It was the potency of the English 'three-deckers' above all which persuaded Venetian, French and Swedish observers that it was English guns which would finally put an end to Dutch commercial greatness.

Yet in this era of furious sea-wars with the Dutch, English sea-power in the end proved much less effective than expected. England was superior in naval power but failed to win the naval conflict. In the First War England won the big battles in the North Sea, but despite this failed to win any commercial or maritime concessions whatsoever from the Dutch. In the Second War the English were eventually beaten and induced to sign a peace by which Surinam, the English foothold in the Banda Islands, Pulorun, and the former English West Africa base of Cormantine were handed over to the Dutch in exchange for New Netherland, which the Dutch considered indefensible in any case. England also conceded to the Dutch the much argued-over principle of 'free ship, free goods', which meant that England now abandoned all right to stop and search Dutch vessels suspected of trading with her enemies or breaking her laws.[53] Finally, in the Third War, in which the Dutch were all but overwhelmed by a joint Anglo-French attack, it seemed at first impossible that England should fail to make massive gains at Dutch expense. Yet not only, by 1674, was Charles II induced to make peace with the Dutch without having captured anything, but he failed even to recover Surinam, Pulorun or Cormantine, surely one of the most astounding results in the history of maritime conflict!

Why then in the end, despite all initial expectations, did England's naval might prove an ineffective instrument against Dutch world trade primacy? The answer is that the Dutch overseas trading system rested on a degree of leverage over markets and shipping resources, as well as financial power, which enabled the Dutch Republic to put such pressure on England that it proved impossible to sustain the naval offensive for long enough to do the Dutch real damage or to force them into maritime concessions. The First Anglo-Dutch War has traditionally been regarded as a victory for England. But this is only true with regard to the naval battles in home waters. Further afield the boot was very much on the other foot with extremely grim consequences for England's trade and shipping. The Dutch, in alliance with Denmark, closed the Sound to English shipping, shutting down the whole of the English Baltic trade for as long as the war lasted.[54] They had the upper hand in the Mediterranean also and, after their victory over the English at the battle of Liverno in March 1653, shut down the whole of the English trade with Italy and the Levant.[55] In the East Indies and the Persian Gulf the Dutch East India Company swept the English off the sea.

In the Second War the Dutch again closed the Baltic to England and paralysed England's trade with the Mediterranean. Again the Dutch Company had matters all its own way in the East Indies and on the coast of India. But this time there was also a new form of pressure: the Dutch mounted a highly effective privateering campaign of their own which, from the early stages of the war onwards, captured more, and more valuable ships, from the English than vice versa.[56] In the Third War, attacked by both the French and the English, the Dutch States General kept all the merchant and fishing fleets in port making thousands of men redundant and forcing them, to feed their families, to sign on with the privateers. This time the Dutch privateers hunted the English in large packs off the east coast of Britain, in the Channel, around the coasts of Spain and Portugal, off Virginia and New England, almost everywhere. The result was the greatest disaster in England's maritime history. Daniel Defoe later stated that 'in the last war with the Dutch we lost 2,000 sail of ships great and small in the first year'.[57] This was an exaggeration. But the real total for the whole of the war was certainly well above 700;[58] and although the disaster was excised from the national record and is rarely if ever mentioned in modern history books, it had a tremendous, demoralizing impact at the time. In effect, England accepted in 1674 that she could not break the Dutch system by force.

To sum up, England's response to her post-1647 'maritime crisis', caused by the restructuring and strengthening of the Dutch overseas trade system in the wake of the Dutch-Spanish peace, was a sustained outburst of aggressive mercantilist deliberation, writing and legislation. Some of the legislation had far-reaching effects and did strengthen England's shipping and especially her colonial trade. Also the role of privilege in English trade was at least somewhat reduced and new elements, including the Jews, began for the first time to play a significant role. But it is also true that large parts of the English mercantilist programme, including the tightening of public regulation of manufacturing and packaging, and the establishment of Dutch-style financial institutions, failed to yield much result. Ultimately the English mercantilist challenge to the Dutch system, backed up though it was by superior naval force, proved to be largely ineffective.

Notes

1. For a general analysis of the Dutch role in world trade during the seventeenth century, the reader is referred to my *Dutch Primacy in World Trade, 1585-1740* (Oxford, 1989).
2. S. Groenveld, *Verlopend getij. De Nederlandse Republiek en de Engelse Burgeroorlog, 1640-1646* (Dieren, 1984), pp.11-12; S. Groenveld, 'The English Civil Wars as a Cause of the First Anglo-Dutch War, 1640-1652', *Historical Journal*, XXX (1987), 545, 551.
3. C. Wilson, *Profit and Power. A Study of England and the Dutch Wars* (2nd printing, The

Hague, 1978), pp.25-30; J.E. Eliaz, *Het voorspel van den eersten Engelschen Oorlog* (2 vol., The Hague, 1920), II, pp.92-6.
4. J.K. Federowicz, *England's Baltic Trade in the Early Seventeenth Century* (Cambridge, 1980), pp.92-6.
5. J.I. Israel, 'The Phases of the Dutch *straatvaart*. A Chapter in the Economic History of the Mediterranean', *Tijdschrift voor Geschiedenis*, XCIX (1986), 12-17.
6. P.J. Blok, 'Koopmansadviezen aangaande het plan tot oprichting eener compagnie van assurantie (1629-1635)', *Bijdragen en Mededelingen van het Historisch Genootschap*, XXI (1900), 47f.
7. H. Taylor, 'Trade, Neutrality and the "English Road"', 1630-1648', *Economic History Review*, 2nd ser. XXV (1972), 239.
8. J. Schreiner, *Nederland og Norge, 1625-1650. Trelastutforsel og handelspolitik* (Oslo, 1933), pp.48-50; J. Schreiner, 'Die Niederländer und die Norwegische Holzausfuhr im 17. Jahrhundert', *Tijdschrift voor Geschiedenis*, XLIX (1934), 323-6.
9. J.I. Israel, *The Dutch Republic and the Hispanic World, 1606-1661* (Oxford, 1982), pp.354-6.
10. M.P. Ashley, *Financial and Commercial Policy under the Cromwellian Protectorate* (Oxford, 1934), p.160; Israel, 'Phases of the Dutch *straatvaart*', p.17.
11. Israel, *The Dutch Republic and the Hispanic World*, pp.346-7, 416-26.
12. *Bronnen tot de geschiedenis van den Levantschen handel* (ed. K. Heeringa, 3 vol., The Hague, 1910-17), I, p.112; John Thurloe, *A Collection of State Papers* (7 vol., London, 1742), II, pp.144-5.
13. British Library (BL) MS Sloane 3662, fo. 58; V. Harlow, *A History of Barbados, 1625-1685* (Oxford, 1926), pp.65-70.
14. R. Davis, 'English Merchant Shipping and Anglo-Dutch Rivalry in the Seventeenth Century', National Maritime Museum pamphlet (London, 1975), p.31.
15. J.E. Farnell, 'The Navigation Act of 1651. The First Dutch War and the London Merchant Community', *Economic History Review*, 2nd ser. XVI (1963/4), 450.
16. R. Baetens, 'An Essay on Dunkirk Merchants and Capital Growth during the Spanish Period', in *From Dunkirk to Danzig. Shipping and Trade in the North Sea and the Baltic, 1350-1850* (ed. W.G. Heeres *et al.*, Hilversum, 1988), p.121.
17. B. Worsley, *The Advocate or a Narrative of the State and Condition of Things between the English and Dutch Nation, in relation to Trade* (London, 1652), p.7.
18. *Calendar of State papers. Domestic, 1651*, p.300.
19. T. Violet, *The Advancement of Merchandize or Certain Propositions for the Improvement of the Trade of this Commonwealth* (London, 1651), p.7; Ashley, *Financial and Commercial Policy*, pp.161-2.
20. Public Record Office, London (PRO) SP 105/150, fo. 167, resolution of the Levant Company Court, 17 Jan. 1647 (1648); the Company renewed its complaint about importing 'indirectly ... from the Netherlands' the following year, see *Calendar of State Papers. Domestic, 1649-50*, p.12.
21. Thurloe, *State Papers*, III, p.142.
22. The parliamentary expedition sent to reduce Barbados to obedience in 1651 captured twenty-four Dutch vessels found trading there, five of them Zeelanders; eighteen more Dutch merchantmen trading with the island, or *Barbados-vaerders* as they were called in Dutch, were seized in 1655 and another six in 1658; Israel, *Dutch Primacy*, p.239.
23. Harlow, *History of Barbados*, pp.93-4.
24. Sir George Downing to Lord Chancellor Clarendon, The Hague, 22 April 1664 in T.H. Lister, *Life and Administration of Clarendon* (3 vol., London, 1838), III, p.308.
25. *A Brief Narration of the Present Estate of the Bilbao Trade* (?London, ?1650), p.9; Taylor, 'Trade, Neutrality and the 'English Road', p.240; J.I. Israel, 'Spanish Wool Exports and the European Economy, 1610-1640', *Economic History Review*, 2nd ser. XXXIII (1980), 205, 208.
26. *A Brief Narration*, p.2.
27. Thurloe, *State Papers*, I, pp.200-1; see also Wilson, *Profit and Power*, p.31.
28. Thurloe, *loc. cit.*; see also *A Brief Narration*, pp.1-3, 9; and Henry Robinson, *Certain Proposals in Order to the Peoples Freedome and Accommodation in some Particulars, with the Advancement of Trade and Navigation of this Commonwealth in generall* (London, 1652), p.11.
29. Worsley, *The Advocate*, p.7.
30. *A Brief Narration*, p.3.
31. Robinson, *Certain Proposals*, p.11.

32. Child speaks also of the 'exact making of all their native commodities, and packing of their herring, codfish and all other commodities...', Sir Josiah Child, *A New Discourse of Trade* (1672) (London, 1693), pp.2-3.
33. T. van Tijn, 'Pieter de la Court. Zijn leven en zijn economische denkbeelden', *Tijdschrift voor Geschiedenis*, LXIX (1956), 316-25.
34. Worsley, *The Advocate*, p.9.
35. Robinson, *Certain Proposals*, p.11.
36. *A Brief Narration*, p.3.
37. C.H. Firth and R.S. Rait, *Acts and Ordinances of the Interregnum. 1642-1660* (2 vol., London, 1911), II, pp.451-5.
38. Child, *A New Discourse of Trade*, preface; see also pp.8, 10.
39. *Calendar of State Papers. Domestic, 1650*, pp.178, 183; Robinson, *Certain Proposals*, pp.10, 18-19.
40. J.I. Israel, *European Jewry in the Age of Mercantilism, 1550-1750* (Oxford, 1985), pp.2-3.
41. Firth and Rait, *Acts and Ordinances*, II, p.405.
42. Thurloe, *State Papers*, I, p.200: Violet, *The Advancement of Merchandize*, pp.10-11.
43. *Ibid.*, pp.2-3.
44. D. Katz, *Philosemites and the Readmission of the Jews into England, 1603-1655* (Oxford, 1982), pp.225-9; Israel, *European Jewry*, pp.158-60.
45. *Ibid.*, p.160.
46. *Calendar of State Papers. Domestic, 1650*, p.180.
47. Israel, *Dutch Primacy*, p.285.
48. *Ibid.*, pp.285-6.
49. Gugliemo Berchet, *Cromwell e la Repubblica di Venezia* (Venice, 1864), p.73; *Calendar of State Papers, Venetian*, XXVIII (1647-52), p.256; Wilson, *Profit and Power*, p.65.
50. Groenveld, 'The English Civil Wars', pp.561-4.
51. *Ibid.*, p.561.
52. C. Boxer, 'The Anglo-Dutch Wars of the 17th Century, 1652-1674', National Maritime Museum pamphlet (London, 1974), pp.4-6, 15, 25.
53. Ashely, *Financial and Commercial Policy*, p.172; this important concession was spelt out in detail under the Anglo-Dutch maritime agreement of February 1668; see H.C. Diferee, *De geschiedenis van den Nederlandschen handel tot den val der Republiek* (Amsterdam, 1908), p.325.
54. Israel, *Dutch Primacy*, p.211.
55. 'Our losses here have been so visible to all Europe, Asia, and Africa', reported the English consul at Livorno in January 1654, 'that they will not believe but our condition is as bad at home'; Thurloe, *State Papers*, I, p.656.
56. J.R. Bruijn, 'Dutch Privateering during the Second and Third Anglo-Dutch Wars', *Acta Historiae Neerlandicae*, IX (1976), 89; Israel, *Dutch Primacy*, pp.278-9.
57. Daniel Defoe, *An Enquiry into the Danger and Consequences of a War with the Dutch* (London, 1712), p.4.
58. Bruijn, 'Dutch Privateering', p.89; J.R. Bruijn's research on this subject has totally transformed our perceptions of the role of Dutch privateering in the Anglo-Dutch Wars; nevertheless, as he himself admits, the figures he gives for Dutch prizes taken from the English are, certainly, considerably too low; see Israel, *Dutch Primacy*, pp.298-9.

5

Economic Policy, Trade, and Managing the English War-Economy, 1689-1712

D. W. Jones

Historians have had perhaps rather more to say about what states have done to promote trade than about what trade has done to promote states. However, for England's great war-effort of the late seventeenth and early eighteenth centuries, the contribution of trade ultimately proved to be crucial for that successful projection of military power abroad whereby England gained Great Power status for the first time. State action, on the other hand, was relatively powerless in securing what was required.

That trade had to be crucial for England's war-effort is clear enough. Following William of Orange's momentous expedition of November l688 to become William III of England, England (with a population of 5.2m) entered the Grand Alliance against Louis XIV of France (population 20m) and commenced what became known for her as the 'Nine Years' War', sending funds and troops for war in Europe. To start with, until the Irish emergency was over, this mainly meant sending funds abroad to subsidize the Duke of Savoy in Northern Italy and various German princes to fight alongside the Dutch in Flanders (though England did already have some thousands of her own subject troops there). From 1692 onwards, however, a major build-up of English troops plus further foreign mercenaries began, so that by the years 1695-7, counting officers and troops, the English army in Flanders stood at some 68,000 strong (of whom some 48,000 were subject officers and troops, the rest foreign mercenaries). The Succession War in the 1700s was to witness a similar increase, but greater in scale. After being quickly re-established in 1702 at some 52,000 strong (officers and men), England's Flanders army grew to reach some 69,000 by 1710-11, the only difference now being that proportionately more were foreign mercenaries, and fewer subject officers and troops. Whilst in pursuit of the chimerical 'No Peace without Spain', side by side with huge subsidies paid to Portugal, Savoy, and the Archduke Charles (the Austrian candidate for the Spanish Succession), English troops were sent to fight in Portugal and Spain, Catalonia becoming a major theatre of operations from 1708 onwards. By the peak years of 1710-11 England was paying, either directly on her own army establishments or indirectly through subsidies, for some 171,000 officers and men fighting abroad in Europe.[1]

The trouble was, however, that none of these commitments could be provided for by direct supply from England's shores. In part this was because the green fodder, required for the horse when summer campaigning, had to be secured locally wherever it was to be found; the quantities involved were simply too vast to be supplied from magazines in the rear.[2] In part, also, this was because it was obviously better for the officers and men to be able to buy freshly baked bread (instead of bisket) and fresh (instead of salted) meat locally; moreover, in the Low Countries the English army could avail itself of the services of a whole host of local, and notably Jewish, entrepreneurs well versed in the business of supplying armies and whose supplies were exempt from local excises.[3]

But in much the greater part, the impossibility of direct supply was simply a matter of the sheer weight and bulk of the supplies that would have been involved. The weight of supplies required by the Flanders army can be estimated at some 245,000 tons annually and, allowing for the bulk of the beer, hay and oats especially, an estimated 441,000 ship-tons would have been needed to ship them out.[4] This can be compared with the 475,000 tons that sufficed to carry the whole of England's foreign trade at this time.[5] True, supplying Flanders would have involved but short-haul voyages. Yet even if we assume that ships in a supply shuttle could have been worked to make fully twice the number of voyages annually made in peace-time trade, the requirement still stands at some 44,000 tons of shipping, or some twelve per cent of England's total mercantile tonnage of the late 1680s.[6] The position with Catalonia was even more hopeless: on the same assumptions, some 88,000 tons of shipping would have been the requirement. In any case, quite apart from giving the French the best of all possible targets to attack, attempting to ship the quantities involved would have been far too costly and time-consuming, and probably beyond the port facilities of the day.

Given the evident impracticality of direct supply, therefore, England had to adopt the only practical alternative – namely, the remitting of funds abroad across the foreign exchanges so that her officers, troops, foreign mercenaries, and allies abroad could then purchase the supplies they needed locally as best they could. But this was doubly dangerous for remitting abroad in this way courted grave economic risks that would not have applied had direct supply been undertaken. Direct supply would obviously have meant that the taxes and loans raised in England to pay for the military commitments abroad would also have been spent in England. Accordingly, the continued stability of England's output and employment would have been guaranteed as this spending would have served to take up the savings extracted by the taxes and loans out of English consumption. At the same time, the physical shipping out of the supplies would also have obviated any need for foreign exchange and thus guaranteed the continued stability of England's balance of payments as well. But raising taxes and loans in England and then remitting them across the foreign exchanges to be spent abroad risked instability on both these counts. Spending abroad and not at home where the savings had been made risked a deficiency of home spending and so a fall in home output and employment; remitting across the exchanges risked a balance of payment deficit and so a money outflow leading to a money squeeze at home, to reduce further home output and employment.

To be sure, these dangers would have been considerably reduced had England possessed large and secure trade surpluses in her trade with Europe. For quite apart from the fact that the required foreign exchange would then have been available, the counterpart of such surpluses has to be the saving whereby not all the import that could have been consumed, was actually being consumed. Were the government able to transfer its taxes and loans across such surpluses, therefore, its taxes and loans would, in effect, have appropriated this saving, and not current spending, leaving current output and employment undisturbed. Much the same effect could also be achieved by England's East India trade in which each year, as the fruit of past investments of bullion (silver mainly) shipped out to India, imports came in from India of which a substantial proportion then went out for sale as re-exports to Europe. In Europe these sales normally just balanced the bullion that had to be purchased for shipment back to India to initiate new cycles of the trade. Now should these latter investments be halted at a time when the government needed to remit taxes and loans, the foreign exchange required to do so would thus become available once the East India re-export earnings were no longer offset by the usual bullion purchases. Meanwhile, current output and employment would again remain undisturbed, the taxes and loans having this time appropriated, in effect, the saving previously covering that bullion investment now no longer being undertaken.

There are also further possibilities, of course. Perhaps the spending abroad itself might help. Thus, to boost English exports, some of it might come back for supplies bought from England (e.g., butter, cheese, and grain for making the army's bread and beer, say); equally, to reduce imports, some of it might divert abroad a part of England's erstwhile import consumption (e.g., wines and linens, say, consumed now by the officers and men serving overseas). Either, or both, would help restore England's employment and balance of payments position. Furthermore, one or two initiatives by the government are conceivable. The government might attempt to pre-empt supplies of foreign exchange or arrange loans abroad as ways of easing its exchange problem; equally, as ways of promoting English exports, it might introduce export bounties or attempt to oblige its subsidies to be received in English goods.

However, with the possible exception of the East India trade immediately before the Succession War, none of these possibilities was at all hopeful. The remittances were so large that those of the 1690s, standing at more than £1.2m annually over the years 1694-6, were roughly double the total of England's trade surpluses in the 1680s; while those of the 1700s, standing at more than £2.0m over the years 1708-11, were rather more than double the trade surpluses of the boom years of interwar trade, 1699-1701.[7] Moreover, it was highly unlikely that in war anything like these surpluses could be preserved. For at the same time as England was maintaining armies and allies abroad on forward military operations, most of the time she was also employing her navy forward, whether covering the Irish operations of the years 1689-91; covering and participating in two huge, if wholly abortive 'Descents' on the French coast in 1692 and 1693; attacking French corn ships over 1693-4; then going on extensive southern European and Mediterranean operations first over the years 1694-5, and then even more extensively during the Succession War, in 1702 and between 1704 and 1708.

Nothing could have been more dangerous for England's trade, in which her European earnings depended importantly on being able to ship in sugars, tobaccos, dyestuffs and East India textiles from her Atlantic colonies and trading stations in India, and then on re-exporting a substantial proportion of these for sale in Europe. True, we have already noted how the East India re-exports were usually offset by the bullion purchased for shipment out to India. But this was certainly not so in the case of the Atlantic re-exports together with the New England and Newfoundland cod sold direct in the Iberian peninsula (with the proceeds remitted back to England). Each year, the sum total of what all these sales earned for sterling was greater by some £800,000 than the naval stores, linens and metalwares that had to be bought to run the Atlantic trades each year: hence the seriousness of a large naval mobilization committed primarily to forward operations. (The naval stores were to build, equip and re-equip the ships upon which these trades were so dependent, and the linens and metalwares were for shipping back to the colonies.)[8] Naval manning requirements were bound to starve the Atlantic trades of the men required to serve them. Moreover, a dangerously unseasonal pattern of sailings could well be imposed upon trade if ships were not allowed out before the end of the naval manning season in early May (thus bringing them into tropical waters during the hurricane season);

and if ships were obliged to return before the beginning of the naval season in February (and thus force their return through stormy, wintry, European waters). In the meantime, given the forward operations, far too few ships-of-the-line were likely to be spared to defend departing or returning ships against the privateering attack which the French were only too likely to launch against English commerce.

During the later 1680s at least, though not immediately before the Succession War (when it no longer applied), the position was made even more vulnerable by the extent to which England's trade balance, to the tune of some £250,000 annually, had become dependent on the surpluses Ireland had in her trade with Europe, and notably so with France.[9] Ireland was in deficit on her trade with England and had rents to remit to English absentee landlords. Accordingly, Ireland settled these debts by making over her European surpluses to England and thus helped pay for England's European imports. But a war against France was bound to bring Ireland's trade with France to an end no less than England's; the surpluses previously made over to England would therefore be lost. In the event, also, there was to be the Irish rebellion and a campaign to suppress it that had severe effects on Irish trade throughout most of the 1690s.[10] Nor for the later 1680s was the position as far as the East India trade any more encouraging. Following an interloping attack on the Company controlling the India trade which competitively drove investments in the trade to wholly uneconomic levels over the years 1682-5, there was then a slump in the India trade.[11] So once war came in 1689, there was very little, if any, scope for a favourable East India 'balance' effect to operate. (For the Succession War, on the other hand, the position, as we shall shortly see, was much more promising once there had been a massive competitive investment in two rival companies over the years 1698-1701 immediately preceding the war.)

Where England's balance of payments was likely to fail her, therefore, the hope that much of England's spending abroad might either come back to England or divert imports away from her shores turns out to be equally unpromising. Much the greater part of spending went on providing feed for the horse, and fresh bread, beer (very bulky) and meat for the men, all of which had to be bought locally. To be sure, there was spending on butter and cheese and on grains to make the bread and beer, together with woollens for the clothing of the foreign mercenaries, all of which, in principle at least, could thus have been bought from England to boost English exports. Further, the consumption of wines and linens by the officers and men could also, in principle at least, have reduced imports by diverting erstwhile import consumption away from England's shores. At most, however, such spending could not have amounted to more than some 36% of total spending in the 1690s, or to more than just some 25% in the 1700s.[12] (This latter, much lower, proportion simply reflects the much larger spending in southern Europe during the Succession War and of which, either because of distance or because so much of it comprised subsidies, much less could realistically be expected to come back for English goods.)

In practice, however, far less than even these relatively small proportions could be expected to be achieved. The only provision laid down by the government was to require the army's bread contractors in Flanders to export annually out of England a quantity of grain equivalent to the amount they used in making the army's bread. (In the 1690s, though not in the 1700s when no stipulation was made, it was specified that the bread itself was to be made out of Prussian rye.)[13] But at best the value of the grain involved could not have amounted to more than some £90,000 annually.[14] For all other supplies in Flanders, the Dutch were far better placed to provide what was required, using the rivers to do so; also, French luxury goods, including wines, were readily available in the Low Countries throughout the 1690s and 1700s and these, prohibited in England, were only too likely to entice much of the officers' spending.[15] From time to time, the government did attempt to get the Duke of Savoy, in return for the subsidy he received from England, to clothe his troops in English woollens; but he appears to have done so only during the years 1695-6 and 1708-11, while the amounts involved (included in the proportions given above) would not have made, and did not make, any decisive difference.[16] The situation was similar with the clothing of England's foreign mercenaries directly on her establishments (also included in the proportions given above): as we shall shortly see, direct action on this score seems to have proved unnecessary, as the foreign mercenaries were clothed in English woollens anyway. (The clothing of England's own subject troops, plus the Imperialists hired to serve in Catalonia, we must note, comprised purely internal transactions; this clothing was arranged and paid for at home and shipped out in bales that were not included in the trade statistics.)[17]

We are thus left with what the government might be able to do to save the exchange and/or promote exports. Neither was promising. Saving the exchange would have meant either borrowing abroad or recourse to the sort of pre-emptive techniques whereby in an earlier age pressure had been exerted on the London Merchant Adventurers to make over the proceeds of their cloth sales abroad to army paymasters there, in return for reimbursement at an agreed rate in England.[18] But quite apart from the fact that the Merchant Adventurers no longer controlled any branch of the cloth trade,[19] the vastness of the remittances now made it essential that the government should enter the exchange market only in equal competition with everyone else. Otherwise the procuring of essential imports by private individuals would be hopelessly disrupted; in any case, it was only in this way that, as the huge remittances demanded, access could be gained to what the *whole* of trade was earning. When the government attempted on a modest scale to contract for the export of some of the Cornish tin it was buying to ease the slump in the Cornish tin industry, and for the proceeds of sale (as earlier with the Merchant Adventurers) to be made over abroad, talk of such exports reduced prices on the continent to wholly uneconomic levels.[20] Nor was borrowing likely to provide a means of escape: the newly established Revolution Finance was far too unknown a quantity to have attracted much foreign lending whereby pounds could thus have been recycled back to England on the model, say, of the petro-dollars of the 1970s.[21]

The likelihood of promoting an export boom, finally, was equally unpromising. For whatever the government might attempt to do, it could not change the fact that by the later seventeenth century all major English exports faced stern competition in Europe. True, provided prices remained low enough, English grains could be expected to benefit from the reintroduction in 1689 (though there is no suggestion that this was connected with the war) of the corn export bounties first introduced in the 1670s; moreover, for malt exports excise was rebated to the exporter from 1697 onwards.[22] But it was only barley and malt that had not been part of that great grain trade that had supplied Europe with wheat and rye from Danzig and Riga since the early sixteenth century. Even with a substantial degree of subsidization, therefore, English wheat and rye exports could hardly be expected to make much progress unless something wholly untoward happened to the great Baltic producers.

The case is very similar with England's woollen textile exports (though there was never any question of subsidizing these). By the later seventeenth century these also faced stern competition in Europe. In the Low Countries there were great centres or regions of production established at Leiden, and in and around Tilburg, Helmond and Eindhoven in the southern extremities of the Dutch Republic and in and around Verviers in the vicinity of Liège. Further afield there were the even greater production centres of Dresden, Leipzig and Zwickau in Saxony; of Bautzen, Gorlitz and Zittau in Lusatia (belonging to Saxony); and of Lissa, Fraustadt, Glogau and Breslau in Silesia.[23] Again, therefore, unless something untoward happened to these producers, there was little prospect that English woollens sales to Europe could be much increased. To put the same thing another way: in the likely event of the destruction of England's pre-war trade surpluses, it was unlikely that there would be an increase in England's inherently more secure domestic exports. Some form of compensation for the erosion of those trade surpluses was going to be needed in the 1690s, and even more in the 1700s.

The central importance of trade for England's war-effort must now be clear. Because so little of the foreign military spending could or would come back to England, and because England's pre-war balances would probably be reduced or even destroyed, any successful projection of English arms abroad required an export boom. Only such an export boom could re-absorb into employment those resources put out of employment in England when taxes and loans were spent abroad and not at home. And only such an export boom could also provide the foreign exchange whereby the taxes and loans could be transmitted across the foreign exchanges without bullion export, and thus an ensuing money squeeze. On the other hand, it is also clear that the English state was relatively powerless to engineer such a boom. The relevance of state action during the wars was limited largely to matters of management, and to the management in particular of the inherently contradictory character of the chosen war strategy. Throughout, the forward naval deployment constantly threatened to destroy that very trade performance upon which the successful forward deployment of the armies and allies abroad depended. In short, the situation was one where though bad management could well lead to disaster, good management could not of itself produce success. Again, only an export boom – and one generated by fundamentally changed market circumstances abroad – could supply that.

This analysis is borne out by the evidence. Serious mismanagement produced a near-disaster in the 1690s, just as a remarkable export boom coupled with a fortuitous gain on the East India balance created a near-miraculous success in the 1700s, despite the fact that England's commitments were roughly double those of the earlier decade. The near-disaster of the 1690s was perhaps predictable. To accommodate naval manning requirements, draconian controls on men and tonnage were imposed on trade, limiting the Atlantic trades to under half the men and tonnage they had employed in the 1680s.[24] Voyages were made dangerously unseasonal when no ships were allowed out before the end of May and when they were obliged to return before February.[25] On the other hand, far too few ships-of-the-line were allocated to commerce protection. As a result, severely reduced trade levels suffered heavy losses from storms and at the hands of the French privateers. English re-exports to Europe, and the important balance earned there by her Atlantic trades, were halved. In the meantime, since nothing untoward had happened to foreign competitors, exports grew very little.[26] Nor did England's spending abroad help much: very little of this came back for goods at home or diverted imports away from England's consumption. As Richard Hill, Deputy Paymaster of the army in Flanders graphically described towards the end of 1695, it was the Dutch who were supplying the bulk of requirements while in his opinion more spending was going on the French goods available in Flanders than ever came back for English and Irish supplies.[27]

Bearing in mind, too, the loss of the Irish balance, it is hardly surprising that in the 1690s there was a serious depreciation of England's exchange; nor that, after having first been drawn out of the country in the late 1680s by the so-called Dutch *schellingen* plague of these years,[28] silver bullion flowed out of the country culminating with a massive £700,000 outflow in 1694. England of course ought to have been brought to her knees, when so little of the spending abroad was absorbing the savings made at home, and when the bullion outflow should have been producing a severe money squeeze. Clipping the coin, however, enabled England to escape internal collapse, at least until the years 1696-7. For it was by clipping the coin that England was able to get hold of the bullion she otherwise could not have obtained, and thus pay debts abroad that otherwise she could not have met. At the same time, because clipping rapidly became an industry in the land, enough new income was generated to take up the resources released at home by the spending abroad. Finally, passing on newly clipped coin at face value meant that a money squeeze was also avoided, for in this way no reduction of the effective money stock occurred.[29] To be sure, confidence was lost late in 1694 and a damaging recoining had to take place over the years 1696-7. The ensuing shortage of circulating media inflicted a serious crisis in home employment in 1697; for four months between early July and late October 1696, remittances to the Flanders army broke down altogether. Still, England managed to survive these years, by which time Louis XIV was ready to sue for peace, especially once William had retaken Namur in 1695. At home, in the meantime, 1695 was a year of inflationary hyperactivity triggered by the currency crisis; it was this which served to keep the country going for one more vital year.

Nothing could contrast more strikingly with the 1690s than the position during the 1700s. The 1700s should have been a re-run of the 1690s — but worse. For now not only did the even greater remittances (roughly double those of the 1690s) risk even greater bullion export and unemployment, but the reformed coinage meant that there could now be no clipping to provide a means of escape from these dangers. But in fact quite the opposite actually happened, as is perhaps best attested by the remarkable stability of England's exchange rates, and by the very minor bullion outflows during the Succession War. Improved management did contribute something, insofar as the draconian controls on shipping of the earlier war were not re-introduced. Also, Navigation Act requirements were relaxed to permit the employment of a higher proportion of foreign seamen (only the East Coast coal trade having been allowed to do so in the 1690s).[30] No 'Descents' like those of 1692 and 1693 were attempted, and it was easier to provide cover for trade when so many military and naval movements — notably to the Iberian peninsula and into the Mediterranean — now ran parallel with major branches of English trade.[31] It is also possible, though by no means certain, that commerce protection improved somewhat, and reduced losses at the hands of the privateers. However, many of the old problems did recur and it may well be that the lower intensity of the French privateering attack was the crucial factor.[32] (Judging from the closing two-and-a-half years of the Nine Years' War, the French fitted out more privateers in the 1690s than they did at any time in the 1700s.)[33]

Nonetheless, better management meant solely that more of England's pre-war surpluses were preserved and maintained than had been the case during the 1690s. For that massive *increase* in England's surpluses which was both required and attained during the 1700s, we must look not to management, but to other developments wholly outside the English government's control. Thus it was very fortunate that immediately before the Succession War there had been a contest between two rival East

India companies for the control of the trade.[34] As a result, a veritable silver mountain of investment had been built up in India. This contest dated back originally to the early 1680s, while the effectiveness of the opposition attack on the established company owed much to the slump in the European diamond trade once Louis XIV had retrenched his purchases in the late 1670s.[35] Once diamonds (usually the only permitted means) were no longer a profitable way of repatriating accumulated gains from India, the company's servants became ever readier to co-operate with interlopers as an alternative, sending goods home with them. Following the great competitive investments of 1698-1701 there was bound to be retrenchment, while throughout the Succession War, conflict with Spain made silver difficult to get hold of.[36] Thanks to the resulting fall in bullion investments, therefore, and the fact that there was a great deal of silver still out in India to generate a flow of imports for some considerable time, what had during 1699-1701 been a significantly negative balance of bullion purchases against East India re-export sales turned into a moderately positive one throughout the 1700s (1709 solely excepted). In most years, indeed, this turn-round contributed the equivalent of between a third and a half of the improvement in the balance enjoyed by Marlborough.[37]

For the rest of this improvement, however, it is to the impact of an unprecedented decade of European war and the opening up of gold production in Brazil that we must look. In 1698 communications between Sao Paulo and the newly established mines were improved so that thereafter ever-increasing quantities of gold, amounting to over a million pounds' worth in some years of the 1700s, reached Lisbon.[38] English exports benefited enormously from the ensuing boom in Brazil, and since English imports from Portugal grew very little during the 1700s, so did England's balance of payments. Equally clear are the beneficial effects for English exports of European war in the 1700s. One aspect of this was that, as England was numbered amongst the greatest producers of 'military' textiles – that is of such woollens as kersey, bays and broad-cloths suitable for making uniforms, plus serge for linings – and was reputed the best,[39] English woollens were bound to benefit from the unprecedented mobilization of the 1700s. (They had also benefited in the 1690s, but mobilization had not then been as great.) In the 1700s, all European armies, including the Dutch, who had needed to mobilize very quickly between 1701 and 1702 once the French were in control of Spanish Flanders, grew further in size; moreover, Peter the Great's Russian army now needed to be uniformed, systematically, for the first time.[40] England dominated all this business, despite Dutch attempts to preserve the business of clothing the troops paid for by Holland and Zeeland for their own indigenous woollens producers.[41] Indeed, it proved unnecessary to follow up English moves of early 1703 to ensure that foreign troops in Flanders, paid for by the English, were clothed in English woollens: it was happening already.[42]

A second, and even more important aspect of war in the 1700s was the way in which it crippled England's competitors and so, for the duration of the Succession War, permitted a dramatic expansion of English exports way beyond anything that even the expanded market for military textiles produced.[43] To oppose the threat of Peter the Great and Augustus of Saxony, Charles XII of Sweden had landed at Narva in 1701 and, having defeated the Russians, marched south right across Estonia, Livonia and Courland (calling at Riga), to reach the vicinity of Warsaw by the end of the year. Between 1702 and 1706 he then operated (at different times) both the length of the Vistula (flowing down to Danzig) and across many of its important tributaries; meanwhile, Peter the Great took the opportunity to occupy Estonia, Livonia and Courland (Riga's hinterland). Little wonder, therefore, that quite apart from the malt and barley exports that now inundated the Republic thanks to the export bounties,[44] English wheat and rye exports should also have made progress both in the Republic and in Portugal thanks to the disruption of Baltic supplies from Danzig and Riga. In Portugal, English grain sales were also assisted by the fighting in Alentejo and Campo Maior which disrupted grain production there and cut off supplies previously coming in from Spanish Estremadura.[45]

English woollens also benefited for similar reasons. In Saxony, woollens production was burdened by the heavy taxes (including a general excise introduced in 1705) levied by Augustus, and by the forcible recruitment of weavers into the Saxon army, which caused a strike at Gorlitz in 1704 (and as it also did later in 1707-8).[46] Then, after Charles XII had struck westward late in 1704, disrupting Silesian production, late in 1706 and following Rehnskjiold's great Swedish victory over the Saxons at Fraustadt, Charles marched right across Silesia, passing close to the woollen textile production centres of Lissa, Fraustadt, Breslau and Glogau, and entered Saxony. He occupied the Duchy with its great woollen textile production centres of Bautzen, Gorlitz, Zittau, Leipzig, Meissen and Dresden for nearly a year, before then marching East in 1708 to meet defeat at Pultava in 1709.[47] (Peter in the meantime was forced by Charles's march to abandon Estonia, Livonia and Courland and to devastate their resources before leaving, making them of no use to the returning Swedes.)[48] A similar situation pertained in the Low Countries where, hard up against the Republic's borders, the French were in control of Spanish Flanders at the beginning of the Succession War. In 1702 Marlborough had campaigned straight through the important region of textile production surrounding Eindhoven, Tilburg and Helmond with devastating effects for production. The following year he laid siege to Verviers, Liège, and Limburg with similar results for textile production there.[49] Little wonder, again, therefore, that in the 1700s there should also have been such a striking expansion of English woollens exports to the Low Countries and Germany.

* * * * *

Thanks to an extraordinary coincidence of fortune, therefore − clipping in the 1690s and, in the 1700s, East Indian affairs, Brazil gold, Peter the Great, Charles XII, Augustus of Saxony and a war crisis in the Low Countries − England was able first to survive in the Nine Years War and then triumph in the Succession War, becoming a great power for the first time in the space of little more than two decades. For without the lucky coincidences of the later decade especially, English trade would not have been enabled to achieve that real transfer of resources upon which England's great war effort abroad ultimately depended. In this, the English state could do little to achieve what was required, though trade was soon to reap its own reward. Over the years 1715-40, and largely based on precisely those markets of Brazil and Spanish America to which access could well have been imperilled had the Spanish Succession passed uncontested to the French, English exports grew more than they had ever done for at least a century and a half. However, the concern of this article has been specifically the interrelationship between English military power and trade during the wars of the Grand Alliance, rather than the longer-term legacy. And in this connection, bearing in mind England's dubious unilateral peace negotiations with the French and the Restraining Orders of 1712, it is no doubt comforting for Dutch historians to learn that Albion was at least as lucky as she was perfidious.

Notes

1. For a reconstruction of England's military commitments, see D.W. Jones, *War and Economy in the Age of William III and Marlborough* (Oxford, 1988), pp.7-11.
2. G. Perjes, 'Army Provisioning, Logistics and Strategy in the Second Half of the 17th Century', *Acta Historica Academiae Scientorium Hungarica*, XVI (1970), 6, 8, 12, 14-7; D. Chandler, *The Art of Warfare in the Age of Marlborough* (London, 1976), p.17.
3. V. Barbour, *Capitalism in Amsterdam* (Baltimore, 1950), pp.30-1; Bodleian Library, Oxford, MS. Eng. Hist. d 146(1), fo. 7.
4. Jones, *War and Economy*, pp.31-3.
5. R. Davis, *The Rise of the English Shipping Industry in the Seventeenth and Eighteenth Centuries* (London, 1962), p.200.
6. *Ibid.*; Jones, *War and Economy*, p.33 and note 16.
7. *Ibid.*, pp.37-9.
8. *Ibid.*, pp.54-5.
9. *Ibid.*, pp.55-7.
10. *Ibid.*, pp.140-l; L.M. Cullen, *Anglo-Irish Trade 1660-1800* (Manchester, 1968), pp.40-1; *idem*, *An Economic History of Ireland since 1660* (London, 1972), pp.27-34.
11. Jones, *War and Economy*, pp.225, 286-301.
12. *Ibid.*, pp.112-14.
13. Salop County Record Office, Shrewsbury, 112/75, 186; B[ritish] L[ibrary], London, Add. MS 38,707, fos 162-5; P[ublic] R[ecord] O[ffice], London, T 48/12; T 64/132.
14. BL Add. MS 10,123, fo. 106.
15. Jones, *War and Economy*, p.115.
16. *Calendar of Treasury Books (CTB)* (ed. W.A. Shaw, London, 1904-61), XXII, 22; XXIII, 24-5; PRO T1/106/6, 130/131.
17. Jones, *War and Economy*, p.35 and note 25.
18. D.W. Jones, 'The 'Hallage' Receipts of the London Cloth Markets, 1562-c.1720', *Economic History Review*, 2nd series, XXV (1972), 581-2 and notes.
19. W.B. Stephens, *Seventeenth Century Exeter* (Exeter, 1958), pp.85-9; I William and Mary, c. 32.
20. Jones, *War and Economy*, pp.89-90.
21. For the limited amounts that appear to have come in, plus the history of the government's borrowings abroad, see *ibid.*, pp.21, 22-3, 25-6, 89, 225 and note 18.
22. I William and Mary, c. 12; 8 & 9 William III, c. 22.
23. Jones, *War and Economy*, pp.61-4.
24. Davis, *Shipping Industry*, pp.59, 396; PRO CO 9/12, fos 108, 151, 222, 24950, 279; 13, fos 1-2, 143.
25. *CTB* IX & X: index s.v. 'Embargo'.
26. For the general position in the 1690s, see Jones, *War and Economy*, pp.128-36, 145-61.
27. BL Add. MS 10,123, fos 124^r-124^v.
28. E. Enno van Gelder, *Munthervorming tijdens de Republiek* (Amsterdam, 1949), pp.133-4; J.G. van Dillen, *Van Rijkdom en Regenten* (The Hague, 1970), pp.442-3.
29. For an account of the clipping trade, see Jones, *War and Economy*, pp.228-34.
30. 2 William and Mary, sess. 2, c. 7; 2 & 3 Anne, c. 11; 6 Anne, c. 64.
31. Thus between April 1703 and October 1707, it had been possible to provide 29 convoys for the Portugal trade alone (*Journals of the House of Lords*, XVIII, 407).
32. The fullest listing of losses is to be found in the House of Lords Records Office, London: Lords MS 2401 (1707), annexed paper O.
33. This conclusion is based on comparing the figures to be found in the following sources: J. Delumeau, 'La Guerre de course Française sous L'Ancien Régime', in 'Course et Piraterie': Papers of the San Francisco Conference (1975), issued by the Commission Internationale D'Histoire Maritime, Paris, pp.274-5; and figures supplied for the Succession War alone by J.S. Bromley in 'The French Privateering War 1702-1713', in *Historical Essays 1600-1750, presented to David Ogg* (ed. H.E. Bell and R.L. Ollard, London, 1963), pp.302-26.
34. See note 11 above.
35. North Yorkshire Record Office, Northallerton, Letter Book of John Cholmley, *passim*.
36. *Records of Fort St George: Despatches from England 1701-1706* (Madras, 1925), pp.55-6, 60, 65, 76; *1707-1710* (Madras, 1927), p.59.
37. For the overall balance of payments position in the 1700s, see Jones, *War and Economy*, pp.217-24.

38. V. Magalhaes Godinho, 'Portugal and her Empire, 1680-1720', *New Cambridge Modern History*, VI (ed. J.S. Bromley, Cambridge, 1970), p.534; H.V. Livermore, *A New History of Portugal* (Cambridge, 1966), p.206; C.R. Boxer, 'Brazilian Gold and British Traders in the First Half of the Eighteenth Century', *Hispanic American Historical Review*, XXXIX (1969), 429; M. Morineau, 'Or Brésilien et Gazettes Hollandaises', *Revue d'Histoire Moderne et Contemporaine*, XXV (1978), 15.

39. Jones, *War and Economy*, pp.202-3.

40. *Ibid.*; A.I. Jucht, '''Russkaya promylennost'' i snabzenie armii obmundirovian i armuniciez', *Poltava, k 250-letiiu Poltavskogo srazhenia. Sbornik Statei* (Moscow, 1959), pp.211-27.

41. *Groot Placaet-Boek* (The Hague, 1658-1796), V, pp.132-3, 134-6, 145-7, 162-4, 183-5, 195-6, 196-8.

42. *CTB* XVIII, 133, 209; PRO T1/84/60.

43. Jones, *War and Economy*, pp.204-9.

44. PRO T1/103/57; BL Loan 29/45R, fo. 230^v.

45. Godinho, *op. cit.*, p.527; PRO T1/136/40.

46. Josef Leszczynski, 'Die Oberlausitz in den ersten Jahren des nordischen Krieges (1700-1709)', in *Um die polnische Krone: Sachsen und Poland während des nordischen Krieges* (ed. J. Kalisch and J. Gierowski, Berlin, 1962), pp.73-9, 82, 92.

47. R. Hatton, *Charles XII of Sweden* (London, 1968), pp.201, 209; N. Davies, *God's Playground: A History of Poland* (2 vol., Oxford, 1981), I, p.498; Leszczynski, *op. cit.*, pp.82-7.

48. M.S. Anderson, *Peter the Great* (London, 1978), pp.54, 57.

49. W.S. Churchill, *Marlborough, his Life and Time* (4 vol., London, 1933-38), II, pp.136-8; *The Marlborough-Godolphin Correspondence* (ed. Henry L. Snyder, 3 vol., Oxford, 1975), I, p.98.

6

The Limitations of Dutch Economic Policy, 1780-1850: the Incompatibility of Aims and Visions

P.C.H. Overmeer

Ever since the emergence of the nation-state, governments have shown a tendency to increase their grip on the economy.[1] The ability of the state both to stimulate economic developments and to obstruct them has frequently been presented in a rather exaggerated light by historians. Traditionally, they have admired the state as a subject of study and have tended to overestimate its power in economic matters. Nowadays the state is studied as a complex, dynamic system of political institutions, made up of the central government, lower authorities, bureaucracy, laws and regulations. We have come to understand that political and administrative organization can be an instrument on the one hand, but may on the other prove simultaneously to be an obstacle to the actual exercise of influence over economic development.

Since the exposure of the nineteenth-century myth of *laissez-faire*, economic historians have grown rather suspicious of the state. They concentrate on factors of production and environment, and generally adhere to the liberal tenet that political measures tend to obstruct the economy. Nonetheless, Dutch historians still find it hard to resist the temptation of blaming a weak state and institutional impotence for economic decline and stagnation in the period between 1780 and 1850. The historiography of that stagnation and sluggish industrial development after 1813 has now finally shifted the emphasis away from psychological factors to economic ones, but the various different labels that have been attached over the years to the economic policy of this period – mercantilist, late mercantilist, early liberal, liberal – clearly indicate the lack of historiographical consensus, and the varying estimates of the role of the state in the economy.

When the agents of economic policy wanted to change the economic structure they discovered sooner or later that there was a twofold time-lag: one between changes in the economic structure and changes in the economic process, and another between new ideas and political action. Changes in the economic process are only gradually felt in society, and only eventually lead in turn to new ideas and new political action. All the state can do is to react to medium-term or secular impulses in the economic process; the short-term demands of vested interest confuse the issue even more. Political decisions aim to alleviate tensions occurring in the short term between innovative and traditional forces in society and in the economy. In these ways the time-lags and the complex interaction between the economy, society and the state complicate our search for the limitations of economic policy between 1780 and 1850.

Besides, as modern economists point out, the nature and workings of an economy may also restrict the effects of the objectives and policies of central government.[2] In the period before 1850, only to a very limited extent were political decisions capable of affecting the lives of private citizens in the more remote corners of a state's territory. Certainly the government had its aims and general wishes, but it is difficult to demonstrate their pursuit and realization: it implies that the government had at its disposal a policy-making body, economic-political instruments and statistical data. Moreover, fiscal revenues to the treasury are virtually the only standards by which we can assess the failure or the success of 'policy'.

The political upheavals during the period between 1780 and 1850 obviously made it much more difficult to develop a consistent economic policy. Even so, the central problems with which the state was confronted were the same throughout: financial policy focused almost exclusively on the issues of the national debt and poverty. Moreover the formulation of theories concerning economic policies was so inconsistent that it was virtually impossible for politicians to provide sensible and *ad hoc* regulations on a day-to-day basis, while maintaining a coherent political line in the long term.

Increasing demands on the state, 1780-1813

The Stadtholder William IV's proposal in 1751 to turn the Republic into a limited *porto franco* was a first (and promising) attempt by the Dutch state to exert control over the economy, but the vested interest of the Amsterdam merchants ensured that 'liberal' commercial policy continued, and later was even complemented with protectionist measures.[3] William Petty was probably right when he stated that Dutch prosperity should not be attributed to 'the excess of their understandings':[4] the reasons for their economic prosperity were not entirely clear to them. But the disastrous economic results of the Fourth Anglo-Dutch War (1780-84) forced a re-evaluation of priorities. Deep dissatisfaction with the disparity between the various sectors of the economy was manifested most clearly in the recently founded *Oeconomische Tak* (Economic Section of the Holland Society of Sciences). Its numerous branches in the towns and villages, especially in Holland and Zeeland, discussed economic themes in a broad sense. Initiatives were put forward for job-creation, and essay competitions were held to stimulate reasoned solutions to the economic problems of the day. The *Oeconomische Tak* advocated a 'patriotic' or altruistic attitude on the part of capitalists, industrialists, and the unemployed alike. The production of goods of optimum quality and the consumption of Dutch-produced goods were acts of patriotism, and a national duty. The emphasis the *Oeconomische Tak* laid on a positive mental attitude shows how much value was attached to psychological factors in economic recovery, and attention was correspondingly drawn away from economic factors. The *Tak* was able to do no more than provide well-intentioned recommendations about such issues as pauperism, industrial premiums, and training, and did not set out to be of a scientific, but rather of a practical nature.

One of the founding members of the *Oeconomische Tak*, H.H. van den Heuvel, did have an understanding of economics. The founding of the Society had been at the suggestion of the enlightened Spanish economist and statesman P.R. Campomanes, and in 1780 Van den Heuvel published a translation of one of Campomanes' books, the *Discorso sobre el fomento de industria popular*. Campomanes was a Spanish patriot, and wished to restore Spain's sixteenth-century fame and wealth by means of the firm leadership of the enlightened despots Charles III and Charles IV. He pointed to the necessity of links between the economic sectors in furthering economic development. Each individual sector had to be carefully assessed in terms of its contribution to the prosperity of the nation as a whole. The branches of industry which had close links with agriculture were highly valued because they provided employment, and because they produced consumer goods for the entire population, as opposed to luxury items.[5] In Campomanes' work Van den Heuvel was able to read that active interference by the state in the economy could lead to positive results, but that on the other hand the economy has laws of its own.

Campomanes taught Van den Heuvel that there are at least three political fallacies regarding the economy. Firstly, politicians hold misconceived ideas concerning the concept of wealth.[6] Secondly, politicians are unaware of economic realities, so that it is quite possible for economic measures to have worse effects than the original deficiencies they were meant to counteract. Thirdly, politicians fail to regard the economy as a structural entity, consisting of interdependent components. Characteristically for the eighteenth century, Campomanes compares the economy to the human body: the various parts must develop simultaneously and in equal proportions, and there may be no excessive growth of a single component part, for this would result in deformities that would hamper the movements of the other parts. It is the function of the body politic, so he claims, to pay systematic attention to all sectors of the economy and to focus on those sectors which, in their turn, give the body politic its power, because the weaker sectors benefit from the progress generated by the stronger ones.[7]

An Orangist author of the same period, Elie Luzac, also used the metaphor of the human body, and showed an almost naive faith in the state's ability to diagnose and alleviate the body politic's economic afflictions.[8] Another contemporary, F.W. Pestel, advocated a voluntarist concept of the state's role: for him, the pursuit of prosperity and happiness depended on harmony and co-operation, but above all on constant political action and on enlightened legislation. The state should be like a purposeful enterprise, in which the government and its subjects were bound together by mutual respect.[9] This line of thought, however, offered few solutions to the problems of the period up to 1795: pauperism, the grain crisis, the national debt, and the financial predicament of the East and West India Companies required decisive action on the part of the state.

In 1795 there began a period of stop-go policies as far as central economic control was concerned in the Netherlands, with centralization being reversed in favour of provincial autonomy on orders from Paris, and then being reversed once more. Neighbouring countries had enjoyed economic expansion, and a policy of political and fiscal centralization had steadily continued. The structural process of building the nation-state had simply not taken place in the Netherlands, although the Dutch Republic had paid increasing attention to the state's fiscal capacity before 1795.[10]

Fritschy has made a comparison between England and the Dutch Republic from the point of view of state finance and defence expenditure. She strongly questions the thesis that the Dutch system of state finance points towards institutional impotence. The notion still persists — as a result of the Patriots' and the Batavians' accusations — that defence, especially the navy, was being neglected and that this was indicative of an impotent political system. But defence expenditure per head of population in the Republic proves in fact to have been higher than in England. As regards the components of state finance and national revenue, the Republic was actually less backward than England at the end of the eighteenth century. Fritschy suggests that the absence of central financial institutions, and the secrecy surrounding government finance, actually assisted government solvency.[11]

It was mainly the need to survive that forced the Batavian Republic to develop an economic policy. The attention paid to the acceleration of the circulation of goods is apparent in the greater care devoted to the upkeep of roads and waterways, the removal of toll barriers in the Generality Lands, the abolition of the guilds, the attempts to come to a uniform system of weights and measures, and to harmonize the various local monetary systems.[12] Given the enforced autarchic tendency of the economy, the Batavian dissatisfaction with the one-sidedness of the economic structure and policy, together with their socio-political attack on the position of the wealthy,[13] may strike us as somewhat contrived. The Batavian politicians concentrated on rebuilding the state, and were fascinated by the concepts of law and the role of the state imposed by the French. Still it is remarkable that 'Dutch' arguments in favour of freedom and decentralization retained their dominant influence: traditional and modern views were fused in a creative mix in the discussions about possible alterations to the political structure and the financial system, in order to bring about a more balanced economic development of the various regions. This became very apparent in the work of the Commission which drew up a draft constitution in 1796, and in the debates in the National Assemblies.

A separation of powers within a unified state was advocated to prevent the abuse of power and to protect civil liberty, but this had consequences for legislation and for the organization of financial policies. The delegate from Holland, P. van de Kasteele, opposed the continuation of autonomous financial regulations in the various provinces. Civil liberties were not equally present in all provinces, and therefore they should be promoted by putting an end to financial and economic disparities. He rejected the claim that separate provincial financial regulations were justified by differences in economic structure. These differences, he felt, should not be exaggerated. It was in fact a uniform system of legislation and of internal financial administration that would further the coherence between agriculture, industry and trade. The national economy would benefit by 'the unification of separate interests to one general interest.[14] The Patriot C. Zelissen stressed that diversity of production and demand would enable the building of a national economy, independent of other countries.[15] In the debates in the Commission on the constitution and the National Assembly, the metaphor of the circle was frequently used, put forward by Zelissen in a 'psycho-political sense'. The various radii of the circle, representing individual acts of will, come together in the centre, from which the total energy of society is activated to further general prosperity. In this concept the state is 'the representative moral person, for all its members'. The links between the people and the state, between individuals and government, must be close and direct.[16]

This Rousseau-esque circle combined both unitarist and democratic principles. The metaphor also affected the rearrangement of the territory of the Republic, in which the former provinces were abolished, and departments and municipalities were introduced. The desiderata were the reorganization of the former provinces into eight departments, equal distribution of the population and, as far as possible, equal access to trade facilities and waterways.[17] The metaphor of the circle had to be transformed into that of several overlapping circles, because it was realized that for the time being tax collection had to continue in its old ways, until fiscal unification had been achieved and made practicable. This rearrangement also satisfied those who wanted no more than an improved system of federal government. They preferred the metaphor of the ellipse, which has a single centre, but a double focal point. They felt that the distribution of power between the political centre on the one hand and the provinces on the other would create better conditions to deal with difficult tasks: 'the ellipse can carry a heavier burden'.[18] In 1801 the replacement of the provinces by the departments as mere administrative districts was revoked; Napoleon wanted peace and quiet in his satellite states and therefore was prepared − for the moment − to allow the Dutch to continue in their own traditions. The old system of provinces was reinstated (still under the name of 'departments'), with a high degree of administrative independence. It is true that after the 'Departmental Law' of 1807, centralization gradually increased, but each of the eight departments consolidated their separate regulations dating from the Batavian period by developing their own varieties of constitutional obligations concerning internal security and the economy.

Those Batavian politicians unwilling to renounce their conviction that a single unitary governing body leads to a more energetic and decisive handling of political affairs had to admit that a centralist political system, when combined with an authoritarian government, might also impair the operation of the state. This became apparent in the tiresome debates in the spring of 1799 about the Instruction for the Agent for Finance, one of the eight 'intermediary persons' who were subordinate and accountable to the Executive Government.[19] It was pointed out that the principle that 'political measures must come second to financial ones' was being undermined. Confusion arose from the paradox that the national government had decreed that departments should continue their own separate systems of tax collection, so as to safeguard their own as well as national revenues, but was simultaneously pressing for the creation of a centralized financial administration which would set up a new framework for national revenue and expenditure. It was some time before it was understood that unitarist legislation could be combined with administrative decentralization.[20] Two of the main advocates of a powerful central government, C.F. van Maanen and R.J. Schimmelpenninck, argued that unity does not necessarily imply that there can be no 'corporations and authorities' separate from the central government. They stressed that freedom of action regarding the local and domestic interests of the departments and municipalities should include all that could not be considered as 'general, national affairs'; however the local authorities should be bound by the laws and the constitution, to safeguard individual liberty and the unity of the nation.[21] This implied that justice should ideally take precedence over political power and the exercise of authority.

After years of debate it began to be understood that the limits to state power are determined by its effectiveness.[22] But the Batavian governments refused to accept this when it came to the unification of the fiscal system, a logical consequence of the amalgamation of the provincial debts. The reconstruction of public finance was too essential a precondition for the founding of the new state: finance was considered to be the principal sinew of the state: its power and healthy functioning were standards by which to judge a government.[23] Fiscal reform had two secondary objectives besides the reconstruction of public finance: firstly, a reduction of the tax burden on wages would assist the activities of entrepreneurs in the manufacturing and processing industries, stimulate efforts to increase agricultural production (by fertilizing the soil), and promote initiatives by individuals and local government to improve road and waterways.[24] Secondly, there was the social objective of income redistribution.

With our modern understanding of the limitations of administration,[25] we can understand why J.H. Appelius, I. Gogel, and their assistants failed to make a success of the fiscal unification. Our knowledge of how the political system and the civil service worked in practice (centrally and in each of the departments) in the Batavian period is not sufficient to allow us to identify the precise reasons for the failure of the levy on capital, and of the national system of taxation introduced in 1805. Nonetheless, some comments may be made.

First there was the problem of the limited time available: the rapid political changes did not permit a consistent financial and economic policy. There were also severe administrative constraints: in 1798 an investigation was launched into the state of provincial finances, but a clear picture of the balance-sheet of income and expenditure is simply not available, because up to that point no proper accounts had been kept. In 1801 things become somewhat clearer: in that and subsequent years it appears from the national budget that expenditure amounted to eighty million guilders, with a budget deficit of between forty and fifty per cent.[26] The departments continued to be responsible for the collection of taxes and their internal management, and thus the inertia of the formal structures was perpetuated. Furthermore there were deficiencies in supervision and monitoring: the number of officials available was very small. This impeded realization of the three incompatible aims of finance, which were (in order of importance) cuts in expenditure, reform of the tax system, and improvement of tax administration.[27]

The first aim, cuts in expenditure, was imposed on the basis of lessons learned in the past. The aversion to bureaucracy was universal: the surplus of officials and their inefficiency was blamed as a waste of money. In 1800 the ministries in The Hague employed some 300 officials, but after the new constitution of 1801 this number was reduced considerably.[28] Any increase in government solvency would probably have led to a larger civil service, rather than a reduced one. The encouragement of the economy, an objective laid down in the State Regulation of 1798,[29] could only be realized with a great deal of difficulty. The economic initiatives which *were* launched succeeded only in spite of the political system, in spite of the absence of consensus and in spite of the shortage of funds, but largely due to the energy of individual politicians and officials with outspoken ideas. An example is J. Goldberg, the Agent for the National Economy from 1799 to 1801, who travelled the country in order to draw up a quantitative survey of the situation in which industry found itself; another is Jan Kops, who set up the departmental Agricultural Commissions, which provided advice to farmers, but also for the government regarding agricultural production and the reclamation of land.[30] Kops kept abreast of agricultural developments in surrounding countries; his actions were motivated by the fear that the Dutch would lag behind in agricultural management and technology.

Appelius and Gogel came up against the administrative limitations of the tax system, but they were well aware that there was sufficient private capital among wealthy citizens to fill the gaps in the budget. Their attempts to convert the tax on capital, which had been levied by means of a quota for each district, into a form of personal taxation, form the most shining example of the irreversibility of the Batavian unification. Fiscal unification resulted from the necessity for the state to operate; it did not result from an understanding of economic theory. Indeed, it is doubtful whether Gogel or Appelius could have provided a straight answer to the question of what the effects on the economy would be of a rapidly introduced national system of taxation. G.K. van Hogendorp pointed out the risks of increasing the taxation of wealth and the damage it might do to the willingness of capitalists to invest.[31] Finally Gogel was forced to acknowledge the 'narrow margins' of revolutionary fiscal policy.[32]

The government's insight into the economy may have been limited, but the exchequer was still able to reap the benefits. Further research into the workings of the political system after the *Staatsregeling* of 1798 may facilitate a critical evaluation of political actions concerning the economy in the Batavian period. The government lacked both a coherent view of the economy and adequate policy instruments. In the crisis situation between 1795 and 1813 it could do no more than provide *ad hoc* solutions. A question in point is whether the makers of economic policy might have benefited from the theoretical insights of the science of economics, which was just emerging.

The hazy framework of economic thought

Two factors impeded the reception and the influence of theoretical insights into economic policy during this period: the persistence of a specific Dutch attitude to the economy, and economic thought itself.

The unique character of the Republic's commercial prosperity in the seventeenth and eighteenth centuries was recognized by foreign economists like Adam Smith, and was considered to be an example of increased prosperity resulting from free trade and civil liberty. To them Holland was a reference point in criticizing the economic and political aspects of mercantilism. They sympathized with what might be called 'the Dutch model', an idiosyncratic type of economic order that can be described as follows: a coastal nation with a small home market and a shortage of raw materials, consequently dependent on general trade for the prosperity of other economic sectors.[33]

Contrastingly, most other countries first tried to develop their agriculture and industry, and then expected trade to export their surplus production. The success of the Dutch model was considered 'proved' by the early liberal economists, who embraced a philosophical historical approach which held that each country has its own destiny on its road towards progress.[34] The success of the Dutch model was also attributed to the free operation of the Dutch political institutions.

The first specifically Dutch concept was the notion of the inseparability of economic and political liberty. The Dutch took it for granted that there was a clear relation between the international and the internal dimensions of the economy. As late as the liberal era of the nineteenth century they were advocating free trade on the basis of history; even by then there was little inclination to take into account the insights of the new science of economics. Dutch theory about the financial and economic obligations of the state continued to be of an eclectic and fragmentary nature, and to this day it has remained characteristically 'applied' economics. These typically Dutch approaches date back as far as the sixteenth century, to Pieter de la Court with his rejection of impediments to the freedom of production and trade, and to Isaac de Pinto where monetary subjects are concerned. In Holland economic theory remained subordinate to political thought.[35] But there was a second Dutch notion. It concerned the position of the small Republic in future world trade. It began to be said that Holland had become a second-rate nation; Van Hogendorp realized that there had been a relative commercial decline, but maintained that, given the increase in international trade, the Dutch share could be restored by means of an anticipatory liberal trade policy, in order to outdistance competing nations that had not yet converted to liberal free trade.[36]

Dutch authors and politicians discovered an inconsistency in the policies of the neighbouring states: on the one hand they concentrated on their national economies and continued to favour the notion of the favourable trade balance, which was the rational argument for maintaining a protectionist policy. On the other hand, they realized that it was necessary to stimulate foreign and international trade in order to export the surplus products of their expanding economies, to acquire the raw materials for their industries, and, in times of shortage, to import grain − usually from Amsterdam.

These two characteristically Dutch notions about the economy in the Netherlands acquired many supporters, among them many policy-makers. The contrasting views that existed among the various Dutch political factions did not imply that they differed in their economic views. It is essential that we should be aware of these contemporary views in order to avoid anachronistic judgments, for at this time economics was still a very young science.[37] A number of points about classical liberal economic thought will help place in perspective the dilemmas faced by the policy-makers.

In the first place, the classical economists were highly interested in the role of the state. Free initiatives of individuals or groups followed their courses within a framework of laws and conventions which differed from country to country and according to the economic situation. Classical economics contained explicit 'policy prescriptions': its attitude towards *laissez-faire* was of a 'very relativist and conditional kind'.[38] It recognized the need for intervention by the state, especially in defence, the colonies, poverty, education and the monetary system.[39] And both the later mercantilists and the liberal economists acknowledged a particular economic role for the state in areas like the infrastructure.

Secondly, strict classical economists did not distinguish clearly between the aims and the means of economic policy. Smith saw that the adjustment of means to ends can often be explained in terms of unintended consequences. For Ricardo it was the task of economic policies to facilitate the economic process (*Prozesspolitik*), but Smith and other economists focused mainly on economic order (*Ordnungspolitik*). In their view economic policies should be aimed at the upkeep of the constitutional framework, within which liberty – including economic liberty – could be realized. Beyond that they were hardly able to indicate any priority of objectives, although excessive inequalities should be prevented from threatening social peace.[40] In the period of restoration after 1815 there was a hesitant form of co-operation between King and States General, arising out of a traumatic fear of war and revolution; consequently the *Ordnungspolitik* approach prevailed among the makers of economic policy on the European continent in general, and also in the Netherlands.

Thirdly, there was a problem about the attitude of governments towards interest groups. In the Netherlands the notion that a process of improvement would gradually result in a transition from discord to harmony of interests was supported by Van Hogendorp. But in the mean time there was a great deal of rivalry between the various groups of manufacturers and merchants.

Finally, it should be realized that the state's concern with the economy was predominantly of a financial nature, although there was little consensus among the classical economists on financial policy. There was a general sense of panic concerning the national debt; David Hume formulated it as follows: 'Either the nation must destroy public credit, or public credit destroy the nation.'[41] Smith was not optimistic about the means available to reduce the burden of debt. He was aware that the growth of commerce automatically implied the growth of the financial institutions and of public finance.[42] In the Netherlands R. Metelerkamp feared that relative commercial recession was a first step on the road towards a total decline, resulting from their financial and fiscal impotence.[43] However, others such as W.M. Keuchenius did not share this pessimism. He argued that the Dutch supply of capital was considerable and the circulation of money, within and across the borders, was lively. Dutch investments in domestic and foreign national debts were so lucrative that, in comparison with other nations, the Netherlands need not be unduly worried about its national debt.[44] The economists concerned themselves with the negative effects of the national debt and of the fiscal system on private investments and consumption. They felt that government loans and direct taxation were greater threats to the accumulation of capital than indirect taxes. They were also critical where public expenditure was concerned, for according to Smith and Ricardo it did not contribute to the social product. This view was fuelled by rumours of corruption and inefficiency on the part of the state and by the suspicion that civil servants' work was unproductive. The classical economists were also worried, as were the politicians, by the dilemma between the growing demands for education and employment and the desirability of a minimal national budget.

These four points concerning early nineteenth-century economic thought show its incomplete and inconsistent nature. The influence of these views in politics was therefore bound to be very weak; moreover, politics only becomes receptive to theoretical insights when they have become part of conventional wisdom, and that stage was not reached until economic theory became economic propaganda, and subsequently economic dogma. Significant popularization of economic science hardly took place in the Netherlands before 1850.

Economic policy after 1813: incompatible aims, incalculable effects

After 1813 the limited Dutch state continued the practice of the Batavian governments in the context of a larger political unit: the United Kingdom of the Netherlands, which included the southern (Belgian) Netherlands. The fifteen-year period (1815-30) was too short to inspire many to believe in the idea of a Great Netherlands nation, but it stirred King William I's dynastic sentiments. After some years of uncertain and capricious policy, in 1824 he finally decided upon the national economic concept of the Netherlands Trading Company, in which southern industry and northern general and colonial trade would join forces in order to increase the national product. Although misunderstood in commercial circles, the plan showed considerable vision and formed the economic basis of a strong nation within an international community that strove together for peace and prosperity.[45] The Belgian Revolution of 1830 prevented the realization of this vision.[46]

William I's economic policy is characterized by I.J. Brugmans as 'late mercantilist',[47] although a more recent study considers his policies cameralistic.[48] As yet little is known about the aims, visions and effects of legislation in William's reign. In the preambles to Acts of Parliament, in speeches from the throne, and in other official documents a general formula is followed, stating that the government aims to lay a sound economic foundation for national unity between North and South, that continuity should be maintained with an eye to revenue, and that some changes are proposed for the benefit of future generations. Other aims are mentioned as well: control over public expenditure, the acquisition of adequate public revenue, the fight to reduce poverty and to improve the infrastructure.[49]

Economic policies must always be regarded in the light of what is politically feasible, the response of the nation and the wishes of interest groups. Being an enlightened despot, William I felt that the States General existed in order to guard the King from acting arbitrarily, but that it was not its function to impose the will of the majority: 'all decision-making must take place from top to bottom, and not, conversely, from the bottom upwards.'[50] Although terms of office in the Second Chamber were not usually extensive and most Members received income from other offices, the States General did provide some opposition, and to portray the Second Chamber as totally compliant would be incorrect. Of all the bills proposed in the period between 1815 and 1830, twenty-five per cent were rejected. But the opposition was hardly coherent, and neither was there a stable government majority. There were two opposition factions which disagreed on free trade, but united in support of the accountability of government finance, the extension of the influence of the States General, and the observation of constitutional rights. The King was obliged to make concessions to appease the roughly seventeen per cent of Members who were active in industry and in capital investment, and to make allowances in the areas of fiscal and financial legislation; these restrictions on the King's room for manoeuvre tended to result in attempts to influence voting, and in government by decree.[51] Members showed little interest in the new science of economics. Another limitation on the reality of what might be achieved by economic policy was, alongside the States General, the Amsterdam Chamber of Commerce, founded in 1811. Although the King himself had not completely abandoned the idea of a central staple market, the Chamber's continuous insistence on it irritated him, and the government was even less inclined to ask the views of the remodelled Chamber of Commerce and Factories after 1816.[52] Its new members were not representative of Amsterdam trade, and commercial circles sent their requests directly to the government, often showing their envy of the increasing prosperity of Antwerp and Hamburg. The modern liberal elements in William I's economic policy were not welcomed in Amsterdam, which (unlike Rotterdam) supported the entrepôt system, rather than a gradual introduction of free trade. For the Amsterdam commercial world, 'liberal' meant the reduction of trade barriers, which was not identical to free trade.[53]

The Chamber failed to reconcile and harness individual interests, and thus missed the opportunity of influencing economic policy. The King realized that the state should protect both the diversity of interests in the various economic sectors, and the various activities of individual enterprises, in order to stimulate the prosperity of the nation. He put the interests of the state before those of the merchants, which accounts for the rather cool relations between the King and Amsterdam.

Economic policy can only operate within a complex system of parameters, and is conditioned by what is politically feasible, by the effectiveness of political institutions, the economic environment, the national economic structure, trends in international trade, international relations, and of course by financial constraints, which allowed little scope for stimulating the economy. William I's policies are proof of this complexity, and this may be illustrated by examining a short-term policy area, the infrastructure, and in the mid-term, the relationship between economic and financial policies.

The infrastructure

A. van der Woud maintains that there was no such thing as a central plan to assist the economy by supporting the national infrastructure. The government simply lacked the knowledge required: much of the country was virtually terra incognita, and away from the western towns was only thinly populated.[54] It was left to those with a vested interest to build roads between the minor towns and villages.

William I spent the years from 1795 to 1813 in England, where he was no doubt impressed by the dense system of canals which afforded industry such a large internal market.[55] To carry out a similar plan in the Netherlands was not feasible: the geographical and topographical knowledge was lacking, and the interface between the state and various lower authorities was ill-defined. It was not until the constitutional revision of 1848 that the provinces acquired a form of financial autonomy and a role of their own concerning the building of interprovincial roads.[56] As far as waterways were concerned, the King took personal charge, but his autocratic behaviour hindered local and private initiative. Plans for building new canals like the Noord-Holland Canal had existed before 1813, in order to safeguard the economic position of old centres, and it is not the case that the new canals were indicative of a new, national economic policy.[57] However, compared to other countries, the Netherlands was active in stimulating regional integration. From 1813 onwards efforts were made to standardize government provisions in the various regions, and to reduce the differences in tax burden that existed between them, which resulted in increased central fiscal power.[58] For an explanation for the relatively late industrialization of the Netherlands, historians have traditionally looked towards regional differences in wages and standards of living and the functioning of the labour market. There is an ongoing debate about the relative economic integration of the Dutch regions in the nineteenth century,[59] but as far as the infrastructure is concerned, very little contribution to a national economy was apparent before 1850.

In the short term, the improvement of the national infrastructure was not always compatible with earnings and employment in the local economy: new canals and highways were often a threat to various forms of local employment and income. Transport imperfections created jobs for people: loads needed to be transshipped, local markets were required, and so were ferries and inns. Moreover the revenue produced by the new national road system (there was a turnpike every six kilometres) went directly to the central government. In this context Van der Woud speaks of 'the advantages of stagnation': foot-dragging rendered the developments gradual and smooth. The towns and their inhabitants tenaciously maintained their hierarchical status, preserving their distinctive identities.[60] In short, William I's dynamic policy aimed at creating a national economic unity was supplanted by a series of only gradual transformations.

Economic and financial policy

In the period after 1813 Western European governments struggled with the national debts they had run up during the war period, and with the reconstruction of their economies now that peace had come. The Netherlands had to formulate a response to the defensive protectionism of its neighbours. It is revealing to note the order in which William I tackled the problems: first the amortization of the national debt; then the launch of a commercial policy, in which he tried both to accommodate the interests of the various economic sectors and to create a coherent liberal tariff system (between 1816 and 1821); and finally in 1821 (just before the trend in international trade took a favourable turn) the provision of state support to industries which had to be able to hold their own in the face of international competition. The order may have indicated a priority of objectives.

The achievement of the government's aims ultimately depended on whether they could be paid for; consequently a healthy state of government finance was essential. In 1819 William I introduced the system of decennial budgets for regular expenditure; he channelled funds intended for the Amortization Syndicate (1822) into building canals and roads, and into industry by means of the National Fund for Industry of 1821 and the Société Générale, founded in 1822. In 1838, the States General was given access to the figures, which showed the growth of the national debt since 1830, and it was clear that further government direction and stimulation of the economy would have to wait until the economy was stronger and was providing more revenue for the state. More readiness among the owners of capital to invest in the development of industry was also required.[61]

In order to stimulate owners of capital to invest more in the domestic economy, in 1816 the King made it necessary to obtain his consent before subscribing to foreign loans. He was a considerable investor himself and consequently well aware of the difficulties involved in trying to prevent the export of capital, and of the inevitable truth that capital goes where maximum profits can be obtained. Apparently the Dutch economy did not yet provide such opportunities. At the same time he had to maintain investors' willingness to subscribe to the Dutch national loans. By 1824 the royal consent had become a mere formality, but as late as 1854 angry criticism was expressed at the inefficiency and mercantilist errors behind the measure.[62]

What W. Roëll called the 'complex system of wheels that keeps the great financial machine moving'[63] caused considerable irritation. Van Hogendorp had a sound understanding of the relations between financial and economic policies, and expressed the view that government intervention facilitating the free play of market forces was preferable, and that the application of different types of measures would result in conflict between the various objectives. He was of a mind with Ricardo who stated in the House of Commons that agriculture, industry and commerce prosper most when the government does not interfere with them. Government interference is only inevitable where the levy of taxes is concerned, in order to produce the income necessary to pay for the operations of the state. It is the task of the science of political economy to make recommendations to the government as to what fiscal measures are best.[64]

Van Hogendorp could not fully understand William I's aims: he had only incomplete statements, and did not understand the political choices the King was faced with in the light of the conflicting interests of North and South, and of the various economic interest groups. He urged William to make individual interests subordinate to the interests of the nation as a whole. He agreed with the argument of employment behind many state interventions, and supported the application of the principle of 'equity and efficiency' to the system of direct and indirect taxation. However, in Van Hogendorp's view economic policy's influence on the development of the national economy depended on the ultimate objective, which the government should bear in mind: the free movement of goods and capital, within and across the national borders. His feelings about the payment of premiums to industry were also based on conforming to market forces. He thought the level of the premiums could gradually be reduced as the competitiveness of the receiving industry increased, and as the liberalization of the tariffs of other countries progressed. He came to this conclusion not just because he feared reprisals if protectionist tariffs were maintained, but also because premiums resulted in 'unnatural' prices and distortede competition.[65]

Economic policy needs to take note of the trade cycle, but politicians of the time were unaware of many of the things that modern research has made clear to us. For example, Dutch agriculture, modern and productive though it was, was not going through a very favourable development at this time, partly as a result of the generally stagnating international economy. But in the Netherlands an attitude of romantic admiration prevailed about agricultural potential, especially in the eastern provinces.[66] It is a remarkable fact that no economic considerations are known to have been expressed by the government or anyone else about the relationship between the crop failures of 1816 and 1817, and the boom in the international grain trade. The first crisis of modern capitalism in trade and banking was experienced in England in 1825, but was largely attributed to factors of a political and institutional nature.[67]

The international balance of power was considered to be a decisive influence on the economy, and in the first few decades of the nineteenth century the Netherlands could still persist in largely ignoring her continental neighbours. As long as industrialization in the continental countries had not got under way, the maritime nations retained an advantage, and economic relations with France and Prussia were as yet relatively unimportant. France had in any case withdrawn into itself after Napoleon's defeat. There was some gratitude that certain institutions which had obstructed economic progress, such as the guilds, had been abandoned under French influence, but in terms of foreign policy a relationship hardly existed. Relations with Prussia were structurally bad, as was shown in negotiations concerning the Rhine issue.[68]

In its policies concerning foreign trade the Netherlands was strongly conditioned by the economic scope Britain was prepared to grant it. Dutch Atlantic orientation made Britain the 'most natural ally'. In the period between 1813 and 1831, during which the European Concert of the five main powers, dominated by Britain, proved increasingly incapable of a sustained approach to international problems, and consequently after 1822 William I was in a position to shape his own policy more independently,[69] to the point where Van Hogendorp warned against arrogance in the Dutch commercial treaties.[70] He followed the debates in the House of Commons, and the liberal course taken by Grenville, Canning, Wallace and especially Huskisson, concluding that in Britain the realization was growing that industrialization would lead to an increased dependence on foreign grain.[71] According to Van Hogendorp this created opportunities for the Dutch grain trade — and hence the national economy — to regain its strength. Therefore he advocated an anticipatory liberalization of the Dutch tariffs to allow the Netherlands — on the basis of its favourable situation and commercial qualities — to regain its relative share of world trade.[72]

At the end of the second decade of the nineteenth century the British began to feel that protectionist policies obstructed economic growth and modernization, although French historiography does not generally agree that between 1815 and 1852 protectionist policies retarded economic development in France.[73] For its part, the Netherlands clung to the 'Dutch model', which maintained that the other economic sectors would benefit from a prospering trade.

Before 1859 commercial policies were primarily determined by the way the international political situation was assessed. In both the Dutch Corn Law of 1835 and in the tariff and shipping laws of 1845 and 1850, British commercial policy in particular was anticipated, in the hope of creating growth opportunities for the national economy.[74] The rationale for the Netherlands, which had undergone such a considerable decline in international politics, was provided by the mythical notion of the Netherlands as one great *porto franco*. After the harsh reconstruction of government finances by F.A. van Hall in 1844, the state was finally able to design an economic policy, but by then liberalism was taking control, as it did in the neighbouring countries. Central government's role in the field of economic policy became more modest, if at the same time it became more outspoken.

Before 1850 the interference of the limited Dutch state, especially its financial policy, often hampered economic development. Effective government support for industry mainly benefited the South. The national economic concept of the triangle of trade, industry and colonies spawned only a brief revival in the North. In 1830, the Belgian Revolution forced the government to revise its overall economic objective, which was to provide an environment suitable for economic activity. For a small country like the Netherlands, economic growth in Britain and Germany provided the indispensable stimulant for its economic development.[75]

Some conclusions

It is too early to arrive at a definitive assessment of the economic policy of the period between 1780 and 1850. We need more information about the economic structure in order to judge the effects of policy. At present a number of traditional views are being questioned, like the notion of economic decline in the eighteenth century, and economic stagnation before 1850.[76] Further research into economic policy at all levels of government may increase our understanding of the scope of these matters.

Some of the objectives of policy were incompatible, and in some cases policy may have had results which were far from the original objectives. In this context it is likely that future research will reveal that economic policy, given Dutch liberal practice, followed the market so closely that the policy objectives regarding the creation of jobs could not possibly have been realized. In the second half of the nineteenth century the Dutch tradition of market promotion became more explicit, probably to the benefit of longer-term economic development.

Before 1850 the politically possible was limited by the vitality of the republican tradition of civil and political liberty. With the backdrop of the traumas of the French occupation, active state interference and political compulsion remained such sensitive points that the Dutch governments after 1830 were forced to compromise. This made it extremely difficult to set a consistent political course.

Economic policy should not simply be interpreted as direct interference in the economic process. Until 1850 economic policies may not have been particularly effective, but in the end they did produce the intended result: to stimulate the cohesion between the various economic sectors on a national scale. In this sense the policy was effectual rather than effective. It was by no means efficient, as a result of administrative limitations and of financial policy, which disturbed the market. In the restoration period after 1813, the government's main aim was to stabilize the social and political order and to guarantee state revenue. To achieve this it was essential to inspire confidence among the social and financial elite; the requisite conservative budget policy hampered state initiatives.

Finally, the international balance of power restricted the Dutch government's scope for action to the formulation and implementation of its own national economic policies. Convinced of the positive effects of a flourishing trade on the other economic sectors, it tried to increase its control of external, international factors. The emphasis on the dominant influence of international forces on the Dutch economy provided, and continues to provide, the government with a rationale for increasing the international integration of the Dutch economy.

Notes

1. G. Ardant, 'Financial Policy and Economic Infrastructure of Modern States and Nations', in *The Formation of National States in Western Europe* (ed. C. Tilly, New Jersey, 1975), pp.164-242.
2. P. Hennipman, 'Doeleinden en criteria der economische politiek', in *Welvaartstheorie en economische politiek* (ed. J. van den Doel and A. Heertje, Alphen aan de Rijn/Brussel, 1977), pp.17-113.

3. Joh. de Vries, *De economische achteruitgang der Republiek in de achttiende eeuw* (Amsterdam, 1959), pp.56-7, 118-24. See also J. Hovy, *Het voorstel van 1751 tot instelling van een beperkt vrijhavenstelsel in de Republiek (Propositie tot een gelimiteerd portofranco)* (Groningen, 1966); P.W. Klein, 'De Nederlandse handelspolitiek in de tijd van het mercantilisme: een nieuwe kijk op een oude kwestie?', *Tijdschrift voor Geschiedenis*, CII (1989), 189-212; and also Klein's article in this volume.

4. Cited by N. Pierson, 'Beschouwingen over Holland's welvaart bij Engelsche economisten der zeventiende eeuw', in *Verspreide Geschriften* (Haarlem, 1910), II, p.225.

5. B.-A. Pierrelle, 'Campomanes, ministre de Charles III d'Espagne', in *Etudes d'histoire économique et sociale du XVIIIe siècle* (ed. A. Decoufle, et al., Paris, 1966), pp.95-148; and a review of L. Rodriguez's *Reforma e Illustracion en la Espana del XVIII: P.R. Campomanes* (Madrid, 1975), in *Revue Historique*, CCLIX (1978), 217-8.

6. Pierrelle, 'Campomanes', p.113.

7. *Ibid.*, p.116.

8. Cited by I.B. Leeb, *The Ideological Origins of the Batavian Revolution* (The Hague, 1973), p.161.

9. I.J.H. Worst, 'Staat, constitutie en politieke wil', *Bijdragen en Mededelingen betreffende de Geschiedenis der Nederlanden*, CII (1987), 498-515.

10. H. de Wit, 'Tussen praktijk en theorie: een schets van belastingen en belastinghervormingsplannen in de 18e eeuw in de Republiek en enkele andere Westeuropese staten', in *Fiscaliteit in Nederland* (Zutphen, 1987), pp.79-92.

11. W. Fritschy, 'Overheidsfinancien als uiting van het "institutioneel onvermogen" van de 18e eeuwse Republiek', *Economisch- en Sociaal-Historisch Jaarboek*, XLVIII (1985), 19-47; *idem, De Patriotten en de financien van de Bataafse Republiek: Hollands krediet en de smalle marges voor een nieuw beleid (1795-1801)* (The Hague, 1988).

12. R.T. Griffiths, 'The Creation of a National Dutch Economy, 1795-1909', *Tijdschrift voor Geschiedenis*, VC (1982), 513-37.

13. P.C.H. Overmeer, *De economische denkbeelden van Gijsbert Karel van Hogendorp (1762-1834)* (Tilburg, 1982), Chapter VIII.1; and S. Schama, *Patriots and Liberators: Revolution in the Netherlands, 1780-1813* (New York, 1977), pp.304-5 and 494-524.

14. *Het Plan van Constitutie van 1796* (ed. L. de Gou, The Hague, 1975), p.75.

15. C. Zillesen, *Wijsgeerig onderzoek, wegens Neerlands opkomst, bloei en welvaard* (Amsterdam, 1796), p.276.

16. *Ibid.*, paragraphs 96-8, 261-74.

17. *Dagverhaal der handelingen van het Vertegenwoordigend Lichaam des Bataafschen Volks* (The Hague, 1798), II, pp.892-9.

18. *Plan van Constitutie*, p.80.

19. *Dagverhaal*, vol. III, pp.734-41, 850-3, 1169-79.

20. The jurisdiction of the Departmental Courts of Justice concerning fiscal legislation had not yet been made uniform. See *Dagverhaal*, vol. III, pp.684-8. On administrative decentralization, see *Dagverhaal*, vol. II, p.1019.

21. *Het Ontwerp van Constitutie van 1797* (ed. L. de Gou, The Hague, 1974), II, pp.140-3 (24 April 1797).

22. *Ibid.*, vol. I, p.71.

23. E.g. *ibid.*, vol. I, p.19.

24. *Ibid.*, vol. I, p.147-8.

25. C.C. Hood, *The Limits of Administration* (London, 1976), pp.3-73.

26. Verbal communication from H. Boels, who is preparing a dissertation for Groningen University on the Batavian period.

27. *Ontwerp Constitutie 1797*, vol. I, p.149.

28. Information from H. Boels.

29. W.J.C. van Hasselt, *Verzameling van nederlandse staatsregelingen en grondwetten* (Amsterdam, 1918), Staatsregeling 1798, e.g. articles 51-9.

30. J.M.G. van der Poel, *Heren en boeren: een studie over de Commissiën van Landbouw (1805-1851)* (Wageningen, 1949), Chapters III and IV.

31. Overmeer, *Economische denkbeelden*, Chapter VII.

32. W. Fritschy, 'De "smalle marges" van een revolutionair fiscaal beleid', in *Fiscaliteit in Nederland* (Zutphen, 1987), pp.93-108; and *idem, De Patriotten*.

33. E.g. G.K. van Hogendorp, *Gedagten over 's Lands Finantien* (1802), p.44.

34. Overmeer, *Economische denkbeelden*, pp.83-9.

35. *Ibid.*, p.133 and *passim*.

36. *Ibid.*, Chapter VIII.

37. G. Stollberg, 'Zur Geschichte des Begriffs "Politische Oekonomie"', *Jahrbücher fur Nationalökonomie und Statistik*, CXCII (1977-78), 1-35.
38. D.P. O'Brien, *The Classical Economists* (Oxford, 1978), p.272.
39. *Ibid.*, Chapter 10.
40. W. Barber, *The History of Economic Thought* (Harmondsworth, 1967), pp.48-9.
41. Quoted in D. Winch, *Adam Smith's Politics: an Essay in Historiographic Revision* (London, 1978), pp.126-7.
42. *Ibid.*, p.135-6.
43. R. Metelerkamp, *De toestand van Nederland in vergelijking gebragt met die van enige andere landen van Europa* (Rotterdam, 1804).
44. W.M. Keuchenius, *De inkomsten en uitgaven der Bataafsche Republiek voorgesteld in een nationaale balans* (Amsterdam, 1803), Chapters 1 and 2.
45. J.A. Bornewasser, 'Koning Willem I', in *Nassau en Oranje in de Nederlandse geschiedenis* (ed. C.A. Tamse, Alphen, 1979), pp.236-40.
46. See H.R.C. Wright, *Free Trade and Protection in the Netherlands, 1816-1830: a Study of the First Benelux* (Cambridge, 1955), p.213.
47. I.J. Brugmans, 'Koning Willem I als neo-mercantilist' in *idem*, *Welvaart en historie: tien studiën* (The Hague, 1970), pp.38-50.
48. A. van der Woud, *Het lege land: de ruimtelijke orde van Nederland, 1798-1848* (Amsterdam, 1987), p.537-47.
49. See *Troonredes, openingsredes, inhuldigingsredes, 1814-1963* (ed. E. van Raalte, The Hague, 1964); and Hennipman, 'Doeleinden'.
50. Bornewasser, 'Koning Willem I', p.247.
51. P.W. Meerts, 'Kamerleden, 1815-1830: een verkenning', *Belgisch Tijdschrift voor Nieuwste Geschiedenis*, XVI (1985).
52. Joh. de Vries, *Met Amsterdam als brandpunt: hondervijftig jaar Kamer van Koophandel en Fabrieken, 1811-1961* (n.p., 1961), pp.6, 18-25; and J.C. Westermann, *Kamer van Koophandel en Fabrieken voor Amsterdam* (Amsterdam, 1936), I, pp.213-16.
53. T. de Jong, *De krimpende horizon van de Hollandse kooplieden* (Assen, 1966), p.264.
54. Van der Woud, *Het lege land*, pp.196, 310.
55. *Ibid.*, p.118.
56. *Ibid.*, pp.58-9, 70, & 28-9.
57. *Ibid.*, pp.132-5.
58. C. Goedhart, 'Anderhalve eeuw gemeentefinancien in ons koninkrijk: enkele hoofdlijnen', in *Bedrijf en samenleving* (Alphen, 1967), pp.65-8.
59. See R.T. Griffiths, *Achterlijk, achter of anders? Aspecten van de economische ontwikkeling van Nederland in de 19e eeuw* (Amsterdam, 1980); J.A. de Jonge, 'The Role of the Outer Provinces in the Process of Dutch Economic Growth in the Nineteenth Century', in *Economische ontwikkeling en sociale emancipatie* (ed. P. Geurts & F. Messing, 2 vol., The Hague, 1977), II, pp.51-67; and Jan de Vries, 'Regional Economic Inequality in the Netherlands since 1600', in *Disparities in Economic Development since the Industrial Revolution* (ed. P. Bairoch & M. Levy-Leboyer, London, 1981), Chapter 18.
60. Van der Woud, *Het lege land*, pp.547-51.
61. H. Riemens, *Het Amortisatie-Syndicaat: een studie over de staatsfinanciën onder Willem I* (Amsterdam, 1935), p.222; and H. van den Eerenbeemt, 'Bedrijfskapitaal en ondernemerschap in Nederland, 1800-1850', in *Economische ontwikkeling en sociale emancipatie* (ed. P. Geurts & F. Messing, 2 vol., The Hague, 1977), II, p.27.
62. R.V. Heyliger, *De Nederlandsche wetgeving op de vreemde geldligtingen* (Leiden, 1854); I.J. Brugmans, 'Koning Willem I', pp.43-4.
63. Cited by N. van Sas, 'Een Amsterdamse realist: Willem Frederik Roëll, 1767-1835', in *Figuren en Figuraties* (Groningen, 1979), p.88.
64. B. Gordon, *Political Economy in Parliament, 1819-1823* (London, 1976), p.16; Overmeer, *Economische denkbeelden*, Chapters III.3 and VII.
65. *Ibid.*, Chapters VI.4, VI.5, & VIII, especially pp.215-221. See also H.R.C. Wright, *Free Trade*, pp.134-8.
66. E.g. G.K. van Hogendorp, *Bijdragen tot de huishouding van staat in het Koninkrijk der Nederlanden* (15 vol., The Hague, 1818-25), IV.
67. Overmeer, *Economische denkbeelden*, pp.389-90; and B. Hilton, *Corn, Cash, Commerce: the Economic Politics of the Tory Governments, 1815-1830* (Oxford, second ed., 1980), pp.202-31.
68. N. van Sas, *Onze natuurlijkste bondgenoot: Nederland, Engeland en Europa, 1813-1832* (Groningen, 1985), pp.205-11, 345.

69. *Ibid.*, pp.336-47.
70. Overmeer, *Economische denkbeelden*, Chapter VIII.3.
71. Gordon, *Political Economy*, pp.116, 140.
72. Overmeer, *Economische denkbeelden*, pp.105-16.
73. W. Goroll, *Die Auseinandersetzung um Freihandel und Protektionismus im Frankreich des 19. Jahrhunderts (1815-1892)* (n.p., 1977).
74. E.L. Kramer, *De graanwet van 1835* (Rotterdam, 1940), p.118f; and N.W. Posthumus, 'Het internationale element in de handelspolitiek van Nederland', *Socialistische Gids*, VII (1922), 121-44.
75. J. Bläsing, *Das goldene Delta und sein eisernes Hinterland, 1815-1851: von niederländischen-preussischen zu deutsch-niederländischen Wirtschaftsbeziehungen* (Leiden, 1973).
76. J.L. van Zanden, 'De economie van Holland in de periode 1650-1805: groei of achteruitgang? Een overzicht van bronnen, problemen en resultaten', *Bijdragen en Mededelingen betreffende de Geschiedenis der Nederlanden*, CII (1987), 562-609; R.T. Griffiths, *Industrial Retardation in the Netherlands, 1830-1850* (The Hague, 1979); and *idem*, 'The Creation of a Dutch National Economy'.

7

Hobson Lives?
Finance and British Imperialism 1870-1914

Peter Cain

In the mid-1970s, two of the most prominent historians of the British Empire introduced a collection of their writings with the following statement:

> Let it be agreed then that the theory of 'economic imperialism' is dead, and that there is no further point in trying to discuss British imperial history within the framework it has created. Whatever the motives for British empire and expansion in the nineteenth century, they cannot in the main be ascribed to an 'economic taproot' of powerful interests seeking to find markets for 'their surplus goods and capital'. Hobson's theory has collapsed before numerous and notable onslaughts. Time and again it has been shown not to fit the facts.[1]

Among the 'numerous and notable onslaughts' on Hobson was the work of Gallagher and Robinson, and of D.K. Fieldhouse. They argued, firstly, that the export of capital, which Hobson took to be the chief motive force behind imperialism, was not a new feature of British economic life in the late nineteenth century and could not, therefore, be invoked to explain the extension of British authority at that time. Moreover, insofar as capital export was a major feature of the British economy, most of the flow of funds overseas was to the white-settled parts of the world and only marginal amounts went to Africa where the major imperial gains were made.[2]

Opposition to Hobsonian explanations has been widened over the years into an objection to all attempts to explain imperialism in terms of changes in the metropolitan economy or in the nature of its impact overseas. In his most recent statement Robinson, the outstanding contemporary theorist, rejects all 'Eurocentric' approaches in which, he claims, imperialism is defined almost 'wholly in terms of metropolitan drives projecting on passive peripheries.'[3] In his view imperialism can only be understood as an 'interactive process' in which a wide variety of European 'inputs', both economic and non-economic, conjoin with an equally varied range of collaborative forces outside Europe to produce a complex spectrum of imperial relationships. Imperialism was not a simple function of British or other European capitalist development: European economic inputs into the periphery were not significant enough to produce imperialism in themselves. In the white colonies where British economic inputs were of relatively greater significance the imperialist element in the relationship faded away in the late nineteenth century; in Africa and Asia, where the economic link with the metropole was weaker, the extension of imperialist authority was greatest.[4]

Purely Eurocentric theories *are* inadequate and there is some force in the claim that, 'when imperialism is looked at as an inter-continental process, its true metropolis appears neither at the centre nor on the periphery, but in their changing relativities.'[5] Nonetheless, Robinson's approach can lead to a serious underestimation of the extent of the European economic input into the rest of the world after 1870. Robinson also fails to appreciate the dynamism of western capitalism and the changing nature of western economies, frequently writing as though the economic structure of Britain and Europe was the same in 1914 as it had been in 1870. The result is that the metropolitan economic contribution to imperialism is frequently underrated. If Hobsonian theories of imperialism ignored the periphery, Robinsonian approaches sometimes fall into the opposite trap of leaving European impulses too far out of account.

In recent years, a substantial body of scholarly work on different aspects of Britain's overseas presence has been produced which directs attention back to the metropolitan economy as a powerful influence upon the nature and direction of imperial expansion. At the same time, there have been attempts, on the part of economic historians trying to understand the complexities of the British economy of Hobson's day and its international ramifications,[6] to re-explore and re-assess Hobson's ideas. As a result, new life can be infused into Hobsonian explanations of British imperialism, as the rest of this essay is intended to show.

Fundamental to the Hobsonian view of imperialism was the assumption that the advanced capitalist nations of his time were all disfigured by a maldistribution of property and income, which meant underconsumption for the masses and oversaving by the rich. Hobson argued that, had the latter tried to find outlets for all their savings within the domestic economy, rates of return on investments would have fallen to very low levels and threatened the stability of the capitalist order. Salvation could be found through the export of excess savings in the form of foreign investments: finding outlets for these savings and protecting them when found was, in Hobson's view, what imperialism was about.[7] Unfortunately, when faced with the problem of showing how economic malfunction led to political action, he all too often fell back upon crude conspiracy theory; some of the best-known of his writings on this theme are full of an anti-Semitic prejudice which makes them ethically unsound as well as academically uninteresting.[8]

However, there are much more sophisticated approaches to policy-making in Hobson's work which, while they emphasize the ultimate control of the financier over the foreign and imperial policy of the nation, do open up some fascinating vistas on the nature of the interconnections between the workings of British economy and decision-making at the centre. This strand in Hobson's thinking deserves far more attention than it has yet received. Within this context one line of enquiry to which Hobson himself alluded in *Imperialism: A Study*, his most famous book first published in 1902, and to which he later returned more systematically in a long-forgotten article, concerned the possibility of explaining the peculiarities of British imperialism by relating them to regional differences in economic and social structure within the nation. Hobson distinguished here between the heavy industrial areas, broadly the North, and the parts of the country in which services were the dominant economic force, mainly the South of England. He argued that the South was the home of a 'moneyed class', a large non-industrial middle and upper class, where incomes often came from a *rentier* interest in home and foreign investments. Imperialism was largely an endeavour to find openings for the surplus savings of this 'moneyed class' whose power was enhanced because they were culturally and socially integrated into the gentlemanly circles which held the major share of power in

Britain. Hobson thought of Northern industrialists as largely outside this particular set of power relations; but he could see that overseas investments were closely linked to the export of industrial commodities, giving some industrialists and their workforce powerful reasons to support policies which were chiefly designed to benefit the 'moneyed class' of the South and the politicians, soldiers and administrators with whom they had close social and cultural affinities.[9]

In pointing to a link between service and financial interests on the one hand and provincial exporting industries on the other, Hobson was referring to a loose alliance between the two sides rather than claiming a growing organic unity between them. The 'monopoly capitalism' or 'finance capitalism' described by Marxists such as Hilferding, though useful as a way of understanding the economic foundations of German and American imperialism, was not, as Hobson realized, applicable to the British case. He also believed that if foreign investment had benefits for the export sector of industry in Britain in the short term it would eventually harm manufacturing, partly by perpetuating underconsumption in Britain and partly by stimulating the development of industry in the 'backward' parts of the world subject to imperial domination.[10]

In order to test a Hobsonian theory of imperialism it is first necessary to review the importance of foreign investment to the economy of Britain in the later nineteenth century and to ascertain as far as is possible who the investors were. Conventional assessments of British overseas investments all show that sustained flows of funds abroad were very much a phenomenon of the later nineteenth century and the Edwardian period, with total assets owned rising from around £200m in 1850 to £700m by 1870, and reaching £4bn just before World War One.[11] At the latter date, the assets brought in a return of about £200m per annum, equivalent to about ten per cent of the national income. These magnitudes have recently been questioned and, it is argued, the figure for total assets owned abroad in 1913 should be written down by about one third, with adjustments being made for earlier dates accordingly.[12] Even if the downward revision was universally accepted as reasonable, the rise in foreign investment after 1850 would still be one of the most marked features of later nineteenth-century economic development. In fact, the assault on orthodoxy has been received somewhat sceptically by the experts even though it is admitted that the conventional totals are based upon inadequate data.[13] Besides this, the discussion on the extent of British investments overseas has largely been concerned with portfolio investments − where British capital was placed in foreign-owned firms. But it is now becoming accepted that the amount of *direct* investment − involving the establishing of British firms abroad − has been much underrated in the past.[14] Any downward revision of the figures for portfolio investment must, therefore, be compensated for by a more generous assessment of direct forms of capital export. Given the present state of research, it is reasonable to accept the well established figure for British foreign investment as roughly accurate.[15]

Hobson thought of foreign investment as largely a product of the South of England, and a study of the geographical distribution of stockholders in imperial and foreign enterprises does show a remarkable concentration of overseas investors around London and a marked lack of interest in foreign or imperial enterprise amongst provincial industrialists, save those in Lancashire and parts of Scotland. Similarly, although merchants showed a predeliction for foreign investment, studies of the occupational structure of overseas investors have shown that manufacturers as a group were far more interested in domestic than in overseas stocks. Also, insofar as manufacturers did show an interest in overseas endeavours, those who did so were predominantly from the London area. By contrast, the group with the most decided preference for investment overseas has been recently described as 'peers and gents'.[16] The importance of aristocratic money in overseas enterprise reflects the steady decline in the profitability of agriculture after 1870, but the preponderance of London and of non-industrial sources of finance relates to the increasing import-ance of the service sector in Britain in the late nineteenth and early twentieth cent-uries. Service output and employment grew at a faster rate than industrial after 1870 throughout Britain, but the part of Britain where services were the dominant mode of employment was the South-East.[17] With the highest per capita income in Britain, the South-East region generated a very high level of savings, which were cut off socially and institutionally from industrial employment and looking for safe outlets. Domestic opportunities for investment of this kind were limited after 1870 and rates of interest on government bonds, railway shares and other suitable stocks would have fallen to very low levels indeed without the opening up of overseas oppor-tunities.[18] Thus funds naturally flowed abroad into government bonds, public utilities and similar investments which were expected to bring a secure and steady return and which found a home in an area much wider than the bounds of the British empire.

As Hobson believed, British foreign investments of his time were a feature of the latest phase of the development of the economy and, at around five per cent of the national income on average between 1850 and 1913,[19] were not the 'comparatively insignificant' item which Robinson claims.[20] Also, the bulk of the investors came from the South-East of England and they were part of the non-industrial elites who formed the 'gentlemanly capitalist' class at the apex of the British social and political heirarchy.[21]

As for the economic effects of the foreign investment itself, there is some evidence to suggest that such heavy flows overseas were inimical to industrial development in Britain. The great surges of foreign investment in the 1880s and during the Ed-wardian period were accompanied by low rates of output of manufacturing growth and investment in general, even though the traditional export areas benefited from overseas flows of funds. By contrast, very low levels of foreign investment in the 1890s were parallelled by a revival in manufacturing growth despite a severe slow-down in industrial exports.[22] Evidence of this kind has recently been used to provide a more directly Hobsonian view of the British economy in the late nineteenth and early twentieth centuries. Kennedy, for example, has recently claimed, with great force, that whatever benefits heavy foreign investment may have conferred on the major export industries and their regions, its effects on domestic investment as a whole were adverse. He believes that home investment was lowered partly because free trade encouraged Britain's debtors to pay their dues by exporting manufactured goods to her, thus lowering profits and discouraging investment. This is not an argu-ment Hobson could have accepted since he was always an ardent free trader, who saw protectionism merely as a device used by vested interests to improve their own position at the expense of the mass of consumers. But Kennedy also argues that home investment was in part low because high levels of foreign investment led to a maldistribution of income in favour of *rentiers* and lowered effective demand for industrial commodities.[23] It is also worth noting here that Hobsonian explanations for the ebbs and flows of overseas investment have also recently been brought back into the front line of discussion. Michael Edelstein's analysis of overseas investment flows is principally drawn up on neo-classical assumptions about the downward tendency of the rate of investment in response to limited home opportunities; but he does pinpoint two periods in the late 1870s and in 1901-03, when 'desired' savings overshot 'desired' domestic investment opportunities considerably. In his considered opinion, these bouts of Hobsonian oversaving may have triggered off the great foreign investment booms of the 1880s and 1905-13.[24] Without foreign outlets, these savings would have been kept in idle balances and severe depression could have resulted. Kennedy and Edelstein's work is highly controversial and the relationship between home and overseas investment is a particularly hotly disputed area of recent research.[25] But their work, along with that on the geographical and occupational origins of investors, does mean, at the very least, that a Hobsonian analysis of the economy has serious claims to attention. It remains now to be seen to what extent these ideas can be applied to specific episodes in British imperial history before 1914.

It is sensible to begin with Africa. The partition still occupies a central place in discussion of both British and European imperialism although, as we shall see, this centrality ought not to be taken for granted. The African tropics can be briefly dealt with since no Hobsonian explanation of the extension of British authority seems plausible. Hobson does imply, without clearly stating it, that tropical Africa received significant draughts of British capital before partition.[26] Lloyd has made an attempt to rescue Hobson by trying to show that, even if British investments in tropical Africa were very small, they may have played a disproportionately important role in partition via the creation of the Chartered Companies, such as the Royal Niger and the East Africa Companies, which were vital to the extension of the British presence in their respective hinterlands.[27] This, though ingenious, obscures the nature and purpose of the Chartered Companies to some degree. However, the failure of the Hobsonian theory here does not necessarily mean that the outcome of the partition in West and East Africa was determined mainly by the strategic considerations stressed by Robinson and Gallagher in *Africa and the Victorians*.[28] There were strong economic pressures, related to changing conditions in European markets, making for involvement but the pressures emanated more from the provinces, from provincial merchants and the manufacturers, than they did from the City of London and its financial institutions.[29]

The occupation of Egypt in 1882 presents a much more interesting test of a theory of financial imperialism. Although he never wrote about the occupation in any great depth, Hobson thought of it as a classic case since the prime cause of the Egyptian crisis was, he believed, the latter's heavy indebtedness to English and French investors who were pressing their 'Governments to foreclose upon the property', because of fears that the Egyptians could not, or would not, pay their creditors.[30] He was willing to admit that the desire to retain control of the Suez Canal was a complicating factor in the crisis but he also came to the emphatic conclusion that 'the political motive [for occupying Egypt] lay idle until it was stimulated into action by the more energetic and constructive power of the financier.'[31]

In *Africa and the Victorians*, Robinson and Gallagher lay far more emphasis upon strategic considerations. What emerges most clearly from this study of the 'official mind' in the build-up to the occupation is not only a perception of a slackening British interest in the Egyptian economy as the latter slid into crisis in the mid-1870s, but also the determination of British officialdom not to be manoeuvred into action by outraged holders of Egyptian stock. Robinson and Gallagher see French initiatives — stemming mainly from bondholder pressure — as crucial in pushing Britain into a reluctant confrontation with the Egyptian problem for fear of a loss of influence at Suez; and they insist that there was no real intention to intervene directly in Egypt until the middle of 1882 when riots in Alexandria finally convinced the authorities that law and order had broken down. Only then did it become essential to fill the void left by the collapse of the Khedival government on which the British had relied, and to curb the militaristic nationalism of Urabi Pasha and his supporters now threatening Egypt with anarchy.[32]

A closer inspection of the workings of the official mind in recent years has undermined many of Robinson's and Gallagher's assumptions and given more credence to Hobson's point of view. From the British perspective, Suez never approached the Simonstown base at the Cape in importance, nor was its security raised as an issue until the crisis in Egypt was on the brink of resolution by force. The attempt to portray the French as the forward party, with the British reacting to them, also fails to convince. French pressure for economic control in Egypt was strong in the very early days of the crisis but French financial anxieties were eased in the late 1870s precisely because of enhanced participation by London finance and a greater British political involvement. By the early 1880s, French interest had switched to Tunisia leaving the British with a fairly free hand in Cairo. Nor can it be claimed that Egyptian anarchy forced British intervention. The rise of the nationalist forces, which threatened the European-supported power structure in Cairo, was accompanied by remarkably little social upheaval; the new political forces, once they began to gain power, had no intention of repudiating Egypt's external economic obligations, still less of driving the considerable European population out of the country. So, since neither the French nor the Egyptians themselves can be said to have forced the British into action, the causes of British intervention need to be explained with reference to the perceptions and the actions of the British themselves.[33]

British interests in Egyptian trade were extensive. Holdings of Egyptian stock were similarly important and increased in the late 1870s as the French withdrew. The Conservative government, which had to address the Egyptian problem before 1880, was unflinchingly determined that all debts should be paid, and played a vigorous part in reorganizing the latter's finances. Under the cover of the government's unofficial but determined involvement, British investment in Egypt increased significantly at the turn of the decade.[34] There is little doubt that the Suez Canal purchase, and government involvement in setting Egyptian finances to rights, encouraged British investors to take up Egyptian stock and led them to believe that the state had a duty to intervene on their behalf if the worst should occur.[35] Unfortunately the impositions of British officials, practising a brutal Gladstonianism in cutting public expenditure, overseeing debt repayment and making Egypt creditworthy again in the eyes of London and Paris, led to a sustained nationalist reaction. By 1879, the British government seems to have assumed that Egypt would have to be taken under direct control since 'orientals' clearly could not be trusted to run a country on sound economic principles.[36]

Gladstone's incoming administration of 1880 made no such initial assumptions and was inclined at first to look with favour on the insurgent nationalists as representing a liberal nationalism with which Britons could sympathize. In Egypt, by contrast, British officials under pressure to relax their rigid policies of financial orthodoxy came increasingly to see Egyptian assertiveness as 'anarchy' and 'disorder'.[37] They eventually convinced the government in Britain, preoccupied with Irish affairs, of the justice of their case and of a threat to the capitalist order of Egypt. Similar anxieties amongst British investors and traders involved in Egypt pushed the government in the same direction, until the riots in Alexandria – which the British mistakenly assumed were inspired by Urabi Pasha's supporters – then provided an excuse for intervention.[38]

It is not necessary to ignore the fact that Egypt presented Britain with a strategic problem at Suez in order to argue that the crisis there was principally one of economic management and control, and that intervention was eventually undertaken on the assumption that Britain had to intervene directly in Egypt if the financial problem were to be solved. Once the collaborators who supported the Khedival regime had lost their authority, neither the official mind in Egypt nor its counterpart in Britain could believe that the nationalists were capable of maintaining the law and order which sustained the capitalist system. The sticking point for the British was undoubtedly the claim of the Chamber of Notables, the nationalists' 'parliament', that it should be consulted on budgetary questions. Wilfred Blunt, the British aristocratic apologist for Urabi, recorded the following conversation with Lord Granville, the Foreign Secretary, in March 1882. Granville asked,

> 'Will they give up the claim of the Chamber to vote the Budget?' I told him I feared it was hopeless to expect this, as the deputies were all of one mind. 'Then', he said, 'I look upon their case as hopeless. It must end by their being put down by force.' I told him I could not believe the English Government could really intervene on such a plea, to put down liberty. But he maintained his ground and I left him much dissatisfied.[39]

Many Liberals felt a strong urge to avoid the embarrassing question of a connection between the campaign to suppress Urabi and Britain's economic interests. It was for fear of such embarrassment that Granville was persuaded to strike out of the document explaining Britain's conduct to other interested powers a passage admitting that Egyptian attempts at financial control had been the prime reason for Britain's hostility to the new men in Cairo.[40] It was for the same reason that the defence of Suez and the strategic importance of Egypt was emphasized in British explanations of their action, even though the Canal did not play a prominent part in the discussions which preceded the intervention.[41] Political discomfort also had a role to play in shaping the radicals' own response. The Egyptian crisis was the first occasion on which the radicals marked down City usurers as the chief architects of imperialism.[42] Perhaps their zeal in identifying finance and its allies in the press, the bureaucracy and the military, also owed something to the natural desire to hide the uncomfortable fact that considerable support for the adventure had come from the radicals' traditional strongholds in the industrial provinces, where fears for the future of the Egyptian market were strong.[43] It needed Hobson, twenty years later, to come to terms as a radical himself with the evidence that financial imperialism in London was often in alliance with industrial imperialism in the provinces.

Hobson was right to believe that the Egyptian crisis was a good example of financial imperialism but he misunderstood the way in which finance 'controlled' policy. 'Finance', he argued in a famous passage, manipulates the patriotic forces which politicians, soldiers, philanthropists and traders generate: the enthusiasm for expansion which issues from these forces, though strong and genuine, is irregular and blind; the financial interest has those qualities of concentration and clear-sighted calculation which are needed to set Imperialism to work.[44]

In truth, during the Egyptian crisis financiers were no better placed than politicians to understand clearly what was going on in Egypt at any time; it was often the ill-founded anxieties of financial interests, whether in Egypt or in the City, rather than 'clear-sighted calculation', which increased the desire to intervene. Financiers could not manipulate Salisbury or Gladstone in the manner Hobson assumes. On the other hand, a huge chain of financial connections had been forged between Britain and Egypt over forty years which had enormous influence in deciding the form which British interest in Egypt would take. These commitments and obligations were the touchstone of Anglo-Egyptian relations, the crucial point about which the whole crisis revolved. In that sense, it is surely correct to say that finance was 'the governor of the imperial engine'.

If Hobson's explanation of the Egyptian crisis has some plausibility, his position on South Africa and the Boer War of 1899-1902 is more problematical. Essentially, Hobson saw the dispute as one between an antiquated government in the Afrikaner republic of the Transvaal and the gold-mining interests who found their profits threatened by government taxation and failure to organize the labour supply efficiently. The British government did not ostensibly go to war for the sake of mining capitalists. Leading politicians wanted a federated South Africa, and public opinion supported aggression against the Transvaal because it was perceived to be racialist and politically illiberal in excluding most of the mining immigrants from the vote.[45] Even Cecil Rhodes, the most famous of the gold millionaires and the inspiration behind the Jameson Raid of 1895 when mining capitalists tried to overthrow the regime of Kruger in the Transvaal, was thought by Hobson to be animated by genuinely patriotic motives as well as by a desire to increase his profits. But Hobson still believed that if 'justice, humanity, prestige, expansion, political ambition all conspired to dwarf the significance of the business motive', then 'persistence, power, direction and intelligible aim' belonged with the mining interests and their financial backers, who had control of the press and access to political power. In retrospect he was inclined to think of the absorption of the Transvaal, and its sister republic, the Orange Free State, as the clearest example of financial imperialism.[46]

Robinson and Gallagher attack this view by pointing to the importance of strategic imperatives in South Africa, particularly the need to keep a secure hold on the naval base at the Cape, a need which presupposed a stable British regime in the South African hinterland. Until the gold discoveries of the 1880s the Transvaal was merely a small, landlocked, poverty-stricken state dependent economically on the British-dominated Cape province. Gold brought the Afrikaners wealth: it also slowly transformed the Transvaal into the economic heartland of South Africa, putting the Cape and its small sister-province, Natal, into the orbit of a state hostile to British control of South Africa. The British response was to press for the enfranchisement of the mining immigrants, in the hope of wresting influence from the Afrikaners, and to push for a federation of the South African states so that the Afrikaner element might be in contained in the same way that the French were contained within the Canadian Confederation. In Robinson's and Gallagher's view, the mining interest had no specific influence on policy, which was controlled by defence-minded statesmen in London. In particular, Rhodes' attempted *coup* of 1895 seemed to them inspired by a desire for imperial *gloire* rather than a capitalist plot to use British power to overthrow a refractory regime.[47]

Much of Robinson's and Gallagher's argument has stood the test of time and scholarly scrutiny. Concern about the Cape was a far more important element in the South African crisis than Suez was in the case of Egypt. On the other hand, a Hobsonian explanation of the Jameson Raid can be constructed on the basis of recent research; and in assessing the British government's overall policy it is more difficult than Robinson and Gallagher imply to divorce the aims and aspirations of the mineowners from strategic necessities as perceived in London.

Blainey suggested twenty years ago that the key to understanding the Jameson Raid lay in the nature of the mineowners' varying economic commitment to gold extraction. Capitalists in outcrop or shallow mining had an assured profitability: those, like Rhodes, involved in deep mining and with expansive and growing capital commitments in London, were anxious about future returns and did have good economic reasons for ousting Kruger's regime.[48] The ensuing debate on Blainey's thesis has revealed that the distinction between supporters of the Jameson Raid and other mineowners rests not so much on a simple division between shallow and deep mines as between those which, whatever their short-term profitability, needed heavy capital investment to maintain long-term financial viability, and those which did not. The conspirators did have materialist motives for their actions: Rhodes' imperial vision was combined with an acute need for a more benign capitalist regime than Kruger could supply.[49]

The Jameson Raid failed. Its main result was to give new openings to extremists on both sides of the conflict. The progress of mining capitalism in the Transvaal had begun to raise up a generation of Afrikaners more inclined to collaborate than Kruger and his supporters: the appearance of the Republic as a borrower in the London market in the early 1890s (courtesy of Rothschilds who, via their Exploration Company, had strong links with Rhodes and other gold capitalists)[50] suggests the beginnings of incorporation into the London financial network.[51] After Jameson, Kruger's anti-British stance seemed justified and, on the British side, the failure of the Raid gave the green light to the more aggressive policies of Milner, and eventually led to conflict in 1899.

After the Raid, the centre of political activity shifted from the mining frontier to governments, from South Africa to London. Even so, the needs of both miners and politicians were congruent. In the late 1870s, and before gold was discovered, the British had tried to federate South Africa, assuming that it was only in a politically united sub-continent that the black tribes could be held in check sufficiently well to allow for the organization of an efficient, native labour force. Without that, it was believed that South Africa would remain economically backward and thus insecure. Strategic objectives, it was assumed, were best supported by economic development and the strengthening of material ties between South Africa and Britain.[52] British policy in the 1890s was different only in emphasis: Milner, Chamberlain and other principals all accepted that Kruger's policy, in harming mining, harmed South Africa not only economically but strategically. Once the war was over Milner, despite his distaste for many of the mining capitalists, was determined to get the industry back to full production as fast as possible and went to extreme lengths to solve the labour supply problem on their behalf. And, in 1910, a South African state was created in which the Afrikaners, now more or less willing collaborators both with British strategic aims and with full-blown capitalism, were expected to work with the British element in South Africa to create a secure state via free economic development. The modern state, the state which offered the possibilities of rapid growth, was also the one which made the Cape secure.[53]

Hobson was wrong to suggest that the mineowners were the chief force behind the incorporation of the Afrikaner republics, though the Jameson Raid did fit the Hobsonian specifications, and he completely missed the significance of the Cape to Britain. For their part, Robinson and Gallagher rather underestimated the extent to which the strategic considerations, which were at the forefront of the official mind, were underpinned by the assumption of the need for a freely functioning capitalism in South Africa and of the corresponding need for a government which could ensure this.[54]

Although his name is linked most frequently with the African partition, Hobson himself regarded the scramble for control of China in the twenty years before World War One as the single most important event in the contemporary history of imperialism. The penetration of China before 1890 had been very limited, but Hobson was convinced that Britain and other industrial powers stood at the beginning of an age when the export of surplus capital would transform China, and other 'backward' nations with complex civilizations. Massive influxes of capital would, he thought, eventually lead to the industrialization of the East under the control of Western capital with the latter losing its own industry.[55] The political battle between the great powers to divide China into 'spheres of interest' was thought by Hobson to be the preliminary to this invasion of European and American surplus savings.[56] He never wavered in his view that the governments of Britain and other powers were working directly on behalf of financial interests who needed the authority of their states to subdue the Chinese and to clear the way for capitalist exploitation.[57] In the wake of the political battle, allocating parts of China and other states in the East to various advanced nations, would come the vast infrastructural investments needed to create the framework for the rapid development of these countries, sheltering under the 'law and order' provided by the intrusion of Western power.

The reality of Britain's penetration of China, and of the Middle East, was rather different. In the heyday of early Victorian optimism, the British assumed that free trade was sufficient in itself to galvanize backward peoples into capitalist development; this benign medicine was forced upon the Turkish Empire in 1838 and upon the Chinese in the wars between 1840 and 1860. The result of free trade was deeply disappointing partly because of the complexities of 'underdeveloped' economies, which could not be unravelled by free trade treaties, and partly because, especially in China, the authorities remained stubbornly unyielding in their hostility to European culture.[58] Successive British governments, carefully monitored by a Parliament deeply suspicious of state expenditures, were reluctant to commit themselves to stronger action to increase penetration.[59] In China, for example, they were only roused into action to support British business in the 1880s when other European powers began to try to undermine British predominance at Peking.[60] But the great turning point came in 1895 when China, defeated by Japan in war, was forced by the latter to pay an indemnity and as a result had to raise foreign loans for the first time. As Chinese military and financial independence failed, so did European penetration increase. British policy was to try to maintain the political and territorial integrity of China by diplomatic and financial action — the latter including the organization of joint great-power loans in 1895 and 1912, which were intended to give all the intruders into China an interest in the political status quo.[61] At the same time, the British ensured that the Yangtze Valley, where British trade was mainly concentrated, was demarcated a 'sphere of interest' and that all major capital projects there — which were the key to political as well as economic control — should be under British authority.[62]

These initiatives were supposed to create the conditions under which British capital would flow into China confirming British predominance there. But capital was slow to come. The joint loans were not difficult to raise since the interest on them was virtually guaranteed by increasing British and other great-power control of Chinese revenues. Capital for railway concessions and similar utility investments was much less in evidence. Without adequate political and military security, British capital would not flow and rapid economic development in China could not occur. On the other hand, security could only be established by a much greater commitment of British power in China. But the latter was regarded as too expensive and as leading to never-ending problems: one India was enough. Without this emphatic commitment, Britain's economic presence in China was bound to remain marginal.[63]

Looked at from another angle, the problem of the British government was that it could not compel British finance to follow it into China or into similar areas such as the Middle East. By contrast, the French government's control over the Paris money market was much greater, and French money was more inclined to go where French governments led. The most remarkable example of this was in the Turkish Empire, where a determined French political push, after the bankruptcy of the Sultan in the 1870s and the takeover of Turkey's finances by European agents, led to an enormous increase in French investment in the Empire and the relative eclipse of British interests there.[64] French economic penetration of China was less successful mainly because France had less political influence in China.[65] But it was not just in the Turkish Empire but also in China that, after the Entente was signed in 1904, the British tried to enlist French co-operation in financing politically sensitive concessions.[66] But, failing this kind of co-operation, when British governments felt that vital diplomatic or strategic matters required economic underpinning, they were often driven to desperate expedients to raise the finance necessary for their policies, because the co-operation of the City was not forthcoming.[67]

The very limited nature of the 'inputs' into China and the Middle East, and the lack of collaboration with capitalism in these areas, suggests that Robinson's 'excentric' approach to imperialism is better than Hobson's arguments in providing insights into British imperialism here. But to understand the process fully, the reasons for this lack of input need to be placed in a wider perspective.

London finance did not flow to Turkey and China because it chose not to do so: there were far richer pickings elsewhere. One of London's great advantages as a money market was its openness and freedom from interference. The City was difficult for governments to control and to use for political purposes, but it was also unparallelled as an international service centre. French governments might find it easier than British to direct Parisian money to Constantinople or Peking, but the French had less success in the free markets of the world economy. Looked at from the British angle, the obverse of the failure to galvanize China and Turkey financially was enormous success in creating a financial empire in Canada, Australia, New Zealand, South Africa and parts of Latin America, which no other great power could match and which made the economic penetration of China and Turkey much less necessary.[68]

Outside South Africa, Hobson did not consider that the white-settled frontier was subject to British financial imperialism. In the chapter on the white colonies which he wrote in *Imperialism*, he recognized only the gradual emergence of political liberty under parliamentary government, though he was anxious lest some overarching imperial federation movement at the turn of the century should lead to both the political and economic subordination of the emergent colonial nations.[69] Robinson, while clearly recognizing an initial economic subordination, believes, as we have already seen, that as the flow of capital from Britain increased in the late nineteenth century the imperialist element in the relationship faded away. This may be true of Canada after Confederation in 1867, since United States influence may have grown relatively faster than British, giving the Canadians the opportunity to play off one economic superpower against another. Even in this case the size of imports of British capital in relation to local savings suggests that the idea of British financial imperialism in Canada in the late nineteenth and early twentieth century would bear further investigation.[70]

In regard to Australia and New Zealand, Robinson's judgement is more questionable. Granting Australasian colonies self-government after 1850 was a clear derogation of imperial power, though it is important to remember that one of the reasons for granting it was that the colonies were perceived to have reached a stage of development where they could function as satellite economies without political supervision from London.[71] Moreover, although it was unintended, the integration of Australasia into the world economy, and into the financial network centred on London after 1850, extended the economic and financial authority of Britain in the colonies.[72] The acute degree of Australasian financial dependence on Britain before 1914 is indicated by the close correspondence between the sterling balances held in London by Australasian and Anglo-Australasian banks and the colonies' money supply. Rises or falls in these balances led to corresponding movements in local money supply and were therefore crucial to the long-term growth path of the colonies.[73] The level of these balances did not simply depend upon trade relations with Britain, important though these were, but on the colonies' ability to borrow in London. These borrowings were not 'small in relation to capital invested', as Robinson asserts:[74] in the 1860s and 1880s, for example, imports of capital from Britain accounted for roughly half of all gross capital formation in the Australian states.[75]

The British penchant for portfolio rather than direct investment in the colonies gave the latter a significant influence on the direction of capital investment; however the weight of the British financial presence and metropolitan control over financial institutions meant that, ultimately, the control of economic policy was not in Australasian hands. In the mid-1880s in New Zealand and the early 1890s in Australia the drying up of the hitherto abundant wells of British capital was partly a consequence of local 'folly'[76] insofar as there had been considerable over-investment in both cases, and exports had failed to materialize sufficiently to allow for easy debt repayment. But the crisis was forced upon the Australians to some degree by the general aversion to foreign lending which followed the Baring Crisis in 1891. The 1890s crisis intensified London control of Australian finance and imposed a Gladstonian straitjacket on local economic policy.[77] Robinson is well aware that 'borrowers anxious to keep their loan status with European stock exchanges were wise to make their financial policies conform to the creditor's requirements',[78] but this rather underestimates the extent to which the colonies' need to apply the 'rules of the game', as set in the City of London, meant that the 'collaborative terms'[79] between periphery and metropole were dictated by the latter.[80] Moreover, it is hard to sustain the claim that the Australasian colonies were largely independent economically by 1919, as Robinson asserts. In Australia, for example, growth was achieved for a while after 1900 without large draughts of British capital but, between 1910 and 1914, as the economy moved towards full employment, the need for capital imports increased sharply,[82] and after 1919 Australia remained a persistent borrower. Her economic well-being depended as much upon the state of her sterling balances in London in the early 1930s as it had done in the 1890s.[83]

The nature and extent of British economic imperialism in Australia and New Zealand[84] was disguised to some degree by the almost automatic response of British investors to Australasian demand for capital before 1890, and by the close cultural links with Britain which muted the development of local nationalist resentment of London's economic dominance. The imperialist element in the connection between metropole and white colonial frontiers was easier to appreciate in Latin America. Between 1860 and 1914, Argentina was transformed through her links with the international economy and, by the latter date, her share of Britain's import trade and her dependence on imports of British capital was as significant as that of any of the white colonies. In 1860, the British presence in Argentina was mainly centred on small firms in the trading sector and confined to the coast. By 1900, British economic power was felt in the interior of the country in the shape of large banks, railway and the utility companies and similar larger organizations. Although not strictly on a sterling standard, as were the Australasian colonies, Argentine dependence on external finance was by 1890 acute, and economic policy was determined by London criteria rather than purely local ones.[85] Like the Australians, the Argentinians faced a financial crisis in the 1890s as British capital dried up. The crisis broke one administration which lacked sympathy with the needs of external capital, and increased the dominance of London-based finance in both banking and the railway sector.[86]

In Brazil, where the economic and political power of local elites rested on the ability to tap foreign finance, a similar loss of local economic independence was evident. The Brazilian economy avoided crises in the early 1890s because coffee exports were bouyant and investors still happy to lend. But as exports declined in the late 1890s, the country ran into a foreign debt crisis for which, with the London Rothschilds as intermediaries, help was received, but only in return for a deflationary package of economic measures designed to cut imports and boost exports, slowing down economic growth in the process. A further crisis just before 1914 was dealt with in the same way and the overall result was increasing control of the banking and transport sectors of the economy by foreign investors.[87]

The white-settled frontier was often subject to British financial dominance in the late nineteenth century and beyond. It received massive benefits from this in terms of economic growth, but its dependence on Britain was not fundamentally different to that suffered by the Egyptians. The main difference between Egypt and the newly settled parts of the world was that the latter had a capitalist structure of greater flexibility which could better adapt itself to crisis. If we think in terms of 'informal' empire as well as 'formal' - to use an earlier concept of Gallagher and Robinson — then it is fair to see the settler societies as subject to a financial imperialism which is recognizably Hobsonian, even if Hobson himself never considered those relationships in this light.

The wheel has come full circle, and there has been a revival of interest in Hobson as a theorist of imperialism. His arguments about the impact of foreign investment on the economy are receiving attention again and, in the light of recent work on Egypt and South Africa especially, his views on the causes of imperial expansion seem much more plausible than they did twenty years ago. Robinson's explanations of imperial interest in the 'sick men' of China and Turkey are rather more to the point than Hobsonian ones, however, and Robinson shows far more awareness of the importance of relationships between Britain and the white-settled frontier, though this can be analysed in terms Hobson would have understood. Some other of his concerns, not dealt with here, have also resurfaced in the recent literature on imperialism. He always argued, for instance, that the creation and maintenance of a formal empire, although it might be beneficial to certain interest groups, was not good business for Britain as a nation. Using the mammoth researches of Davis and

Hutterback on foreign investment as his starting point, O'Brien has recently argued in very similar terms with explicit reference to Hobson's own arguments and conclusions.[88]

So Hobson lives. However, in regard to the central problem of the economics of imperial expansion, it is clear that any deeper understanding of the nature of British financial imperialism must go further than Hobson himself was prepared to travel. Hobson always saw finance as the supreme arbiter of policy, the force which galvanized all others − economic, political, cultural, ideological − into decisive action. This easily becomes a naive, conspiratorial approach to decision-making which hardly fits the complexities of, for example, the Egyptian case already analysed. What is needed is much closer investigation of the role of finance, seen as part of a complex social and political order in Britain, with a view to answering such questions as: why did financial interest play such an important role at the centre of British politics, and why did industry exert less influence on policy than the City? This kind of enquiry can be undertaken by placing the City within the context of the wider 'gentlemanly capitalist' society referred to earlier in this essay and discussed in detail elsewhere.[89]

Notes

1. R. Hyam and G. Martin, *Re-appraisals in British Imperial History* (London, 1975), p.1.
2. J. Gallagher and R.E. Robinson, 'The Imperialism of Free Trade, 1815-1914', *Economic History Review*, 2nd Ser. VI (1953-54); R.E. Robinson and J. Gallagher, with A. Denny, *Africa and the Victorians. The Official Mind of Imperialism* (London, 2nd ed., 1984), chapter I; D.K. Fieldhouse, 'Imperialism: An Historiographical Revision', *Economic History Review*, 2nd Ser. XIV (1961-62); D.K. Fieldhouse, *Economics and Empire* (London 1974), chapter III.
3. R.E. Robinson, 'The Excentric Idea of Imperialism, with or without Empire', in W.J. Mommsen and J. Osterhammel, *Imperialism and Africa, Continuities and Discontinuities* (London, 1986), p.268.
4. *Ibid.* pp.268-9.
5. *Ibid.* p.271.
6. P.J. Cain, 'J.A. Hobson, Financial Capitalism and Imperialism in Late Victorian and Edwardian England', *Journal of Imperial and Commonwealth History*, XIII (1985). [Reprinted in *Money, Finance and Empire 1790-1860* (ed. A. Porter and R. Holland, London, 1985).] For a lively new approach to Hobson see also N. Etherington, *Theories of Imperialism. War, Conquest and Capital* (London, 1984), especially chapters 3 and 4.
7. For a short, early and impressive outline of the theory see J.A. Hobson, 'Free Trade and Foreign Policy', *Contemporary Review*, LXXIV (1898).
8. On the anti-semitism see *Imperialism. A Study* (London, 1988 edition), p.57.
9. *Imperialism*, pp.151, 314-15, 384-5; 'The General Election. A Sociological Interpretation', *Sociological Review*, III (1910), 113ff.
10. On the comparison between Hobsonian and Marxist theories of imperialism see P.J. Cain, 'International Trade and Economic Development in the Work of J.A. Hobson before 1914', *History of Political Economy*, XI (1979); and A. Brewer, *Marxist Theories of Imperialism. A Critical Survey* (London, 2nd ed., 1990).
11. P. Cottrell, *British Overseas Investment in the Nineteenth Century* (London, 1975), pp.11-14, 23, 31.
12. D.C.M. Platt, *Britain's Overseas Investment on the Eve of the First World War* (London, 1986).
13. See, for example, W.P. Kennedy's review of Platt in *Economic History Review*, 2nd Ser. XL (1987), 307-9; and C.H. Feinstein, 'Britain's Overseas Investments in 1913', *Economic History Review*, 2nd Ser. XLIII (1990).
14. P. Svedberg, 'The Portfolio-Direct Composition of Private Foreign Investment Revisited', *Economic Journal*, LXXXVI (1978); M. Wilkins, 'The Free-Standing Company, 1870-1914: an Important Type of British Foreign Direct Investment', *Economic History Review*, 2nd Ser. XLI, 2 (1988).

15. The difficulties of precision in this area are indicated by the fact that L.E. Davis and R.A Huttenback, in *Mammon and the Pursuit of Empire. The Political Economy of British Imperialism, 1860-1912* (Cambridge, 1986), offer three different estimates of British overseas portfolio finance. On the basis of different assumptions they produce accumulated totals of £3.2bn, £3.6bn and £4.8bn for the years 1865 to 1914 (pp.40-1).
16. Davis and Huttenback, chapter 7.
17. C.H. Lee, 'The Service Sector, Regional Specialization and Economic Growth in the Victorian Economy', *Journal of Historical Geography*, X (1984); and the same author's *The British Economy since 1700* (London, 1986).
18. W.P. Kennedy, *Industrial Structure, Capital Markets and the Origins of British Economic Decline* (Cambridge, 1987), p.145.
19. C.H. Feinstein, R.C.O. Matthews and J.C. Odling-Smee, *British Economic Growth 1856-1973* (Oxford, 1982).
20. Robinson, 'The Excentric Idea of Imperialism', p.270.
21. P.J. Cain and A.G. Hopkins, 'Gentlemanly Capitalism and British Expansion Overseas, I. The Old Colonial System, 1688-1850', *Economic History Review*, 2nd Ser. XXXIX (1986); and 'Gentlemanly Capitalism and British Expansion Overseas, II. New Imperialism, 1850-1945', *ibid.*, XL (1987).
22. Feinstein, Matthews and Odling-Smee, Table 9:10 and p.282.
23. Kennedy, *Industrial Structure*, pp.153-63.
24. M. Edelstein, *Overseas Investment in the Age of High Imperialism, the United Kingdom, 1860-1914* (London, 1982), pp.254-6.
25. See the review of the evidence by S. Pollard, 'Capital Exports, 1870-1914 – Harmful or Beneficial?', *Economic History Review*, 2nd Ser. XXXVII (1985); and the same author's *Britain's Prime and Britain's Decline* (London, 1989), especially chapter 2.
26. See, for example, 'Free Trade and Foreign Policy', p.177; *Imperialism*, p.54.
27. T. Lloyd, 'Africa and Hobson's Imperialism', *Past and Present*, LV (1972).
28. Chapters X-XIII.
29. For an introduction to the literature here see P.J. Cain, *Economic Foundations of British Expansion Overseas, 1815-1914* (London, 1980), pp.50-5. See also J. Forbes Munro, 'Shipping Subsidies and Railway Guarantees: William Mackinnon, Eastern Africa and the Indian Ocean, 1860-93', *Journal of African History*, 28 (1987); and the same author's *Britain in Tropical Africa 1880-1960: Economic Relationship and Impact* (1984).
30. J.A. Hobson, *Democracy After the War* (London, 1917), p.89.
31. *Ibid.* p.90.
32. Robinson and Gallagher, chapter 4.
33. A.G. Hopkins, 'The Victorians and Africa: A Reconsideration of the Occupation of Egypt, 1882', *Journal of African History*, XXVII (1986), 370-89.
34. Hopkins, p.379.
35. *Ibid.*, p.381. See also B.R. Johns, 'Business, Investment and Imperialism. The Relationship Between Economic Interest and the Growth of British Intervention in Egypt, 1838-82' (Unpublished PhD thesis, Univ. of Exeter, 1981), pp.75-92, 107, 215, 250-1, 253-4, 281-2.
36. R.A. Atkins, 'The Conservatives and Egypt, 1875-1880', *Journal of Imperial and Commonwealth History*, II (1974), 200.
37. On the 'anarchy' in Egypt see, especially, A. Scholch, 'The "Man on the Spot" and the English Occupation of Egypt in 1882', *Historical Journal*, XIX (1976).
38. A. Scholch, *Egypt for the Egyptians! The Socio-Political Crisis in Egypt, 1878-82* (London, 1981), especially chapter 3; M.E. Chamberlain, 'The Alexandria Massacre of 11 June 1882 and the British Occupation of Egypt', *Middle Eastern Studies*, XIII (1977).
39. W.S. Blunt, *Secret History of the Occupation of Egypt* (1969 ed.), pp.221-2, reporting a meeting on 11 March 1882.
40. M.E. Chamberlain, 'Sir Charles Dilke and the British Intervention in Egypt, 1882: Decision Making in a Nineteenth Century Cabinet', *British Journal of International Studies*, II (1976), 238-9.
41. See Dilke's memo for the Cabinet of 4 July 1882 in S. Gwynn and G.M. Tuckwell, *The Life of Sir Charles W. Dilke* (London, 1917), I, p.465.
42. Blunt, pp.211, 214, 241, 294-5. See also M. Chamberlain, 'British Public Opinion and the Invasion of Egypt', *Trivium*, XVI (1981).
43. Joseph Chamberlain's attitudes are interesting in this context. See R. Jay, *Joseph Chamberlain. A Political Study* (Oxford, 1981), pp.67-9; and Chamberlain's own *A Political Memoir 1880-92* (ed. C.H.D. Howard, London, 1953), pp.70-81.
44. *Imperialism*, p.59.

45. See J.A. Hobson, *The War in South Africa* (London, 1900).
46. Hobson, *Democracy After the War*, pp.84-7.
47. *Africa and the Victorians*, chapter XIV.
48. G. Blainey, 'Lost Causes of the Jameson Raid', *Economic History Review*, 2nd Ser. XVIII (1965).
49. R. Mendelsohn, 'Blainey and the Jameson Raid: the Debate Renewed', *Journal of Southern African Studies*, VI (1980); see also R.V. Kubiceck, *Economic Imperialism in Theory and Practice. The Case of South African Gold Mining Finance, 1886-1914* (Durham N.C., 1979).
50. R.V. Turrell and J-J. van Helten, 'The Rothschilds, the Exploration Company and Mining Finance', *Business History*, XXVIII (1986). This gives a much bigger role to Rothschild in South African finance than does S. Chapman, 'Rhodes and the City of London: Another View of Imperialism', *Historical Journal*, XXIII (1985). Hobson was well aware of the importance of the Exploration Company in *The War in South Africa*, p.197.
51. R.V. Turrell, '"Finance . . . the Governor of the Imperial Engine": Hobson and the Case of Rothschild and Rhodes', *Journal of Southern African Studies*, XIV (1987), 420.
52. N. Etherington, 'Labour Supply and the Genesis of South African Confederation in the 1870s', *Journal of African History*, XX (1979). This should be compared with the account given in *Africa and the Victorians*, chapter III.
53. On these themes see, especially, J.S. Marais, *The Fall of Kruger's Republic* (Oxford, 1961), pp.323-32; D. Denoon, 'Capital and Capitalists in the Transvaal in the 1890s and 1900s', *Historical Journal*, XXIII (1980); and S. Marks and S. Trapido, 'Lord Milner and the South African State', *History Workshop*, VIII (1979).
54. Two recent general surveys of the South African problem which have been found very useful here are S. Marks, 'Scrambling for South Africa', *Journal of African History*, XXIII (1982); and P. Richardson and J-J. van Helten, 'The Development of the South African Gold Mining Industry 1895-1918', *Economic History Review*, 2nd Ser. XXVII (1984). For a different perspective see A.N. Porter, *The Origins of the South African War* (Manchester, 1980).
55. J.A. Hobson, *Imperialism*, pp.304-27. For Hobson's long-standing interest in China see Cain, 'International Trade and Economic Development in the Thought of J.A. Hobson', pp.410-20.
56. This is expressed clearly in 'Free Trade and Foreign Policy', written in 1898.
57. *Democracy After the War*, pp.93-100.
58. For an introduction to the recent historiography see Cain, *Economic Foundations*, pp.61-3. See also E.W. Edwards, *British Diplomacy and Finance in China 1895-1914* (Oxford, 1987); and P. Lowe, *Britain and the Far East. A Survey from 1819 to the Present* (1981).
59. For excellent introductions to the complexities here see D.C.M. Platt, *Finance, Trade and Politics in British Foreign Policy 1815-1914* (Oxford, 1968), Part III, chapters 2 and 4; and D. McLean, 'Finance and "Informal Empire" before the First World War', *Economic History Review*, 2nd Ser. XXIX (1976).
60. D. McLean, 'Commerce, Finance and British Diplomatic Support in China, 1885-6', *Economic History Review*, 2nd Ser. XXVI (1973).
61. D. McLean, 'The Foreign Office and the First Chinese Indemnity Loan, 1895', *Historical Journal*, XVI (1973); K.C. Chan, 'British Policy in the Reorganization. Loan to China 1912', *Modern Asian Studies*, V (1971).
62. L.K. Young, *British Policy in China 1895-1902* (Oxford, 1970), chapter IV.
63. On the broad theme of Western penetration of China see J. Osterhammel, 'Semi-Colonialism and Informal Empire in Twentieth Century China: Towards A Framework of Analysis', in Mommsen and Osterhammel, *Imperialism and After*, chapter 19.
64. On French and British involvement in the Turkish public debt see R. Owen, *The Middle East in the World Economy* (London, 1981), pp.100-10, 192-9.
65. On French finance in China see D. Gagnier, 'French Loans to China 1895-1914: The Alliance of International Finance and Diplomacy', *Australian Journal of Politics and History*, XVIII (1972).
66. E.W. Edwards, 'The Origins of British Financial Co-operation with France in China 1903-6', *English Historical Review*, LXXXVI (1971); K.A. Hamilton, 'An Attempt to Form an Anglo-French "Industrial Entente"', *Middle Eastern Studies*, II (1975).
67. As in their attempts to prevent Russian penetration of Persia. See D. McLean, *Britain and her Buffer State: The Collapse of the Persian Empire, 1890-1914* (London, 1979). For similar problems in Mesopotomia see M. Kent, *Oil and Empire: British Policy and Mesopotamian Oil, 1900-1920* (London, 1976).

68. C. Jones, '"Business Imperialism" and Argentina, 1875-1900: A Theoretical Note', *Journal of Latin American Studies*, XII (1980).

69. *Imperialism*, pp.328-55.

70. In this context it is worth considering that the Canadian Pacific Railway, the key to Canadian expansion westwards after 1870, was frequently dependent for financial survival in the 1880s on City support. See D.C. Masters, 'Financing the C.P.R. 1880-5', *Canadian Historical Review*, XXIV (1943); P. Ziegler, *The Sixth Great Power, Barings 1762-1929* (London, 1988), pp.227-8. One important aspect of British imperialism in Canada before Confederation is dealt with by D.W. Roman, 'Railway Imperialism in Canada, 1847-1865', in *Railway Imperialism* (ed. C.B. Davis and K.E. Wilburn, New York, 1991), pp.7-24.

71. For an introduction to the relationships, see C.B. Schedvin, 'Staples and Regions of Pax Brittanica', *Economic History Review*, 2nd Ser. XLIII (1990).

72. H.J. Habakkuk, 'Free Trade and Commercial Expansion 1853-70', in *Cambridge History of the British Empire*, vol. II (Cambridge, 1940), especially pp.798-9.

73. A.H. Tocker, 'Monetary Standards in Australia and New Zealand', *Economic Journal*, XXXIV (1924); M.W. Doyle, 'An Essay on the Structure of Britain's Extended Economy in the Nineteenth Century', *Revue Internationale d'Histoire de La Banque*, XIX (1979), 101ff.

74. Robinson, 'The Excentric Idea of Imperialism', p.275.

75. Estimates from N.G. Butlin, *Investment in Australian Economic Development, 1861-1900* (Cambridge, 1964), p.29.

76. Robinson's word: 'The Excentric Idea of Imperialism', p.281.

77. E.A. Boehm, *Prosperity and Depression in Australia, 1887-1897* (Oxford, 1971), is the standard work on the depression. For differing viewpoints see Butlin, chapter VI; H. Coombs, 'Balance of Payments Problems: Old and New Style', in *Readings in Australian Economics* (ed. N.T. Drohan and J.H. Day, Melbourne, 1966); and W.A. Sinclair, *The Process of Economic Development in Australia* (Melbourne, 1976), especially pp.148-51.

78. *Ibid.*

79. *Ibid.*, p.271.

80. L.H. Trainor, 'The Economics of the Imperial Connection: Britain and the Australian Colonies 1886-96' (London, Institute of Commonwealth Studies, 1979).

81. Ibid., p.275.

82. See the statistics in N.G. Butlin, *Australian Domestic Product, Investment and Foreign Borrowing 1861-1938-9* (Cambridge, 1962), Table 265, p.444; see also Sinclair, *The Process of Economic Development*, pp.151ff.

83. For the later story see C.B. Schedvin, *Australia and the Great Depression* (Sydney, 1970); and W.A. Sinclair, 'The Depressions of the 1890s and the 1930s in Australia: A Comparison', in *Readings in Australian Economics*.

84. Some indication of New Zealand financial dependence on Britain can be gained form N. Rosenberg, 'Capital Imports and Growth, The Case of New Zealand. Foreign Investment in New Zealand, 1840-1958', *Economic Journal*, LXXI (1961).

85. Jones, '"Business Imperialism" and Argentina'; and *idem*, 'Great Capitalists and the Development of British Overseas Investment in the Late Nineteenth Century: the Case of Argentina', *Business History*, XXII (1980). For an alternative view see D.C.M. Platt, 'Economic Imperialism and the Businessman, Britain and Latin America before 1914', in *Studies in the Theory of Imperialism* (ed. R. Owen and B. Sutcliffe, Oxford, 1972). Also important in this context, and for a wider view of Latin America, are B. Albert, *South America and the World Economy from Independence to 1930* (London, 1983), and C. Marichal, *A Century of Debt Crises in Latin America: from Independence to the Great Depression, 1820-1930* (Princeton, 1989).

86. J.E. Hodge, 'Carlos Pellegrini and the Financial Crisis of 1890', *Hispanic American Historical Review*, L (1970); Jones, 'Business Imperialism', pp.442-3. Compare H.S. Ferns, *Britain and Argentina in the Nineteenth Century* (Oxford, 1960), pp.438-83. See also S. Topick, *The Political Economy of the Brazilian State, 1889-1930* (Austin, 1987).

87. D. Joslin, *A Century of Banking in Latin America* (Oxford, 1963), pp.142-6, 152-9; R. Graham, *Britain and Modernization in Brazil 1850-1914* (Cambridge, 1968), pp.102-5.

88. P. O'Brien, 'The Costs and Benefits of British Imperialism, 1846-1914', *Past and Present*, CXX (Aug. 1988).

89. Cain and Hopkins, 'Gentlemanly Capitalism and British Expansion Overseas, II. New Imperialism, 1850-1945', *passim*.

8

Colonialism or Imperialism?
Dutch Overseas Expansion, 1870-1914

M. Kuitenbrouwer

'Imperialism is no word for scholars', the British imperial historian W.K. Hancock remarked in 1940.[1] Since then many historians have overcome the initial objections of the profession to a term connected with the general theories of Hobson, Lenin and other left-wing authors. Dutch historians have adopted the term too, as a general characterization of the period between 1880 and 1914 and the conduct of the great powers during that period. For the Dutch expansion in the Indonesian archipelago, however, which largely took place at the turn of the century, the concept still meets with strong reservations. Even the term expansion has been placed in italics in this respect.[2] It is not the purpose of this paper to analyse in detail the historiography of imperialism in general, or indeed the Dutch version in particular. The question of the extent to which Dutch expansion in the Indonesian archipelago should be characterized as imperialism will only be dealt with in the conclusion. Rather I shall concentrate on examining the role of the Dutch state and economy in overseas expansion after about 1870. In this context the 'state' will be identified with territorial control, ranging from formal rights to actual occupation, and government policy. The economy is analysed in terms of trade, investment, industrial and non-industrial enterprise. Dutch overseas expansion will be presented as a process of concentration of political and economic efforts on the Indonesian archipelago, a concentration on a widening scale and with cumulative effect, which was in the end quite successful. But, of course, in the age of imperialism a process such as this did not always run an even or balanced course.

Overseas relations before 1870

By 1870 the Netherlands was a small European state which followed policies of informal neutrality and free trade in European affairs. The diverse sectors of its open economy were gradually developing and modernizing, although at uneven paces. The Netherlands already had, of course, widespread colonial possessions and varied economic interests overseas. The possessions included Java, the colonial centrepiece, some enclaves on other islands of the Indonesian archipelago, Elmina on the African Gold Coast, and the West Indian colonies of Surinam and the Antilles. From the time of the Dutch East India Company the Netherlands had inherited a vague claim to sovereignty over the whole Indonesian archipelago, but outside Java this claim was seldom implemented. The Anglo-Dutch treaty of 1824 had accomplished only some territorial exchanges and a rough demarcation of spheres of influence near Singapore. The Dutch government was obliged to guarantee the independence of Aceh, the strategically located sultanate on Northern Sumatra.[3] The treaty was followed by sharp diplomatic conflict over Dutch protection in colonial trade and shipping, and British support for the presence of James Brooke in Northern Borneo. With most Indonesian states Dutch suzerainty was established by contract. Sometimes it was upheld by force and even extended. But these military expeditions seldom had a lasting effect. On the whole the conservative Dutch government followed a policy of so-called 'abstention' towards the outer islands, concentrating on the successful exploitation of Java through the state monopolies of the Cultivation System.[4] Only on Sumatra, rich in mineral and agricultural potential, was a gradual expansion of political control and influence taking place. It led to new protests by the British government, but it also attracted economic interest from the Netherlands. In 1860 the Billiton Company started mining tin on the island of Billiton, largely financed by the elite of The Hague. In 1869 the Deli Company was founded with the support of the powerful Netherlands Trading Company of Amsterdam, in order to cultivate tobacco in Deli on the east coast of Sumatra, in Aceh's former sphere of influence. As early as 1865 the liberal Minister of Colonies, I.D. Fransen van de Putte, had taken the first step towards freeing Dutch policy from the guarantee of Aceh's independence.[5]

But until 1870, political and economic attention in the Netherlands remained focused on Java, where Dutch liberals pursued the abolition of the Cultivation System and of the related protection in colonial trade and shipping. In particular Dutch shipping was slow to adapt to new conditions such as the spread of steam power. When protective measures were gradually abolished, its place in the international ranking list dropped from fourth to eighth between 1850 and 1870. The share of the East Indies in Dutch trade in 1870 was stagnating at 15.9 per cent of Dutch imports and 7.9 per cent of Dutch exports.[6] In that year the Dutch parliament enacted the legislation by which the Cultivation System was largely dismantled. Amsterdam became the financial centre of private plantation production on Java, although initially investments fell short of expectations.[7] Outside the East Indies the overseas presence of the Netherlands was rather limited. Extra-European, non-colonial trade accounted for a mere 4.4 per cent of Dutch imports and 2.3 per cent of Dutch exports in 1870. Dutch governments acted in different ways on behalf of the various overseas interests. In Surinam, where slavery had only been abolished in 1863, the colonial government tried in vain to prevent the former slaves from leaving the plantations. When ships and goods from Curaçao were confiscated in Venezuela, in retaliation against arms-smuggling from the Dutch island, a naval force was sent in 1870.[8] In African Elmina, a permanent financial liability, military involvement also increased as tensions between the British and the Ashanti rose.[9] But from Rotterdam the Dutch African trade was expanding. In addition to the firm operating out of Elmina, the ambitious African Trading Company was organized in 1868, which became the largest European trader on the Congo river.[10] In Asia Dutch governments followed the lead of the larger Western powers in establishing commercial and diplomatic relations. In Japan traditional co-operation with the Shogunate changed to participation in the enforced opening-up of the country by the Western powers. In 1858 a rather 'unequal' commercial treaty was concluded, granting the Netherlands extra-territorial rights. In 1864 a Dutch naval force joined an international expedition against a vassal rebelling against the Shogun. The Netherlands participated in the negotiations between the Western powers and the new imperial government of Japan on future diplomatic and commercial relations, which followed the international intervention.[11] With China a more equal treaty was concluded in 1863, but formal representation was only undertaken in 1872, under growing pressure from industrial and commercial interests in the Netherlands.[12]

Priorities in overseas policy

By 1870 then, Dutch colonial and non-colonial relations were already increasingly influenced by the commercial and political expansion of Britain, France and other Western powers in the overseas world. The construction of the Suez Canal was considered a clear sign of such growing interest. At the opening of the Canal in 1869 it was expected in leading circles in the Netherlands that the importance of Asia in general, and that of the Indonesian archipelago in particular, would increase strongly in the near future.[13] The rise of Germany and Italy as new European powers and the growing influence of the United States in the Pacific added an element of urgency to such predictions. With some difficulty the Steamship Company 'Nederland' was started in 1870 from Amsterdam, followed by the 'Rotterdamsche Lloyd' in 1875, to establish direct communications with the East Indies through the Suez Canal, both receiving small government contracts.[14] But in view of the limited financial, economic and military resources of the Netherlands, the liberal Dutch governments made a number of more general decisions which roughly outlined future priorities in overseas relations. Colonial possessions were considered of great national interest in the case of the East Indies, of some interest in the case of the West Indies, and of no interest whatsoever in the case of African Elmina. Within the Indonesian archipelago Sumatra received clear priority over the other islands in further expansion. Both for economic and political reasons free trade was regarded as the best policy for the East Indies and other parts of the overseas world. All together, good relations with Britain were to be preferred in colonial affairs − and in European affairs as well. On the initiative of the Minister of Colonies, E. de Waal, three more-or-less connected treaties were concluded between Britain and the Netherlands at the end of 1870 and beginning of 1871. The Netherlands ceded Elmina to Britain, and agreed to the free admittance of British trade and subjects in the Dutch-controlled parts of Sumatra. On the other hand Britain consented to all past and future expansion of Dutch control on Sumatra, and permitted the emigration of contract labour from British India to Surinam.[15]

The Anglo-Dutch treaties were strongly debated in the Dutch parliament and press. The liberal majority in parliament narrowly agreed to the cession of Elmina, despite objections from the Rotterdam trading interest that Africa really was the 'continent of the future'. But the treaty on Sumatra was rejected, partly because the repeal of Aceh's independence was not explicit enough. Aceh was considered a 'den of thieves' by liberal speakers, a centre of piracy, slaving, Islamic fanaticism and even cannibalism. On the other hand conservative members of parliament warned strongly against war with Aceh. 'That place is useless to us', predicted a former naval officer who had visited Aceh: 'it will only cost a lot of money and lives'.[16] But a new treaty was negotiated with Britain which clearly gave the Netherlands a free hand on Northern Sumatra. Even before parliamentary approval was granted, Minister De Waal started to put pressure on Aceh to suppress any piracy and slave trade. This pressure was built up by his liberal successor P.P. van Bosse, and by Governor-General J. Loudon, in consideration of the successful development of tobacco cultivation in Deli and the danger of foreign interference, which was actively sought by Acehnese envoys.[17] At the same time Van Bosse and Loudon agreed to abolish all differential rights in the new East Indian Tariff, partly as a pre-emption of territorial aspirations by other powers. 'With a decent trade tariff we keep all enemies ... out of the Indies', Van Bosse, an influential former Minister of Finance, wrote privately to Loudon. In 1872 his liberal successor Fransen van de

Putte carried the new Tariff Act through parliament, where the political case for free trade was acknowledged by the liberal majority.[18] When the open-door policy was implemented, the share of the East Indies in Dutch trade sharply declined, largely to the benefit of British trade. From the British Straits Settlements foreign planters and capital poured into Deli. This did not, however, prevent a prolonged war with Aceh.[19]

When in 1873 news reached Governor-General Loudon that Acehnese envoys had concluded a treaty with the American consul in Singapore, he rashly declared war on Aceh, with the reluctant support of Minister Van de Putte. War was accepted and even welcomed by the liberal majority of the Dutch parliament and public. After the defeat of the first military expedition, a second one led only to the nominal annexation of Aceh in 1874. Many campaigns of 'pacification' followed. Up to thirty per cent of the colonial army, which was enlarged from 28,000 men in 1872 to 39,000 men in 1876, became deployed in Aceh. The long-standing surplus of the colonial budget gave way to a growing deficit, supplemented by war-credits from the Netherlands. Pacification was formally concluded in 1881, but Acehnese resistance continued.[20] In the meantime, territorial expansion in other parts of Sumatra and the Indonesian archipelago came to a stand-still. The Dutch government only reluctantly supported the expedition of the new Geographical Society of the Netherlands to explore the mineral and agricultural resources of Central Sumatra in the late 1870s.[21] In the Dutch West Indies, however, the Dutch government made a firm stand against Venezuela, where ships and goods from Curaçao were confiscated again in 1875, and which had plans to conquer the island. Despite parliamentary suggestions to sell the 'bare rock' to Venezuela, a naval force was sent and diplomatic relations remained broken.[22] But outside the colonial sphere of influence, Dutch overseas trade was largely left on its own. Complaints from the Rotterdam trading interest against Liberia and the Portuguese government in Angola were handled rather aloofly by the Dutch Foreign Office.[23]

The scramble for colonies

When the growing European interest in the overseas world led to a scramble for colonies during the 1880s, situations became more complicated for the Dutch Ministers of Foreign and Colonial Affairs. But on the whole they managed to maintain their priorities, although some policies of concentration became even more defensive. In particular the 'Imperial Course', and the subsequent overseas policies of Britain, seemed to pose problems for Dutch interests in the Indonesian archipelago and in Africa. After the foundation of the British North Borneo Company, the Dutch government, under parliamentary pressure, in 1879 occupied a disputed border-region in Northern Borneo. When the Company was formally chartered, diplomatic conflict with Britain followed.[24] The kidnapping of the crew of the British steamer Nisero by an Acehnese raja led to even greater tensions in 1884. The British government offered mediation in a way which jeopardized Dutch claims of sovereignty over Aceh as a whole. The Dutch government declined the mediation offer, and succeeded in winning over the British government to joint action against the raja, who immediately released the hostages. Together with the serious financial situation and the growing unrest on Java, the Nisero incident caused the Dutch government to concentrate its military presence in Aceh around the capital, with a token naval blockade of the other parts.[25]

In Africa the British occupation of Egypt and the British-supported claims of

Portugal on the Congo coast posed less acute problems. In both cases Dutch governments tried to remain aloof from rivalries between the great powers, while supporting international solutions which safeguarded Dutch interests. In Egypt, where Dutch shipping ranked fourth in the use of the Suez Canal, the Netherlands finally gained admission to the international Suez Convention in 1891, despite initial British reservations.[26] During the Berlin Conference of 1884-1885 the Dutch Minister of Foreign Affairs was mainly preoccupied with the restriction of the formal norm of effective occupation for colonial possession to the west coast of Africa, observing 'that we are in the Indian archipelago in permanent contact with Great Britain, always risking conflict'. But the assignment of the Congo to the Free State of King Leopold II and the confirmation of free trade for the region by the Conference was welcomed with regard to the Dutch trading interest.[27] When Leopold won international support for the restriction of free trade at the Brussels anti-slavery conference of 1890-1891, the Dutch Minister of Foreign Affairs put up obstinate opposition on behalf of the Dutch trading interest. But in the end the Dutch government had to give in and soon Dutch trade declined under pressure from the Free State. African trade from Rotterdam survived, however, by shifting its activities to other parts of the continent.[28]

In the case of South Africa more fundamental tensions developed between the priorities of the Dutch government and the growing sympathy of the Dutch parliament and public for the Dutch-related Boers. While the British annexation of the Boer republics in 1877 had been accepted quite calmly, the successful revolt of the Boers in 1880-1881 created a strong nationalist current in the Netherlands. A national organization was formed to support the independence of the Boer republics and strengthen the Dutch element within them. The Calvinist leader A. Kuyper and some liberal figures drew up plans for a New Holland in South Africa, as a reinforcement of the Old Holland in Europe and as an alternative to the insecure possession of the East Indies.[29] After a visit of Transvaal's president Kruger in 1884, nationalist Dutchmen were appointed to strategic positions in the administration of Transvaal. In 1887 the Netherlands South African Railway Company was founded with capital from the Netherlands, Germany and Transvaal. After the construction of the strategic Delagoa line to the Indian Ocean, the Company successfully expanded its operations and influence in South Africa. More Dutch investments followed and trade developed. Depressed farmers in the Netherlands, however, failed to respond in great numbers to the nationalist calls to emigrate to the New Holland. Dutch governments of all political persuasions kept a safe distance from the nationalist agitation in the Netherlands and the Dutch interests in South Africa. When the Minister of Foreign Affairs finally appointed a consul-general in Transvaal in 1888, he gave him strict instructions to give no offence to Britain in the support of Dutch interests.[30]

The consolidation of the Netherlands East Indies

While the scramble for colonies continued, the Dutch governments adopted a policy of external consolidation in the East Indies. As it became widely recognized that the international norm of effective occupation was hard to meet, a number of bilateral border agreements were reached. To achieve a secure border on Borneo the disputed border region was discreetly ceded to Britain in 1891. On New Guinea an agreement with the British government was reached in 1895 on the border with the Australian part. With Germany an informal understanding on the border with the German part existed, which became gradually formalized after 1902. In the case of Timor the Dutch government exerted considerable pressure on Portugal in order to obtain a favourable agreement in 1893.[31] The circumstance that France and Germany had established colonies nearby, but developed no sharp rivalries with Britain in the area, favoured the Dutch implementation of its formal claims on the Indonesian archipelago. Although some Dutch politicians could hardly believe it, British governments on the whole preferred possession of the East Indies by the Netherlands to possession by larger powers, or to the expansion of their own colonial obligations. In the meantime Dutch political and economic interests remained centred on Java and Sumatra. In 1884 a sharp crisis in Javanese sugar production led to a further concentration and modernization of private enterprise by leading financial institutions and financiers from Amsterdam. The Netherlands Trading Company became the largest of the so-called cultivation banks. The individual planter disappeared and the share of foreign and local capital declined on Java. By 1890, 79 plantation companies with a capital of 67.8 million guilders were located in Amsterdam, 19 companies with a capital of 13.8 million in Rotterdam, and 13 companies with a capital of 13.6 million in The Hague.[32]

To stimulate colonial production, the conservative-liberal government had lowered the export duties on sugar and other crops in the East Indian Tariff, but had raised most import duties in compensation. In protest a Catholic member from the industrializing province of Brabant proposed the re-introduction of differential rights, exclaiming: 'Should everything happen in the interest of the trading cities, to foster the plantations, whose shareholders do not live in the landward provinces, but in the provinces of Holland?' His proposal was rejected, however, by a large majority in the Dutch parliament.[33] While sugar production on Java was slowly recovering, tin mining on Billiton and tobacco cultivation on Sumatra flourished. The Billiton Company regularly paid dividends of more than 100 per cent to its shareholders during the 1880s, the Deli company sometimes dividends of 1000 per cent. New economic ventures were slow to develop, however. With the assistance of the colonial government a start was made with opening up the coalfields of Central Sumatra and with the exploitation of gold mines in Northern Celebes.[34] But state-sponsored initiatives to explore the resources of the non-occupied parts of the East Indies could also be rejected by the Dutch parliament. 'Such resources are there perhaps, but we know for sure they are there in other parts of the Archipelago', the liberal member from Amsterdam and former executive of the Deli Company, J.T. Cremer, observed in 1885.[35] Cremer distrusted in particular the attempts of the colonial government to open up mines for state exploitation. On his initiative the Dutch parliament forced the colonial government in 1890 to withdraw a military expedition from the island of Flores, reportedly rich in tin.[36]

But when foreign (British) influence in the strategic sector of shipping was involved, the mutuality of interests between the Dutch state and economy was readily invoked by Cremer and other leading liberals. Even before the governmental contract with the British-owned shipping company running the intra-insular lines within the East Indies expired, the large shipowners from Amsterdam and Rotterdam cooperated closely with the Dutch and colonial governments in the foundation of the Royal Packet Company in 1888, which received a rather heavily subsidized government contract, with a strong monopoly position in intra-insular shipping. The contract was almost unanimously confirmed by the Dutch parliament as a matter of national interest, for external and internal political and economic reasons.[37]

Territorial occupation and economic expansion

While the international borders of the Netherlands East Indies were being drawn and Dutch control over the internal lines of communication was secured, a process of territorial occupation and economic expansion began in the course of the 1890s. There was a close interaction between the Dutch state and economy in this process, but the first initiatives came from the colonial government. In 1894 Governor-General C.H.A. van der Wijck carried through the military conquest of the Balinese state on Lombok, in the name of Dutch 'supreme authority' and the interest of the non-Balinese population. The conquest was acclaimed by the majority of the Dutch parliament and public, with an outburst of nationalist activities.[38] In 1896 Van der Wijck turned an Acehnese attack on the already extended concentrated lines into the formal decision to occupy Aceh completely. The military conquest was carried out successfully by General J.B. van Heutsz, who, as Governor of Aceh, received the formal surrender of the last sultan in 1903. The colonial army was enlarged again from 34,000 men in 1893 to 44,000 men in 1898. As the military campaign progressed, nationalist pride in the Netherlands increased. Only the Dutch socialists strongly opposed the 'pacification' of Aceh, comparing it to the British conquest of the Boer republics in South Africa.[39] As early as 1898 Governor-General Van der Wijck and the new Minister of Colonies Cremer had decided to end the traditional policy of 'abstention' towards the remaining Indonesian states and bring all of the East Indies under effective Dutch control. The first test-case of the new forward policy was the military annexation of the Sumatran sultanate of Djambi in 1901, which resisted Dutch private efforts to open up its oil reserves.[40]

In the Netherlands quite a strong consensus was reached on expansion in the East Indies between the liberal and clerical parties, which were sharply divided on most domestic issues. It developed around three interrelated policies: first there was the territorial forward policy shaped by Governor-General Van der Wijck and his advisors, based on the example of Aceh. Secondly there was the policy of capitalist development along 'national' lines, consolidated by Minister Cremer. His main legislative work was the Mining Act of 1899, which clearly favoured private exploitation over state exploitation, on the basis of a rather low levy of 4 per cent on gross revenue, while safeguarding the control of the colonial government over lands and concessions. In 1898 Cremer took strong action against the first of many attempts by the American Standard Oil Company to penetrate the developing Dutch oil industry in the East Indies, together with the nationally minded shipowners in the Netherlands.[41] In 1899 he prolonged the favourable contract with the Royal Packet Company, which had effectively proved its value for the Dutch state during the Lombok and Aceh campaigns, and its value for the Dutch economy by stimulating colonial trade and the shipbuilding industry. In addition to its growing intra-insular network the Company opened an external line to China and Japan in 1902 and to Australia in 1907, again subsidized by the Dutch government.[42] Thirdly and finally, the 'Ethical Policy' of a Dutch 'moral calling' towards the indigenous population of the East Indies was initiated in 1901 by the clerical coalition government of the Calvinist leader Kuyper. This policy aimed at the state-sponsored promotion of material and spiritual welfare, ranging from irrigation to popular education by the local government or missionary societies. It was supported not only by most liberals, but also, and very strongly so, by the Dutch socialists.[43]

The policies of territorial occupation and 'ethical' welfare were implemented in particular between 1904 and 1909, by the Calvinist Minister of Colonies A.W.F.

Idenburg and Governor-General Van Heutsz, who were less inclined to the policy of capitalist development than Cremer and Van der Wijck, but continued it in its principal lines. For example, when the annexation of Djambi was followed by fierce competition between Dutch oil contractors, and Standard Oil appeared on the scene, the process of 'pacification' was hindered, and the territory was closed down.[44] But in most cases private enterprise was welcomed in the newly occupied parts of the East Indies. The systematic subjection of all Indonesian states and communities was carried out by political pressure or military force, and it led to the introduction of direct or indirect rule, depending on the local situation. It was backed up by a substantial increase of Dutch colonial officials in the so-called Outer Regions outside Java. In most cases, on Sumatra, Borneo and Celebes, they exercised effective, colonial control. In some cases, like New Guinea, they remained largely 'living coats of arms for passers-by', in the words of one of their prominent members.[45] The colonial army, however, was reduced to 35,000 men in 1909. It had become more mobile and specialized in 'police-actions' against guerilla resistance, which continued in places like Aceh until the First World War.[46] In defending military action, against socialist critics and some liberal and clerical dissidents as well, Minister Idenburg called 'the use of the sword' the 'highest demand of neighbourly love'. As Governor-General of the East Indies he was more accommodating towards the first, moderate movement of Indonesian nationalism, which started on the eve of the First World War.[47]

The economic expansion in the East Indies was state-assisted, but originated from the general growth of both the international and national economies, which developed in the course of the 1890s. Even before the policy of territorial occupation was implemented, the number of Amsterdam plantation companies working in the Outer Regions rose from nine (with a capital of 8.5 million guilders) in 1890, to 58 in 1900 (with a capital of 49.2 million guilders). In the boom year of 1897, 31.5 million guilders was invested from Amsterdam in the sixteen Dutch oil companies active in the East Indies.[48] In 1890 the Royal Dutch Petroleum Company had been founded by a pioneering oil contractor, some financiers from Amsterdam and political figures in The Hague. In 1892 it struck its first well on the borders of Aceh. After a difficult financial start, it greatly expanded its activities on Sumatra and Borneo at the turn of the century, gradually incorporating other Dutch oil companies. In 1907 it amalgamated with the British Shell Company working on Borneo and together they dominated the oil industry of the East Indies.[49] Dutch investments were not only increasing in the Outer Regions, but also on Java. Particularly after the international abolition of protection of beet sugar by the Brussels Convention of 1903, Dutch private capital invested in the East Indies doubled between 1900 and 1913, from 750 million guilders or roughly 7.5 per cent of all Dutch capital, to 1.5 billion guilders or more than 10 per cent of all Dutch capital.[50]

Research on the volume, composition and rates of return of colonial investments is still in progress. But their relative profitability can be inferred from the fact that between 1904 and 1914 Dutch companies working in the East Indies accounted for 325 million guilders or 30 per cent of all domestic share-issues in the Netherlands. The contribution of the East Indies to the Dutch National Income had grown from 2 or 3 per cent in 1870 to 5 per cent in 1890, and to 10 per cent in 1913.[51] As Dutch overseas shipping recovered strongly at the turn of the century, the share of the East Indies in Dutch imports was increasing again, to 15.1 per cent in 1910, but its share in Dutch exports further declined to 4.3 per cent. Between 1870 and 1913 the share of the Netherlands in the greatly expanded East Indian trade had dropped, however, from 77 per cent to 27 per cent of the exports and from 42 per cent to 31 per cent of the imports. The share of the Outer Regions in East Indian exports had multiplied from about 20 per cent in 1870 to nearly 50 per cent in 1913.[52] Although Dutch capital remained predominant in cultivation and mining, British and American investments were also growing, particularly in new products like oil and rubber. In 1912 even Standard Oil was admitted to the East Indian oil industry. As the volume and profitability of investments increased, and the costs of the 'ethical' welfare policy multiplied, political regard for Dutch private enterprise grew less circumspect. In 1910 the Mining Act was amended to introduce the possibility of mixed state and private ownership. In 1921 Djambi was finally opened again to a mixed Dutch oil company of this kind.[53]

Even when the international borders of the Netherlands East Indies were clearly drawn and the Outer Regions were effectively being occupied, the security of Dutch colonial possession remained a matter of great concern. The rise of the United States and in particular of Japan as imperial powers in Eastern Asia caused much alarm in political and colonial circles. The naval defences of the East Indies were gradually strengthened. The international consolidation of the East Indies was also pursued by diplomatic means. The Anglo-Japanese alliance of 1902 made the traditional reliance on informal British protection look less self-evident. During the Russo-Japanese War a rumour from the German Emperor that the British navy was about to take the strategic coal-station of Sabang even caused a real war-scare in Kuyper's clerical government.[54] Between 1907 and 1913 Dutch Ministers of Foreign Affairs tried in vain to move the American government towards a South Sea *entente* which would guarantee the territorial status quo in the region. The open-door policy was now also acknowledged by clerical leaders as a form of political protection. Progressive politicians promoted the 'ethical policy' as an alternative to military defence. 'Where we succeed in winning the love of our subjects, every enemy is powerless', a socialist leader stated. But as the First World War approached some officials and politicians believed that only the 'mutual envy' between the great powers really assured the Netherlands of continued possession of the East Indies.[55]

Outside the East Indies, colonial interests remained important in Dutch overseas relations. Towards Japan they could no longer, of course, be directly maintained. After a number of diplomatic incidents a liberal Dutch government finally acknowledged the rise of Japan in 1896 by concluding a new 'equal' commercial treaty, which even gave the small number of Japanese in the East Indies the same formal status as Europeans.[56] But official Chinese interest in the large number of Chinese immigrants in the East Indies was turned down repeatedly. From the 1880s direct recruitment and transport of contract labour from southern China to the plantations of Deli developed on the initiative of the ever-active Cremer. When there was talk of establishing a Dutch extra-territorial concession in Southern China in the late 1890s, Cremer, as Minister of Colonies, was not unfavourable towards the idea, but turned it down on pragmatic grounds. 'Industrially and commercially it is still felt that the Netherlands is a small nation, whose forces are engaged by its large colonies', he observed in 1898. But during the Boxer Rebellion the Dutch government sent, at his demand, a strong naval force to China, and participated in the international convention which followed the suppression of the rising.[57] In the West Indies an international intervention against Venezuela was informally supported from Curaçao in 1902-1903. In 1908 the clerical Dutch government even threatened actual war against Venezuela, after acquiring the consent of the United States.[58] Occasionally Dutch warships were sent to Morocco, Turkish Arabia or Portuguese Africa to protect 'the legitimate rights of Dutch subjects'. But on the whole the Dutch governments effectively supported overseas trade by subsidizing shipping lines to South America and the Far East, and by the gradual expansion and professionalization of the Consular Service. During the age of imperialism Dutch overseas trade outside the colonies even increased somewhat, to 8 per cent of Dutch imports and 2.4 per cent of Dutch exports in 1910.[59]

The priority of the East Indies in Dutch overseas policy was only put to a test during the Boer War in South Africa. The liberal government came under the heavy pressure of pro-Boer and anti-British public opinion in the Netherlands. Nationalist agitation started with the Jameson raid in 1895. But the liberal Minister of Foreign Affairs J. Roëll delayed sending a telegram of congratulations to Kruger and privately remarked: 'my conviction is that we must concentrate on the *preservation* and further development of the Indies and shoulder no other task. Therefore I remained towards Transvaal always an *interested* and *sympathizing* spectator, nothing more'.[60] His liberal successor W.H. de Beaufort was personally even more interested in and sympathetic to the Boer republics, but he observed Dutch neutrality as strictly as possible during the Boer War. His chief opponent Kuyper essentially continued this policy when he became Prime Minister in 1901. Even the leaders of the pro-Boer movement warned their members against possible 'complications' in the East Indies.[61] Apart from hurt nationalist feelings, some material losses had to be accepted as well, such as the British nationalization of the Netherlands South African Railway Company and the expulsion of its personnel. But after the war the Dutch and British governments negotiated financial compensations for the owners and the employees of the company.[62] Nationalist feelings and designs were increasingly transferred to Dutch expansion in the East Indies.

Colonialism or imperialism

During the age of imperialism the Netherlands successfully built a colonial empire in the Indonesian archipelago, with connections with the Suez Canal, the Islamic pilgrimage-port of Djeddah and the Chinese labour depot of Swatow. Towards Venezuela and in China it occasionally practised something like gunboat diplomacy. In between, an informal expansion of Dutch influence took place in Transvaal. But should this be considered imperialism from an international, comparative point of view? The question is complicated by the multiple, often conflicting meanings of the term, since its adoption by modern historians. In the process of revision of the original economic theories, the emphasis has shifted from economic to political and cultural factors, from formal to informal forms, from Eurocentric to excentric perspectives, from the 'new imperialism' at the turn of the century to earlier phases of overseas expansion. In this way the concept has been accepted by some Dutch historians, who observe in the Indonesian archipelago the emergence in the early nineteenth century of an informal 'frontier imperialism' of local officials and commanders, which gradually developed into the 'ethical imperialism' of the colonial state at the turn of the century.[63] But any use of the term in the case of both the Dutch state and economy remains controversial. At first sight the rejection of the term in these respects seems self-evident. How can a small, neutral European state with an age-long presence in the Indonesian archipelago, losing or ceding its African possessions before the partition of the continent started, with a less industrialized economy than surrounding European countries, be considered imperialist?[64] Imperialism is not the same as colonialism, as has recently been pointed out again from a theoretical point of view by N. Etherington.[65] But to consider the Netherlands as being merely colonialist would neglect the substantial, active and supportive parts played by the Dutch state and economy in the process of expansion in the Indonesian archipelago, and some political and economic side-effects as well in other places overseas. There were shifts towards a Dutch imperialism, which gained momentum at the turn of the century, in a close interaction between the Dutch state, economy and the colonial government. The geographical and chronological deviations from the international pattern of imperialism are mainly the result of the circumstance that the Netherlands was indeed a small European state, which was only (but rather well) established as a colonial power on Java on the eve of the age of imperialism.

The Anglo-Dutch treaties of 1870-71, and the Aceh War which followed, can be considered a first, selective shift towards Dutch imperialism. The Aceh War was much less a local, temporary affair than preceding military campaigns in the Indonesian archipelago, and Dutch economic and strategic interests were much more involved. But it lacked the major impulse of relative economic and potential political decline which characterized the British shift towards imperialism in the course of the 1870s.[66] If it can be considered an early start of Dutch imperialism, the Aceh War soon turned out to be a false start, blocking further expansion on Sumatra or in other parts of the archipelago. As European imperialism spread during the 1880s, the Netherlands retreated further to colonialism, concentrating on existing colonial claims, established economic positions and the naval containment of Aceh. Dutch governments did not adopt the ambitious territorial and protectionist policies of Portugal in Africa, which nearly ruined the Portuguese state and economy in the outcome.[67] But in the Dutch case there were far less pressures or incentives to do so. The decline of East Indian trade and the crisis in Javanese sugar cultivation could be managed by the colonial network in the Dutch economy, with some assistance from the state. The sudden interest in the Boer republics was potentially more implicating, because of its connections with overseas rivalry with Britain, domestic political crisis and economic depression in the Netherlands. But it was resisted by the Dutch governments and did not develop any dominating influence in Transvaal. While staying carefully aloof from the partition of Africa, the Dutch governments successfully consolidated the international borders of the East Indies, with only a small concession on Borneo.

In the course of the 1890s a decisive process of territorial occupation and economic expansion started. But should such an 'internal' process be termed imperialism? There are valid reasons for doing so. In the first place, but least important, the traditional policy of 'abstention' was still operative. Even in 1896 the status of 'semi-sovereignty' of many Indonesian states was compared by a Dutch Minister of Justice to the international status of the Boer republics with respect to Britain.[68] In the second place, but more important, there remained great concern about the preservation of formal possession as Eastern Asia became a central arena of international imperialism. From Lombok onwards external considerations were involved in a number of occupations and in the case of New Guinea at the turn of the century they were even dominant. The door remained open for foreign trade and capital, but it became more guarded.[69] Finally, and most important, leading political and economic circles in the Netherlands which had previously refrained from colonial expansionism, increasingly began to favour it. The first, defensive shift towards imperialism had been the launching of the Royal Packet Company in 1888. When military success was provided by the Lombok and Aceh campaigns, objectives became more ambitious, namely to enlarge the power and prestige of the Netherlands and secure economic advantages by means of a colonial empire. While

117

the 'pacification' of Aceh was still going on Governor-General Van der Wijck and Minister of Colonies Cremer had already decided on the future occupation of the remaining Indonesian states. Their interesting careers show the close interaction between the state and economy in Dutch imperialism, but also its basically colonial character. In the course of becoming an influential member of parliament for Amsterdam, Cremer had played a leading role in the Deli Company, the Deli Planters Union, the Deli Railway Company, a reconstructed cultivation bank during the Javanese sugar crisis, the Royal Packet Company, the railway materials company 'Werkspoor', and its connected shipbuilding company in Amsterdam. After his period as Minister he became president of the Netherlands Trading Company, Dutch delegate in the Suez Canal Company during the First World War, and then Dutch envoy to Washington. After an official career in the East Indies Van der Wijck was a director of the Royal Packet Company before he became Governor-General. Afterwards he became a director of the Royal Dutch Petroleum Company and of many plantation companies. Other politicians like the former liberal Minister of Colonies and of Finance, P.J. Sprenger van Eyk, and the future Calvinist Prime Minister H. Colijn, also established close ties with 'Royal Dutch'.[70]

In the development of a liberal-clerical consensus on Dutch imperialism, nonmaterialist interests naturally played a large role. Religious, nationalist and humanitarian loyalties were mobilized, which gave Dutch imperialism its strong 'ethical' orientation: an orientation which was also present in British, French and American imperialism, however.[71] As a liberal member of parliament and Minister of Colonies Cremer had welcomed the ever-controversial missionary effort in the Outer Regions of the East Indies as a contribution to 'civilization, welfare, law and order'.[72] The Calvinist leader Kuyper was also a main architect of the new imperialist consensus. During the 1870s Kuyper had opposed the Aceh War and during the 1880s he had suggested the cession of Borneo and New Guinea, favouring expansion in the Transvaal. Like most Calvinists he had criticized the high profits of the Billiton Company, demanding a larger share for the state in colonial mining. But during the 1890s he gave decisive parliamentary support to the military conquest of Aceh and the capitalist Mining Act. At the turn of the century he even promoted the establishment of a Dutch extra-territorial concession in China. For Kuyper, private colonial enterprise remained to some extent instrumental to his 'ethical' welfare policy, which he had already introduced in principle in his political programme in 1879. As Prime Minister Kuyper rejected the term imperialism for the military and economic aspects of the 'ethical policy', but he welcomed the word 'expansion'. The other Calvinist leader, A.F. de Savornin Lohman, commented on the military occupation of the Outer Regions: 'one can call it imperialism or not, but there is no other way'.[73]

Conclusion

But what did the colonial empire contribute to the Dutch state and economy? The imperialism at the turn of the century stimulated the nationalist pride of the Queen and of most of the leading political elites. It favoured the national integration of a political society which, domestically, was becoming more polarized by class and 'pillarized' by denomination.[74] On the international level the colonial empire gained the Netherlands admission to some gatherings of the great powers. It gave a certain plausibility to the pretence of some Ministers and diplomats that the Netherlands was really 'the first of the states of the second rank'. But when tested directly by international politics the status of 'middle power' never materialized for the Netherlands. In Asia this was already being demonstrated by the changing relationship with Japan. In Europe it would become even more evident during the First World War, in relation to both Germany and Britain.[75] On the economic side there were also mixed results. Contemporaries greatly valued the economic contribution of the East Indies to the Netherlands. 'What place would the Netherlands still occupy in the ranks of nations, without its possession of colonies?!', Minister Idenburg exclaimed with regard to this contribution in 1903. 'The Indies lost, disaster born', a much-quoted pamphlet stated in 1914.[76] The East Indies did indeed contribute to the growth of national income at the turn of the century, but on a rather uneven scale. The East Indies and in particular the Outer Regions did attract profitable investments, although twice as much Dutch capital remained invested in other, largely Western countries on the eve of the First World War.[77]

The East Indies only partially affected industrial growth in the Netherlands, which increased particularly during the 1860s until 1873 and during the 1890s up to 1913, but remained moderate compared to neighbouring countries.[78] During the first phase, still under protection of colonial trade, the textile industry of the eastern Twente district developed a lasting interest in Java and a fluctuating interest in other overseas markets. During the second phase shipbuilding, railway materials and metal industries in the maritime provinces of Holland were stimulated. But Dutch imports of tropical crops, minerals and other raw materials from the East Indies or other parts of the overseas world remained far more important than exports of industrial commodities to it. These imports were in part processed for domestic consumption, in part manufactured for export, or traded directly to other Western countries. One could say that the overseas world, and the East Indies and the Outer Regions in particular, contributed to the relative growth of the commerce, transport and finance sectors in the seaboard provinces of North and South Holland. Although share-holding in new colonial ventures like the Royal Dutch Petroleum Company did spread through the Netherlands before the First World War, there remained a distinct *Hollands* colonial network in the Dutch economy, with Amsterdam as its permanent, increasingly thriving centre. The political and ideological hegemony of this network seems to have exceeded its real significance for the Dutch economy.[79]

Dutch expansion overseas and Dutch imperialism in the Indonesian archipelago did influence, but not shape, the course of economic development in the Netherlands between 1870 and 1914. Economic development originated from diverse domestic sources and remained largely connected to the development of other Western economies, in particular the German economy.[80] Dutch economic interest in the East Indies never became crucial for the Dutch economy and remained too limited and one-sided to develop the East Indies fully. But that was more or less the case with all colonial empires.

Appendix

Dutch overseas trade in 1870-1910

Imports (in millions of guilders)

	East Indies	Asia	Africa	South America	total overseas
1870	81.0 (15.9%)	10.7 (2.1%)	2.4 (0.5%)	8.9 (1.8%)	103.0 (20.3%)
1875	77.2 (10.7%)	27.2 (3.8%)	3.3 (0.5%)	11.2 (1.6%)	118.9 (16.6%)
1880	56.1 (6.7%)	28.5 (3.4%)	7.0 (0.8%)	10.5 (1.2%)	102.1 (12.1%)
1885	97.0 (9.6%)	45.6 (4.1%)	6.8 (0 6%)	19.7 (2.2%)	169.1 (16.5%)
1890	159.5 (12.3%)	44.0 (3.4%)	9.8 (0.7%)	21.6 (1.6%)	234.9 (18.0%)
1895	202.4 (14.0%)	67.6 (4.7%)	6.9 (0.5%)	46.6 (3.2%)	323.5 (22.4%)
1900	272.5 (13.8%)	46.8 (2.4%)	9.5 (0.5%)	116.6 (5.0%)	445.4 (23.3%)
1905	399.6 (15.5%)	74.3 (2.9%)	11.9 (0.5%)	114.9 (4.4%)	600.7 (23.3%)
1910	493.9 (15.1%)	106.4 (3.3%)	15.6 (0.5%)	136.2 (4.2%)	752.1 (23.1%)

Exports (in millions of guilders)

	East Indies	Asia	Africa	South America	total overseas
1870	31.6 (0.9%)	3.5 (0.9%)	0.7 (0.2%)	4.7 (1.2%)	40.5 (10.2%)
1871	40.9 (0.7%)	3.8 (0.7%)	0.8 (0.1%)	3.2 (0.6%)	48.7 (9.2%)
1880	46.8 (7.4%)	0.9 (0.1%)	1.5 (0.2%)	3.2 (0.5%)	52.4 (8.2%)
1885	45.2 (5.0%)	3.1 (0.4%)	2.8 (0.3%)	2.3 (0.3%)	53.4 (6.0%)
1890	53.2 (4.9%)	9.6 (0.9%)	5.0 (0.5%)	6.3 (0.6%)	74.1 (6.9%)
1895	52.0 (4.4%)	7.7 (0.7%)	5.0 (0.4%)	7.0 (0.6%)	71.7 (6.1%)
1900	63.8 (3.8%)	8.9 (0.6%)	4.7 (0.3%)	8.4 (0.5%)	85.8 (5.2%)
1905	70.5 (3.5%)	16.8 (0.8%)	9.6 (0.5%)	16.6 (0.8%)	113.5 (5.6%)
1910	113.8 (4.3%)	25.5 (1.0%)	12.4 (0.5%)	23.2 (0.9%)	174.9 (6.7%)

Source: Statistiek voor den Handel en Scheepvaart and *Statistiek van den in-, uit- en doorvoer.*

Notes

1. Quoted in N. Etherington, *Theories of Imperialism. War, Conquest and Capital* (London and Canberra, 1984) p.220.
2. I. Schöffer, 'Dutch "Expansion" and Indonesian Reactions: Some Dilemmas of Modern Colonial Rule (1900-1942)', in *Expansion and Reaction. Essays on European Expansion and Reaction in Asia and Africa* (ed. H.L. Wesseling, Leiden, 1978), pp.78-100.
3. H.J. Marks, *The First Contest for Singapore 1819-1824* (The Hague, 1959).
4. C. Fasseur, 'Een koloniale paradox. De Nederlandse expansie in de Indonesische archipel in het midden van de negentiende eeuw (1830-1870)', *Tijdschrift voor Geschiedenis* (1979), 162-187. Between 1831 and 1877 the surplus on the colonial budget produced by the Cultivation System added 823 million guilders to the Dutch state finances, roughly 25% of all income; C. Fasseur, 'Nederland en Nederlands-Indië 1795-1914', in *Overzee. Nederlandse koloniale geschiedenis 1590-1975* (Haarlem, 1982), p.83.
5. *Ibid.*, p.175. Cf. A. Reid, *The Contest for North Sumatra. Atjeh, the Netherlands and Britain 1858-1898* (Kuala Lumpur, 1969), pp.25-6.
6. See the appendix for the trade figures. Cf. M. Kuitenbrouwer, *Nederland en de opkomst van het moderne imperialisme. Koloniën en buitenlandse politiek* (Amsterdam, 1985), pp.29-30.
7. Fasseur, 'Nederland', pp.80-5; J.S. Furnivall, *Netherlands India. A Study of Plural Economy* (Cambridge, 1944/Amsterdam, 1979), pp.160-70.
8. C.C. Goslinga, *Curaçao and Gúzman Blanco. A Case Study of Small Power Politics in the Caribbean* (The Hague, 1975), pp.10-30; R. van Lier, *Samenleving in een grensgebied. Een sociaal-historische studie van Suriname* (Deventer, 1971), pp.131-40.
9. D. Coombs, *The Gold Coast, Britain and the Netherlands 1850-1874* (London, 1963), pp.50-7.
10. H.L. Wesseling, 'Nederland en de Conferentie van Berlijn, 1884-1885', *Tijdschrift voor Geschiedenis*, XCIII (1980), pp.561-4.
11. Kuitenbrouwer, *Nederland*, pp.30-1.
12. *Ibid.*, pp.51-2; F. van Dongen, *Tussen neutraliteit en imperialisme. De Nederlands-Chinese betrekkingen van 1863 tot 1900* (Groningen, 1966), pp.28-46. See on the Dutch

participation in European privileges in Turkey, Egypt and Siam the contributions in *Nederland in de wereld. Opstellen over buitenlandse en koloniale politiek aangeboden aan Dr. N. Bootsma* (ed. P. Luykx and A. Manning, Nijmegen, 1988).

13. From 1858 onwards Dutch diplomats were represented in the administration of the Suez Canal Company; A. Delprat, *De reeder schrijft zijn journaal* (The Hague, 1983), pp.371-2.
14. Kuitenbrouwer, *Nederland*, p. 40; M.P. Bossenbroek, *Van Holland naar Indië. Het transport van koloniale troepen voor het Oost-Indische leger 1815-1909* (Amsterdam, 1986), pp.40-2.
15. Kuitenbrouwer, *Nederland*, pp.43-7. Cf. Reid, *Contest*, pp.56-73; Coombs, *Gold Coast*, pp.57ff.
16. *Handelingen Tweede Kamer* (7 July 1871), p.1102; cf. *ibid.*, pp.1098, 1107, 1127. Reid has observed that there was a strong element of trade conflict with merchants from the British Straits Settlements in Acehnese piracy, which was in decline anyway; no Dutch ships were ever involved. Reid, *Contest*, pp.16-17, 79-83; cf. *Officieele bescheiden betreffende het ontstaan van den oorlog tegen Atjeh in 1873* (The Hague, 1881), pp.5-41.
17. Kuitenbrouwer, *Nederland*, pp.59-64; Reid, *Contest*, pp.83-91.
18. Van Bosse to Loudon, 12 March 1869, collection J. Loudon, Algemeen Rijksarchief, The Hague. Cf. Kuitenbrouwer, *Nederland*, pp.47-8.
19. The negative effects of the abolition of differential rights for Dutch colonial trade were reinforced by the coincidental abolition of domestic sugar duties in Britain in 1874; Kuitenbrouwer, *Nederland*, p.50. Although cosmopolitan in character, the plantation economy of Deli was dominated from the start by the Deli Company. Aceh was falsely seen as the cause of local disturbances which led to a further intensification of Dutch rule in 1872. Neither did the following Aceh War hinder the economic development of Deli. Kuitenbrouwer, *Nederland*, pp.61, 71; cf. J. Breman, *Koelies, planters en koloniale politiek. Het arbeidsregime op de grootlandbouwondernemingen aan Sumatra's Oostkust in het begin van de twintigste eeuw* (Dordrecht, 1987), pp.12ff, 143ff.
20. The risk of foreign interference was not merely a justification for the Dutch declaration of war on Aceh, as Reid has suggested. Concern over American expansion already existed and was shared in particular by Minister Fransen van de Putte, who disliked war, but accepted the need of a Dutch *fait accompli*, even after Washington had denied any involvement. Kuitenbrouwer, *Nederland*, pp.62-8; cf. Reid, *Contest*, pp.91-7.
21. Kuitenbrouwer, *Nederland*, pp.75-6.
22. *Ibid.* pp.57-79; Goslinga, *Curaçao*, pp.59ff.
23. Kuitenbrouwer, *Nederland*, pp.55-6.
24. *Ibid.* pp.77-80; G. Irwin, *Nineteenth-century Borneo. A Study in Diplomatic Rivalry* (The Hague, 1955), pp.202-6.
25. Reid, *Contest*, pp.218-50; Kuitenbrouwer, *Nederland*, pp.103-11.
26. Kuitenbrouwer, *Nederland*, pp.85-8.
27. *Bescheiden betreffende de buitenlandse politiek van Nederland 1848-1919. Tweede periode 1871-1898* (ed. J. Woltring, The Hague, 1967), III, no. 511. Cf. Wesseling, 'Nederland', pp.569-76.
28. Kuitenbrouwer, *Nederland*, pp.91-4; S. Miers, *Britain and the Ending of the Slave Trade* (London, 1975), pp.236-92.
29. G.J. Schutte, *Nederland en de Afrikaners. Adhesie en aversie* (Franeker, 1986), pp.9-73; Kuitenbrouwer, *Nederland*, pp.118-33.
30. *Bescheiden*, VI, no. 188. Cf. Schutte, *Nederland*, pp.101-48; J.J. van Helten, 'German Capital, the Netherlands Railway Company and the Political Economy of the Transvaal 1886-1900', *Journal of African History*, XIX (1978), 369-90.
31. Kuitenbrouwer, *Nederland*, pp.111-14, 156-60.
32. *Verslag Kamer van Koophandel Amsterdam* (1890), 8. Cf. *Changing Economy in Indonesia*, VI. *Money and Banking 1816-1940* (ed. J.T.M. van Laanen, The Hague, 1980), pp.48-50, 92-104; J.S. Furnivall, *Netherlands India*, pp.196-9.
33. *Handelingen Tweede Kamer* (22 March 1886), 1254, 1277.
34. J.Th. Lindblad, 'Economische aspecten van de Nederlandse expansie in de Indonesische archipel, 1870-1914', in *Imperialisme in de marge. De afronding van Nederlands-Indië* (ed. J. van Goor, Utrecht, 1986), pp.246-7; A.I.P.J. van Beurden, 'De Indische "Goldrush", goudmijnbouw en beleid', *ibid.*, pp.179-227; Kuitenbrouwer, *Nederland*, pp.114-18.
35. *Handelingen Tweede Kamer* (17 November 1885), 469.
36. P.J. Jobse, 'De tin-expedities naar Flores 1887-1891', *Utrechtse Historische Cahiers*, I (1980), no. 3.

37. J. à Campo, 'Een Maritiem BB. De rol van de Koninklijke Paketvaart Maatschappij in de integratie van de koloniale staat', in *Imperialisme* (ed. Van Goor), pp.19-71.
38. J. van Goor, 'De Lombokexpeditie en het Nederlandse nationalisme', in *Imperialisme* (ed. Van Goor), pp.19-71.
39. Kuitenbrouwer, *Nederland*, pp.160-4, 190-3. From 1873 the 'pacification' of Aceh took the lives of 60-70,000 Acehnese, 12,500 members of the colonial army and 25,000 Javanese forced labourers; its financial costs amounted to roughly 400 million guilders.
40. E. Locher-Scholten, 'Motieven voor het optreden tegen het sultansbestuur van Jambi in 1901', unpublished paper for the symposium 'Imperialisme in de marge', Utrecht 18 January 1984. Cf. the private correspondence between Cremer and Van der Wijck in the course of 1898, in the C.H.A. Van der Wijck collection, Algemeen Rijksarchief, The Hague.
41. Cremer to Van der Wijck, March 4 and April 15, 1898, collection Van der Wijck. Cf. E.P. Wellenstein, *Het Indisch mijnbouwvraagstuk* (The Hague, 1918), pp.53-84.
42. À Campo, 'Maritiem BB', pp.144-58.
43. E. Locher-Scholten, *Ethiek in fragmenten. Vijf studies over koloniaal denken en doen van Nederlanders in de Indonesische Archipel 1877-1942* (Utrecht, 1981), pp.176-209.
44. Locher-Scholten, *Motieven*. See on Idenburg and Van Heutsz: J. de Bruin and G. Puchinger, *Briefwisseling Kuyper-Idenburg* (Franeker, 1985), pp.14-47; J.C. Lamster, *J.B. van Heutsz als Gouverneur-Generaal 1904-1909* (Amsterdam, n.d.), pp.12-69.
45. The number of Dutch colonial officials in the Outer Regions nearly doubled between 1890 and 1909 to about 300, more than the number on populous Java; A.D.A. de Kat Angelino, *Staatkundig beleid en bestuurszorg in Nederlands-Indië* (The Hague, 1930), II, pp.74, 90, 106-7. See on the expansion of Dutch rule in various parts of the Outer Regions: Lamster, *Van Heutsz*, pp.36-50, 147-77; I. Black, 'The "lastposten": Eastern Kalimantan and the Dutch in the nineteenth and early twentieth-centuries', *Journal of Southeast Asian Studies*, CXXVI (1985), 281-92; H.J. van der Tholen, 'De expeditie naar Korintji in 1902-1903: imperialisme of ethische politiek', *Mededelingen van de Sectie Militaire Geschiedenis Landmachtstaf*, X (1987), 70-92; J.A. Arts, 'Zending en bestuur op Midden-Celebes tussen 1890 en 1920', in *Imperialisme* (ed. Van Goor), pp.85-123; W. Manuhutu, 'Pacificatie in praktijk. De expansie van het Nederlands gezag op Ceram, 1900-1942', *ibid.*, pp.267-317; H. Schulte Nordholt, *Een Balische dynastie. Hierarchie en conflict in de Negera Mangui 1700-1940* (Haarlem, 1988), pp.4-12; E. Locher-Scholten, 'Een gebiedende noodzakelijkheid. Besluitvorming rond de Boni-expeditie 1903-1905', in *Excursies in Celebes* (ed. H.A. Poeze and P. Schoorl, Dordrecht, 1991), pp.143-65.
46. P.M.H. Groen, 'Koloniale politiek en militaire geschiedschrijving', *Mededelingen van de Sectie Militaire Geschiedenis Landmachtstaf*, VI (1983), 93-119.
47. De Bruijn and Puchinger, *Briefwisseling*, pp.47-64.
48. *Verslag Kamer van Koophandel Amsterdam* (1890), appendix G; *ibid.* (1897), 306-8; *ibid.* (1900), appendix F. Cf. T. van Tijn, 'Een nabeschouwing', *Bijdragen en Mededelingen betreffende de Geschiedenis der Nederlanden*, LXXXVI (1971), 83-4.
49. C. Gerretson, *Geschiedenis der 'Koninklijke'* (Utrecht, 1937), vol. I and II.
50. *Changing Economy in Indonesia, III. Expenditure on Fixed Assets* (ed. P. Creutzberg, The Hague, 1977), p.169. Cf. Van Tijn, 'Nabeschouwing', p.84; Lindblad, 'Economische aspecten', p.240; H. Baudet and M. Fennema, *Het Nederlands belang bij Indië* (Utrecht/Antwerpen, 1983), p.36.
51. J.A. de Jonge, *De industrialisatie in Nederland tussen 1850 en 1914* (Amsterdam, 1968), p.356; Baudet and Fennema, *Nederlands belang*, p.35.
52. Lindblad, 'Economische aspecten', pp.254-5; D.H. Burger, *Sociologisch-economische geschiedenis van Indonesia* (Wageningen, 1975), II, pp.78-85.
53. Wellenstein, *Mijnbouwvraagstuk*, pp.119-25; Furnivall, *Netherlands India*, pp.309-12, 325-9.
54. C. Smit, *Nederland in de Eerste Wereldoorlog, I. Het voorspel: 1890-1914* (Groningen, 1971), pp.84-5. Cf. H.J.G. Beunders, *Weg met de vlootwet! De maritieme bewapeningspolitiek van het kabinet-Ruys de Beerenbrouck en het succesvolle verzet daartegen in 1923* (Bergen, 1984), pp.3, 12, 24-45; G. Teitler, 'De Krijgsmacht, in offensief en defensief verband', in *Imperialisme* (ed. Van Goor), pp.71-85.
55. Smit, *Nederland*, pp.201-6; Beunders, *Vlootwet*, pp.9-10, 13-14.
56. Kuitenbrouwer, *Nederland*, pp.53-4, 99, 146-7; H.A.F. Lijnkamp, *De 'Japannerwet'. Onderzoek naar de wording* (Utrecht, 1938).
57. *Bescheiden*, II, no. 512. Cf. Van Dongen, *Neutraliteit en imperialisme*, p.193ff.
58. Smit, *Nederland*, pp.208-12.

59. Kuitenbrouwer, *Nederland*, pp.33, 49, 155. Cf. À Campo, 'Maritiem BB', pp.158-67; C.A. Tamse, 'The Netherlands Consular Service and the Dutch Consular Reports of the Nineteenth and Twentieth Centuries', *Business History*, XXIII (1981), 271-6.
60. Woltring, *Bescheiden*, VI, no. 146.
61. Kuitenbrouwer, *Nederland*, pp.173-90; Schutte, *Nederland*, pp.73-101, 143-71.
62. Smit, *Nederland*, pp.46-51.
63. Cf. Fasseur, 'Koloniale paradox', pp.184-7; Locher-Scholten, *Ethiek*, pp.194-200; Bossenbroek, *Holland*, pp.16-17. These authors all acknowledge, however, political and economic influences from the Netherlands.
64. Metropolitan, political and economic factors in Dutch imperialism were stressed, with due regard for local factors, by Kuitenbrouwer, *Nederland*, pp.202-15. The interaction between the metropolitan economy and colonial state in Dutch imperialism is analysed by Lindblad, 'Economische aspecten', which was published in extended form in *Modern Asian Studies*, XXIII (1989), 1-23. See also *idem, Between Dayak and Dutch: the Economic History of Southeast Kalimantan 1880-1942* (Dordrecht, 1988), pp.7-47, 119-71; and various contributions to *Het belang van de buitengewesten: economische expansie en koloniale staatsvorming in de buitengewesten van Nederlands-Indië 1870-1942* (ed. A.H.F. Clemens and J.T. Lindblad, Amsterdam, 1989). As well as the term imperialism, the significance of Dutch political and economic factors has been denied by Schöffer, 'Dutch "expansion"', pp.79-81. Wesseling first took the same line of argument in his extended review of Kuitenbrouwer, *Nederland*, in 'Bestond er een Nederlands imperialisme?', *Tijdschrift voor Geschiedenis*, XCIX (1986), 214-25, which appeared in slightly altered form in *Journal of Imperial and Commonwealth History*, XVI (1988), 57-70. In further elaborations of the review article Wesseling has reluctantly accepted the term imperialism for the Dutch expansion in the Indonesian archipelago, but still denies the significance of metropolitan factors. Cf. Wesseling, 'The Giant that was a Dwarf, or the Strange History of Dutch Imperialism', in *Theory and Practice in the History of European Expansion Overseas* (ed. A. Porter and R. Holland, London, 1988), pp.58-71; *idem,* 'British and Dutch Imperialism: A Comparison', *Itinerario*, XIII (1989), 61-77.
65. Etherington, *Theories*, pp.1-5, 263-7.
66. P.J. Cain and A.G. Hopkins, 'The Political Economy of British Expansion Overseas, 1750-1914', *Economic History Review*, XXXIII (1980), 484-6. See on the debate on 'mid-Victorian imperialism', C.C. Eldridge, *Victorian Imperialism* (London, 1978), pp.74-122.
67. C. Clarence-Smith, *The Third Portuguese Empire 1825-1975. A Study in Economic Imperialism* (Manchester, 1985), pp.81-116.
68. *Bescheiden*, VI, no. 212.
69. Kuitenbrouwer, *Nederland*, pp.151, 172; Fasseur, 'Nederland', p.178; Locher-Scholten, *Ethiek*, p.196.
70. Cf. the biographical articles in the *Encyclopedie van Nederlandsch Indië* (8 vol., The Hague, 1917-1940).
71. R.F. Betts, *The False Dawn. European Imperialism in the Nineteenth Century* (Minneapolis, 1975), pp.150-85.
72. Kuitenbrouwer, *Nederland*, p.172.
73. *Ibid.*, pp.194-8.
74. See on the tensions of class and denomination at the turn of the century, S. Stuurman, *Verzuiling, kapitalisme en patriarchaat* (Nijmegen, 1983), pp.166-82.
75. Kuitenbrouwer, *Nederland*, p.209; cf. C. Smit, *Tien studiën betreffende Nederland in de Eerste Wereldoorlog* (Groningen, 1975), pp.15-17.
76. H. Baudet, 'Nederland en de rang van Denemarken', *Bijdragen en Mededelingen betreffende de Geschiedenis der Nederlanden*, XC (1975), 438-9.
77. De Jonge, *Industrialisatie*, pp.306-7.
78. According to recent figures the share attained by industry and utilities in the total labour force was 25.1% in 1909, with 27.6% in agriculture and 18.7% in commerce, transport and finance; R.T. Griffiths, 'The Creation of a National Dutch Economy: 1795-1909', *Tijdschrift voor Geschiedenis*, XCV (1982), 528, 531, 533. Cf. De Jonge, *Industrialisatie*, pp.236-9; Griffiths, *Achterlijk, achter of anders? Aspecten van de economische ontwikkeling van Nederland in de 19e eeuw* (Amsterdam, 1980).
79. Baudet, 'Nederland', pp.441-2. The share of commerce, transport and finance in the labour force of the province of North Holland (in which Amsterdam is situated) increased from 21.8% in 1859 to 26.5% in 1909; Griffiths, 'Creation', p.531. Neither the positive nor the negative effects of the East Indies on the Dutch economy should be exaggerated. To argue, for example, that the East Indies restrained further industrialization in the

Netherlands tends to neglect the successful modernization of Dutch agriculture, with a substantial share of the labour force remaining in that sector, and the strong tendency to invest abroad outside the colonial sphere; see for the colonial under-industrialization thesis, À Campo, 'Orde, trust en welvaart. Over de Nederlandse expansie in de Indische Archipel omstreeks 1900', *Acta Politica*, XV (1980), 159-60.

80. Trade with Germany, with Rotterdam as main centre, did increase from 22.2% to 25.0% of Dutch imports and from 44.2% to 48.9% of Dutch exports between 1875 and 1910; cf. H.P.H. Nusteling, *De Rijnvaart in het tijdperk van stoom en steenkool 1831-1914* (Amsterdam, 1974).

9

The Economic Role of the Interwar British State[1]

Roger Middleton

Interwar Britain, like other advanced economies, witnessed a growth of the state and a transformation of its economic role. Unlike other countries, however, in Britain the historiography of these developments is largely subsumed within the debate about the Keynesian revolution. In fact, these two developments are quite distinct, though clearly interconnected. Thus, one objective of this paper is to show that there were forces making for an increased public sector, and greater state intervention in the economic field, which were quite independent of the contemporaneous debate which reached eventual fruition in the Keynesian revolution, if indeed that term may still be applied to Britain after the doubts raised by recent work.[2]

The further objectives of this paper are to examine the forces underlying the growth of public expenditure, which for the interwar period have been subject to little systematic study; and to question the traditional interpretation of the period, where there has been a temptation to view developments as some sort of linear progression from *laissez-faire* to the managed economy. Finally, we conclude with a plea for a more comparative economic history of the growth of government.

The public sector is traditionally measured in terms of the share of public expenditure or taxation in national income (with public expenditure and GDP being measured at market prices). Unfortunately, this approach of measuring what is most easily identifiable and quantifiable cannot incorporate what has been one of the most important features of public sector growth this century: the growth of government regulation of the private sector, which imposes public and private economic costs which do not show up as public expenditures.[3] As Peters and Heisler note:

> To date much of the analysis of the growth of government has been like the search of the proverbial drunkard, who looked for a lost house key under the lamppost, because the light was better there. We have been looking for government growth in forms for which data are more readily available, in quantifiable form, ubiquitous units, and preferably in interval form.[4]

Since this particular process of government growth began in its modern form around the turn of the century, and was greatly intensified in the interwar period, we need to be conscious from the outset that the conventional indicators of public sector size provide but a partial coverage of the channels through which the public sector impinges on the private. This problem is particularly magnified with cross-country studies. One response to this deficiency is that in the current literature on government growth there have been attempts to provide alternative and wider (non-financial) measures of government growth and its impact, such as quantity of laws enacted, the services performed by the state and the degree of regulation imposed upon the private sector.[5] As yet, this development has not been applied to the inter-war period.

An associated problem of the conventional approach to the political economy of government growth has been the temptation to assume that the public sector can easily be differentiated from the private. For example, can a privately owned armaments company which only produces for its country's armed forces (a monopsonistic market) really be said to be in the private sector in the same sense as a sole trader operating in the open market and facing less direct regulation? In reality it cannot.[6] Indeed, it is now agreed that one of the most outstanding features of contemporary economies is the entanglement of the public and private domains, such that many of the most interesting aspects of public sector growth do not involve direct financial transactions which can be captured in the conventional indicators of the public sector. While there is a long history of government relations with the private sector, in particular the armaments industries,[7] this more general process began in earnest in the interwar period, its analysis being complicated by the contemporaneous concentration of British industry and the growth of corporatism.[8]

Against this backcloth we are now in a position to look at the conventional indicators of the growth of the interwar public sector. Figure 1 enables the period to be placed in context by charting the long-term growth of general government expenditure and expenditure on goods and services.[9]

Figure 1 UK general government expenditure and expenditure on goods and services as % of GDP 1890-1985

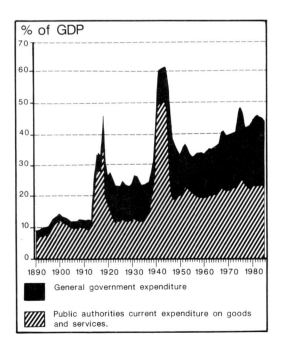

% of GDP

General government expenditure

Public authorities current expenditure on goods and services.

Sources: Chapman and White, 'Long-Term Trends in Public Expenditure', chart 2; 1919 data from Feinstein, *National Income*, tables 3, 14, 39.

At first sight the impact of the First World War looks obvious, a structural break in trend which has typically been described in terms of the Peacock and Wiseman 'displacement effect',[10] whereby war results in a permanent upward shift in the public's tolerance of higher tax rates. Clearly the near doubling of the expenditure ratio, from 0.119 to 0.205 over 1913-20,[11] marked a permanent upward shift; its analysis, however, is more problematic.

The 'displacement effect' has been subject to much criticism, both general and empirical,[12] and attention has now shifted back to a reappraisal of a much older explanation of the government expenditure function, that of Wagner's 'Law of increasing state activity'.[13] On one reading, this posited an upward trend to the expenditure ratio, and, on another, that once a certain level has been reached, there would be approximate stability in the ratio (implying an expenditure-income elasticity of approximately unity). It is this latter reading which has given rise to the permanent income model of public expenditure,[14] a natural extension of Friedman's work on the consumption function and Wildavsky's on incremental budgeting.[15]

This work has in general focused on the postwar period, although Chrystal and Alt have made estimates of the government expenditure function for the period 1900-76 (but excluding the two wars and their immediate aftermath, 1914-20 and 1939-47).[16] Their regressions yield an elasticity measure of 0.53 for logged income or 0.97 when expenditure is lagged one time period. Taking this latter result yields two important conclusions: first, that government expenditure has in fact been remarkably stable over the course of the twentieth century, with its current value in any one year almost entirely explained as a linear function of its value the previous year; and, second, that the trend in expenditure over 1958-76 is an exact extrapolation of that established in 1907-13.[17]

It is important to note at this stage that Peacock's and Wiseman's 'displacement effect' derived from a study of total government expenditure, and not expenditure on goods and services, which is the focus of Chrystal and Alt and of much other recent work.[18] As is clear from Figure 1 and Table 1, the war does indeed cause little in the way of a displacement effect on expenditure on goods and services. If we exclude the war periods, their immediate aftermaths and the beginnings of serious rearmament in the late 1930s, the elasticity of expenditure growth relative to GDP growth pre-war (1904-13) was zero, and that for the interwar period was 1.43 (1920-37) or 1.29 (1924-37),[19] the latter a more acceptable period for comparison as it allows longer for the dislocation of the war and a period where endogenous expenditures are not subject to cyclical sensitivity. Thus there is some evidence for an acceleration in the rate of growth of expenditure on goods and services after the First World War.

The picture is broadly similar for total public expenditure. The overall position is given in Table 1, while Table 2 presents elasticity estimates for 1924-37 along with two sub-periods. The results show that in each case the observed elasticity was greater than unity; and that for total public expenditure the elasticity was historically high. Indeed, the estimate of 1.60 is significantly above the period 1960-76 which has been estimated at 1.21.[20]

This evidence, reproduced from my earlier study,[21] prompted one reviewer to comment: 'It remains unanswered why public expenditure growth in the "Keynesian postwar world" was slower than in the 1920s and 1930s when, until rearmament, budget deficits were resisted, largely successfully'.[22] The broader political economy of this is discussed in a later section; for the present it is sufficient to note that the answer is contained in table 1: that the growth of the interwar public sector is princ-

Table 1
UK: Public expenditure by economic category as % of GDP, selected years, 1900-37*

	Current goods and services	Gross capital formation	Subsidies and grants to private sector	Current grants paid abroad	Debt interest	Total
1900	9.3	1.8	0.5	0.1	1.6	13.3
1913	8.1	1.2	0.9	–	1.7	11.9
1920	8.2	1.7	4.7	0.2	5.7	20.5
1924	9.0	2.2	4.3	0.2	7.9	23.6
1929	9.2	2.6	4.9	0.1	7.7	24.5
1932	10.1	2.8	7.2	0.1	7.8	27.9
1937	11.7	3.3	5.6	0.1	5.3	25.9

Source: Middleton, *Towards the Managed Economy*, Table 3.1; calculated from Feinstein, *National Income*, Tables 3, 14, 39.

* Public expenditure is here defined as current and capital expenditure by central and local government plus capital expenditure by the public corporations.

Table 2
UK: Observed elasticity of public expenditure growth relative to GDP growth (current prices) 1924-37

	central government	local government	total public expenditure
(1924-9)			
Current	1.27	2.84	1.39
Capital	..	4.19	3.83
Total	1.24	3.14	1.61
(1929-37)			
Current	1.46	1.34	1.29
Capital	5.04	2.86	3.49
Total	1.52	1.71	1.53
(1924-37)			
Current	1.41	1.98	1.36
Capital	3.05	2.86	4.03
Total	1.45	1.71	1.60

Source: Middleton, *Towards the Managed Economy*, Table 3.2; calculated from Feinstein, *National Income*, Tables 3, 12-14, 34, 36, 39.

ipally explained by the growth of transfer payments, namely debt interest and subsidies and grants to the private sector. Of the 14 percentage points of GDP rise in the expenditure ratio over 1913-37, fully 8.3 percentage points are accounted for by this factor. In this sense the force of war is reaffirmed, as Peacock and Wiseman meant it, and as is portrayed in the tradition of the social policy literature established by Titmuss.[23]

Thus more than half of the rise in the expenditure ratio was the result of the greatly increased expenditures on debt interest and on subsidies and grants to the private sector. Both categories of expenditure constitute transfer payments, and as such do not represent direct claims on resources (current expenditure on goods and services and public authorities' capital formation). However, whilst transfer payments increased more than direct expenditures over 1913-20 (respectively from 2.6 to 10.4 per cent of GDP and from 9.3 to 9.9 per cent of GDP), over the subsequent period the trends were reversed: between 1924 and 1937 transfer payments fell from 12.2

to 10.9 per cent of GDP while direct expenditures rose from 11.2 to 15.0 per cent of GDP. Thus within the total of public expenditure, and in relation to GDP, the public sector's claim on resources was growing throughout the interwar period.[24]

It remains to compare Britain's experience with that of other European states. The available data are most incomplete (see appendix tables 2 and 3). Nevertheless, it shows that out of this sample of thirteen major states the British public sector, as conventionally measured, was far from being the largest. Indeed, it is probable that Britain ranked sixth, and was certainly smaller than the two major industrial powers, France and Germany, a relative position which has been sustained throughout the postwar period.[25]

The overall course of public sector receipts is shown in Figure 2, with a more detailed breakdown for selected years in Table 3. As with expenditure, the receipts ratio nearly doubled over the course of the war, from 0.124 in 1913 to 0.209 in 1920, largely as a result of the increased yield of taxes on income. While public expenditure was rigorously curtailed in the immediate postwar period, no such development occurred on the taxation side of the account, and the ratio rose gradually − though pro-cyclically − to 0.244 by 1937.

Figure 2: UK public sector receipts as % of GDP 1900-39

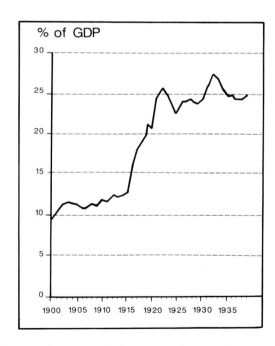

Source: Calculated from Feinstein, *National Income,* Tables 3, 14, 34

This upward trend resulted from increased rates on existing taxes and some widening of the tax base. Over the course of the war taxes on expenditure had remained fairly stable, the aggregate average or effective rate of tax on consumers' expenditure being about 5 per cent. Thereafter, the effective rate exhibited a marked upward trend: from 7 per cent in 1920 to 10.7 per cent in 1937.[26]

The most important development, however, concerned the income tax which 'changed out of all recognition'.[27] Between 1913/14 and 1918/19 the standard rate was increased from 6 to 30 per cent, and whilst it was reduced in the early 1920s it

Table 3
UK: Public sector receipts by economic category as % of GDP, selected years, 1900-37

	Taxes on income	Taxes on expenditure	Taxes on capital	National insurance contributions	Property income	Current grants from abroad	Total
1900	1.0	6.6	1.0	0.0	1.1	0.0	9.7
1913	1.8	7.0	1.1	0.8	1.8	0.0	12.4
1920	10.2	8.3	0.8	0.5	1.1	0.1	20.9
1924	7.9	10.0	1.4	1.4	2.3	0.2	23.3
1929	6.2	10.6	1.7	1.7	3.1	0.5	23.8
1932	8.2	12.0	1.7	2.1	3.3	0.0	27.4
1937	6.2	11.6	1.8	2.0	2.8	0.0	24.4

Source: Middleton, *Towards the Managed Economy*, Table 4.1; calculated from Feinstein, *National Income*, Tables 3, 14, 34.

was to fluctuate in the range 20-25 per cent for the remainder of the period until rearmament in the late 1930s once more forced large increases.[28] Of equal importance to these developments, in terms of the impact of government growth on the private sector, was the huge increase in the numbers subject to income tax. In 1914 these had totalled about one million;[29] by 1919/20 they had risen to 3.9m and had only fallen back to 3.4m by 1935/6.[30] Moreover, between 1912/13 and 1922/3 the proportion of total income tax revenue paid by businesses had fallen from 51 per cent to 35 per cent.[31]

We are now in a position to return to our earlier question, that of explanations of the growth of the interwar public sector. The general issue of government growth has received extensive treatment in the current literature, but this is mainly about the postwar period. Nonetheless, this literature is a useful reference point for our discussion.

Four central hypotheses have been advanced to explain the postwar growth of the public sector in OECD countries:[32]

1. *The open economy*, that is where governments with large foreign trade sectors, finding that the power of domestic macroeconomic policies is thereby limited, reduce the effects of exogenous shocks by increasing the size of their public sector and thus their influence over the domestic economy. This can take a passive (e.g. fiscal drag with inflation) or an active form (e.g. public expenditure as a means of employment creation).
2. *The partisanship of government*. This seeks to explain public sector growth in terms of the ideological complexion of government, with faster growth evident under 'left' governments, with their stress on state intervention and income redistribution, than those of the 'right', with their emphasis upon individualism and lower taxes.
3. *Fiscal illusions*. Here it is argued that complex and indirect systems of taxation create fiscal illusions leading to public expenditures that would be higher than if a simple tax structure prevailed. Therefore, we would expect public sector growth to be most pronounced in those countries which rely on indirect taxes and social security contributions rather than direct taxes.
4. *Bureaucratic pressures*. The view that bureaucracies, and not just politicians, are powerful forces for expenditure growth because by expanding their departmental budgets they are able to increase their prestige and status within the bureaucracy.

These, and other subsidiary hypotheses, have been extensively tested for the postwar period, with − not surprisingly − differing results according to how models were specified. In particular, there are major problems in modelling political variables such as the complexion of government. In so far as a consensus has emerged it would be that there is some support for the open economy hypothesis and that of the partisanship of government. In particular, a strong 'left' tended to stimulate the growth of public expenditure, though this effect was not as strong as that of the 'right' inhibiting the growth of expenditure.

What conclusions can we draw from this for the interwar period? Taking each of the four hypotheses in turn:

1. *The open economy.* Whilst there was no stabilization policy in a Keynesian sense during the interwar period, the Labour government of 1929-31 did use public capital expenditure to offset partially the exogenous shock of the world depression. However, these expenditures were sharply curtailed in the budgetary crisis of 1931,[33] and thus there was no long-term effect. In a more general sense, though, the disturbed conditions of the interwar period, which were primarily the consequence of export instability,[34] did make for government growth (see below).

2. *The partisanship of government.* This hypothesis is much less promising in its application, for we are dealing with a relatively short period, one in which the two Labour governments (1924, 1929-31) were both minority administrations dependent upon Liberal support, and where public expenditure was highly cyclically sensitive, making meaningful comparisons on the basis of party complexion unfruitful. Moreover, whilst in general Labour's ideological position favoured greater expenditure, in practice Snowden's dominance of economic management and the party's fatalistic vision of British capitalism,[35] together with the very limited room for manoeuvre, meant that there was little discernible difference in *ex-post* expenditures between the Labour and Conservative administrations.

3. *Fiscal illusions.* These were not unknown to the interwar period, though they took the form of window-dressing to create the appearance of budgetary orthodoxy,[36] rather than in the more usual sense of the term, that of 'a systematic tendency to misperceive the actual levels of costs and benefits in some tax-spending combination'.[37] Nevertheless, even though there was no political business cycle between the wars, the practical effect of fiscal window-dressing was to sustain expenditure at levels which would have been unsupportable had a true balanced budget rule been imposed.

4. *Bureaucratic pressure.* Whilst this hypothesis, developed from Niskanen's work,[38] has not been directly applied to the interwar case, there is an extensive literature on interwar bureaucracy,[39] and on Treasury control.[40] The broad stance of this work would not support a view of interwar bureaucrats as self-seeking in a way that promoted expenditure growth. On the contrary, Lowe's recent study of the Ministry of Labour demonstrates that, such was the Treasury's control of expenditure and the career prospects of higher civil servants, that the self-seeking official had no interest in promoting expenditure growth.[41] Other evidence, from the Ministry of Health, the largest civil spending department, conveys the same impression.[42] Thus, there is no evidence of institutional entropy, 'the in-built tendency for any organization to run down over time, degenerating from the pursuit of collective goals into the simple pursuit of the individual, private interests by those holding official positions'.[43] Rather, as

Lowe says: 'Inter-war civil servants were the most reluctant of "bureaucrats", acquiring such power as they did because Britain's economic and social problems could only be solved by central government and because, within government, political leadership was largely conspicuous for its absence.'[44]

Thus some progress can be made here by using the reference points of the current literature on government growth. However, the case is still compelling that we should refer to more general economic and political forces. In my earlier study,[45] the general factors which underlay expenditure growth were grouped under two headings: those that were largely exogenous or independent of policy, and those endogenous factors which in large measure were the consequence of policy and of the problems of the British economy.

Under the first heading, account should be taken of the various war-related expenditures, such as pensions and disability allowances, and of certain demographic changes which were to influence the pattern of expenditure. In particular, the falling birth-rate resulted in a rising proportion both of the population who were economically active and of those of retirement age, the net effect being additional demands for pension support and, given excess supply in the labour market, for outlay on unemployment benefits.

With regard to the largely endogenous influences, of particular importance was the continually high level of unemployment, which was to affect total expenditure both directly and indirectly. The direct influence operated through benefit payments and relief work expenditures for the unemployed; the indirect influence was broader in effect and of greater significance.

Whilst it might be supposed that the difficult economic conditions of the period would have served to frustrate demands for further social reforms, and therefore to have acted as a constraint upon the continued growth of expenditure, in fact the opposite seems to have been the case. As was noted by contemporaries, and as has been confirmed by more recent experience, economic failures such as heavy unemployment or a deteriorating standard of living can be a potent force intensifying demands for increased social expenditures. These forces were well expressed in the May Committee report:

> After the heavy sacrifices of the war large sections of the nation looked to the post-war period with the natural expectation of a general improvement in the old conditions of life. The disappointment of many hopes in the economic sphere seemed to intensify demands for improvements from political action and all parties have felt the insistent pressure for promises of 'reforms' as the price of support . . . At election times those desiring increased expenditure on particular objects are usually far better organized, far more active and vocal than those who favour the vague and uninspiring course of strict economy; and as a result candidates not infrequently find themselves returned to Parliament committed, on a one-sided presentation of a case, to a course which on fuller knowledge they see to be opposed to the national interests.[46]

Accordingly, the upward trend of expenditure may be seen as another manifestation of the failure to resolve the unemployment problem. It should be noted, however, that the translation of these demands into increased expenditure was by no means automatically assured. It only resulted because there had occurred certain fundamental changes in political circumstances which were conducive to increased expenditure. The widening of the franchise and the emergence of the Labour Party, the two most conspicuous developments of the early twentieth century, were to create conditions of increased party rivalry and a political atmosphere whereby promises of increased expenditure were a powerful means of gaining electoral support.

We can consider certain implications of the expanded public sector under two broad headings: economic and administrative.

Under the first heading the most important consequence of the enlarged public sector, for both policy and the economy, was a problem which appeared at an early stage and was to bedevil all interwar governments in their budgetary policies, that of the irreconcilability of the balanced budget rule with a budget structure, the characteristic of which was its sensitivity to cyclical fluctuations. In the pre-war period, the interrelationship of the budget with the economy, and the implications of this for budgetary policy, were problems that never raised themselves to any important degree. The enlargement of the public sector brought about by the war, however, changed conditions fundamentally: public expenditure had now reached such a proportion of GDP that this interrelationship could not be ignored. Indeed, in a sense, the history of subsequent developments revolves largely around the authorities' attempts to come to terms with this essential (Keynesian) economic truth.[47]

This problem was magnified by certain interwar developments which also contributed to the upward trend of expenditure. The problem was well put by Hicks:

> It seems probable that the financial crisis of 1931 was largely due to the failure to realize in advance the extent to which social expenditure had become increasingly vulnerable to depression on account of the steady expansion of the unemployment services. Cyclical sensitivity is a matter which should properly be taken into account when new social legislation is introduced.[48]

The second important economic implication was that the enlarged public sector, together with the widening of the tax base and acceptance of higher rates of taxation, all provided much greater scope for income redistribution via fiscal policy. What is interesting about the interwar period is that, at least in an active policy sense, governments did not use their newly acquired influence. There were odd occasions on which Chancellors of the Exchequer were explicit about the distributional consequences of their policies, in particular Snowden's 1931 budgets and Chamberlain's budgetary strategy during 1933-4,[49] and there is evidence of reduced income inequality between the wars, which makes the period 'something of a watershed'.[50] However, as Barna has noted:

> Redistribution of incomes through public finances was not ... a deliberate policy, but accidental to the piecemeal development of the social services. It was an *ad hoc* policy: certain needs had to be satisfied by society as they arose, and as social conscience demanded their satisfaction. The fact that the payment for the social services fell largely on the upper income classes was to some degree an incidental consequence of the British system of taxation. But while this method dealt, to some extent, with the exigencies of the moment, it has not solved any of the problems that called it forth and has left no permanent mark on the initial distribution of incomes. Redistribution was of the nature of a palliative rather than a cure.[51]

Turning now to the administration dimension, the widening of the tax base and expansion of social expenditures had important consequences for the conduct of policy, and a certain relevance to Olson's observations about distributional coalitions in relation to long-term economic growth and efficiency.[52] Current interpretations of the interwar 'Treasury view' hold that the Treasury's resistance to the Keynesian solution for interwar unemployment was partially founded on the belief that the balanced budget rule 'acted as the ultimate constraint on the growth of expenditure, since it moderated and tempered the natural demands of politicians and sectional interests for new expenditure, and provided a "neutral" framework within which competing demands were reconciled'.[53]

Even with the safeguard of the balanced budget rule, the problem of expenditure control was still deemed to be serious within Whitehall. Whilst it was an essential foundation of the liberal state in Britain to contain rent-seeking behaviour by the private sector, the growth of expenditure and the adoption of policy instruments such as the general tariff in 1931-2 posed grave dangers and much greater scope for distributional coalitions to exercise their influence in the way detailed by Olson and the wider public choice literature. However, although interwar governments felt compelled to introduce economic policies such as tariffs which created the opportunity for rent-seeking, much attention was paid to minimizing the practical adverse consequences of their actions.

There has been no formal study of interwar economic policy within this framework,[54] but the general picture is clear from a number of studies. For example, Booth has detailed the way in which unemployment policy in the 1930s was administered in such a way as to prevent the Conservative-led National Government from 'becoming involved in an auction at the polls over the level of unemployment relief';[55] and Hutchinson's study of the Import Duties Advisory Council, the body charged with determining the tariff structure, demonstrates that government was determined that applications for additional protection from special interests should be directed to, and thereby contained by, an advisory body rather than the Board of Trade.[56]

State intervention

We noted in the introduction that our knowledge of the economic role of the interwar British state has largely been conditioned by the Keynesian historiography with its particular research agenda. Thus, whilst there is a wealth of studies on macroeconomic policies,[57] on the likely effectiveness of the Keynesian solution for interwar unemployment,[58] and on the performance of the British economy,[59] there has been little systematic work which relates these issues to the broader growth of the state. The space remaining here precludes such a detailed and lengthy exercise, but it is possible to make a start on developing a taxonomy and identifying questions which need further research.

Without undue characterization, the traditional interpretation and chronology of the interwar British state can be divided into four parts:

1. That the pre-war allegiance to *laissez-faire* gravely handicapped the creation of an efficient war economy, and illustrates the durability of the minimalist state in face of adversity.[60]
2. That the continuing allegiance to *laissez-faire* was responsible for the bonfire of controls and deflationary monetary policies of the early 1920s;[61] evidence that

the war had little short-term impact, upon either micro- or macroeconomic policies.

3. That while the 1920s saw a number of *ad hoc* developments, governments remained wedded to market-based solutions to Britain's problems.[62]
4. That it was not until the 1930s that a more interventionist stance became evident, but even then policies tended to be *ad hoc* and incoherent.[63]

This traditional interpretation has been subject to a number of revisions in recent years:

1. The detailed research of Searle, Emy and others has revealed that the Liberal Party was not wedded to *laissez-faire* by 1914,[64] that its social reform and other policies were informed by a collectivist ideology which had developed as a reaction to Gladstonian individualism.[65]
2. French has sought to demonstrate that the inadequacy of the initial response to war was not a function of the commitment to *laissez-faire* but rather the result of a failure to anticipate the consequences of war for the civilian economy.[66] Thus 'business as usual' was perfectly rational in the light of military strategy in 1914, and, by implication, the war tells us little about the diuturnity of *laissez-faire* in peacetime.
3. Cline has attacked the Tawney theses, that because government viewed wartime controls as a temporary expedient they did not perceive that they might have peacetime applications, and instead tried to demonstrate that it was not the reassertion of orthodox economics in 1919 which stimied the future for state intervention, but the unexpected collapse of Germany in 1918 which made such policies unnecessary.[67]
4. Recently, Booth has questioned the whole tenor of recent writings (notably Peden and Aldcroft) which portray interwar economic policies as haphazard and inconsistent, and which assume that 'Keynesian policies [were] the *sine qua non* of rationality in economic policy-making.'[68]

The first revision has stood the test of time, and seems to have been fully absorbed into the literature.[69]

The second and third revisions are much more open to doubt. French's thesis is flawed in one major essential, that military strategy and conceptions of war were themselves conditioned by *laissez-faire*. The classical economists' view of war stressed its destructive consequences and, at least as absorbed in Britain, led to the conclusion that there ought to be a small peacetime defence establishment and low taxation in order to create a stable economic base from which to conduct a war. Interestingly, French discusses these points but doesn't seem to make the logical connection.[70] Cline's revisionism is more difficult, for undoubtedly there is much of substance in his claim that it was the unexpected termination of the war which influenced subsequent events. However, the wealth of literature on the reconstruction period does point to a reassertion of economic orthodoxy and an extreme reaction against state controls and bureaucracy.[71]

Finally, we have Booth's thesis, where particular elements have not been well received,[72] although there is much in his claim that there was more consistency in Treasury policy of the 1930s than has hitherto been acknowledged.

Even with these revisions, however, the overriding impression created by the literature is that the interwar period saw the gradual erosion of *laissez-faire*; that it was characterized by increased state intervention which eroded the private domain; and that the important questions concern the eventual acceptance of Keynesian demand management which has been taken as synonymous with the managed economy. Thus, typically, we find the interwar period described in terms of progression from a 'participating' to a 'control' system,[73] with these changes being modelled in terms of the development of government instruments and objectives.

There is an alternative view and method which needs exploration: that increased intervention is not incompatible with *laissez-faire*; and that while policy instruments developed between the wars there is an observable consistency in government objectives. Thus, on this view, what is important about the interwar period is the extreme reluctance displayed by government, not to avoid intervention *per se*, but to forego intervention of a form which limited the domain of the private sector by changing the balance of market power. In this sense, Booth is undoubtedly right when he eschews the language of *laissez-faire* and instead talks of evolution from a facilitative to a support system.[74]

Before exploring this avenue we ought first to consider some problems associated with the term *laissez-faire*.

First, our understanding of this term in the interwar context is necessarily conditioned by our perception of its pre-war reality. Ever since Brebner's seminal paper,[75] the pre-war attachment to *laissez-faire* has been subject to much scrutiny.[76] Whilst debate continues it is clear that *laissez-faire* was never pursued literally in nineteenth-century Britain and that by 1914 there was a clear conception of how, even in the absence of technical economic market failure, government could intervene when the social consequences of market outcomes were deemed unacceptable.[77] This has particular importance for a theme to be developed later, that the pressure for greater intervention in the interwar period came not from economic failures *per se* but from their social and political consequences. It is debatable whether this literature has been properly assimilated into our conception of the interwar period, with obvious consequences.

Secondly, the association of the term *laissez-faire* with the classical economists carries with it the danger of assuming some direct connection between economic theory and economic policy. It is now clear that there is no such simple association for the interwar period,[78] and that our expectation that there might be was conditioned by the dominance of the Keynesian historiography.

If then there are problems with the existing terminology and methodology, how might we develop a more realistic approach? Three possibilities suggest themselves.

To begin with, we can salvage something from the instruments-and-objectives approach which has long characterized the literature. Whilst there are dangers in drawing conclusions from a simple temporal comparison of the instruments and objectives of government in the economic sphere, careful specification can illuminate important issues about the balance of political power and its implications for the market order. The following three examples of state activity illustrate this approach.

First, let us take the government-sponsored industrial rationalization schemes, which might be interpreted as a very significant development in the growth of state intervention. In reality they demonstrate that the state was trying to preserve the free market order by facilitating the private sector's own rationalization of particular markets, this by the most careful selection of instruments and intermediaries (like the Bank of England and the Import Duties Advisory Committee) which were not directly under its control.[79] As Hall rightly notes, the 'striking feature of British intervention' has been its highly consensual nature, 'in which state-supported schemes are essentially directed by the private sector.'[80] In the interwar period part of the responsibility for this must be laid at the door of the government's chief industrial adviser,[81] who sought 'to keep government intervention in industry covert and to regenerate employment, ostensibly at least, through the market'.[82] Thus, in industrial policy, whilst there might have been the appearance of the erosion of *laissez-faire*, the private sector's autonomy was not significantly diminished.

Our second example, that of the development of public corporations between the wars, yields similar conclusions: that the state sought to preserve the free market order in the face of changing technical and economic conditions.[83] Thus, there was one very limited case of a transfer of ownership to the public sector between the wars, that of London passenger transport,[84] whereas the creation of the BBC, the CEB and others 'did not constitute precedents for a policy of nationalisation. They were both the result of technical and scientific developments. No transfer of ownership took place.'[85] Moreover, the public corporations were 'removed from direct and continuous *political control* and made subject to political control only of an indirect and spasmodic nature',[86] this administrative structure mirroring our earlier observations about the state's response to its own enlargement.

Our third example concerns central-local government relations and the Keynesian solution for interwar unemployment which focused upon public works expenditures to stimulate employment. Public works were largely under the control of local authorities, and it is clear that an essential foundation of the Treasury's objections to the Keynesian solution was that it would have entailed greater centralization and a transformation of the respective constitutional positions of the centre and the localities. In this respect, therefore, the state (here represented as central government) chose not to enlarge its powers when faced with economic crisis.[87]

Turning from the instruments-and-objectives approach, we might instead take a more agnostic position and reject altogether general explanations of state intervention. Thus, the economic dimension of the interwar state could be perceived in terms of a process of 'muddling through', of conscious empiricism but with little ideological commitment, an approach for which there is a long tradition in the literature,[88] and one which mirrors the conclusions of Hicks and Barna reported earlier.

This approach is perfectly compatible with our current view of pre-1914 *laissez-faire* as far less doctrinaire than was previously imagined; it can also make comprehensible one of the overriding characteristics of the interwar state, namely that the various state agencies appeared to be pursuing different policies at different times with little consistency between them. Thus the interwar state cannot be taken as an homogenous entity, and insofar as a more coherent and planned set of policies did emerge these were the consequence of the Second World War and its aftermath.

Finally, we could adopt a market-based approach to the analysis of government growth. This would retain some of the features of the instruments-and-objectives approach but focus much more clearly on the main factor and goods markets and the way their operation was altered by state intervention. This is likely to have the greatest appeal to the economist, and the following is by way of an introduction to the main themes. It is the beginnings of the analysis which forms the subject of my current research.

First, let us examine factor markets, where we begin with the labour market, which has a long tradition of state intervention. Typically intervention had been prompted by social concerns, but at the beginning of the century attention also turned to the economic efficiency of this market with the establishment of labour exchanges, and suchlike.[89] Pre-war intervention, however, had also affected this market by raising the price of labour (the development of trade union and minimum wage legislation, the introduction of unemployment insurance, etc.), and restricting its supply (the introduction of old age pensions).

Interwar developments built upon these foundations; there were few innovations, though the degree of regulation increased substantially. Two aspects of government policy which affected the market's operation require particular mention.

First, there is the debate engendered by Benjamin's and Kochin's paper,[90] where they argued that interwar unemployment was not due to deficient aggregate demand but largely the consequence of the operation of the unemployment insurance system, with its high replacement ratio (the ratio of unemployment benefits to wages). This thesis, which has not fared well in the face of detailed scrutiny,[91] is a development of interwar concerns about the effect of unemployment insurance on the labour market.[92] For government, however, the most pressing problem was the budgetary cost of insurance benefits. This is not to argue that the economic consequences of the insurance system for the market's operation were not appreciated; rather, that the whole episode illustrates how interwar governments became committed for political reasons to social programmes and then had to bear the adverse economic consequences.

The question of government policy towards the labour market also requires a more general comment. Interwar governments shared the concern of contemporary neo-classical economists that unemployment was exacerbated by real wage resistance.[93] However, they remained aloof from the process of real wage adjustment at the microeconomic level. As Checkland puts it:

It left to the employers the task of restoring due proportions in terms of wages, doing so firm by firm and sector by sector. In this way the most volatile aspect of economic control was kept out of politics. In a sense this was at the expense of business, placing it in a confrontational relationship to labour. But for the state to assume a positive wage-fixing role on any scale would have been to make politicians and bureaucrats the arbiters of the central problem of all economies, namely the distribution of the product year by year.[94]

At the macroeconomic level, of course, government had a considerable influence upon the conditions in which these microeconomic adjustments took place. However, since government had no commitment to macroeconomic management, and little consciousness of its effects before the late 1930s,[95] its alienated position regarding microeconomic operations seemed perfectly tenable. More importantly, it also had considerable political benefits.

Turning now to the other factor market, that for capital, there were important developments in the instruments and objectives of government.[96] In the pre-war period there had evolved a system of financial regulation supervised by the independent Bank of England, and where the principal objectives were to maintain an open capital market (both domestic and external) and to promote London's financial services.

The serious deterioration of the current and capital accounts of the balance of payments occasioned by the First World War was then to force major changes.[97] To begin with, however, the desire to return to normality – characteristic of the early 1920s – suggested that governments might be able to limit their agenda to pre-war objectives, while agreeing that new instruments would be necessary. Thus the gold standard was readopted in 1925 at pre-war parity, but was managed much more than even the pre-war system. Even so, the authorities were still motivated by the belief that the gold standard was sufficient of an automatic mechanism to offer some protection against political abuse of monetary policy,[98] at this time the principal macroeconomic policy instrument.

As is well known, Britain could not sustain the gold standard system, and it was abandoned in September 1931. The full significance of subsequent events has not yet been appreciated, for during the rest of the 1930s the authorities pursued a managed float of sterling calculated to depress its exchange value in order to stimulate exports.[99] Moreover, the 1930s also saw the origins of modern exchange controls and, during the period of the War Loan conversion operation, the capital market was subject to an extraordinary degree of control. Thus, in the capital market, state intervention increased enormously, though the Treasury was careful to maintain the appearance that the Bank of England was controlling events. In reality, as Norman, the governor of the Bank of England, put it:

> When the Gold Standard was abandoned, there took place an immediate redistribution of authority and responsibility, which deprived the Bank of some of its essential functions. Foreign Exchange became a Treasury matter, and perhaps it still remains to be seen what other responsibilities pass with it from Threadneedle Street to Whitehall.[100]

We can close this section of the paper with some brief observations about goods markets. Earlier we noted how government-sponsored industrial rationalization schemes had not resulted in a transfer of market power to the state. On the contrary, the effect of the various schemes in the staple industries was to enhance the position of the private sector, albeit at the cost of diminishing competition by strengthening barriers to entry and promoting cartelization and concentration.[101] Thus government did indeed undermine the free market, but not in the conventional manner; rather it gave free reign to private sector operators who proved perfectly adept at producing the same result.

This general development was accompanied by greatly increased state intervention in specific goods markets. This is evident in the field of tariffs, where the Dyestuffs (Import Regulation) Act, 1920, and the Safeguarding of Industries Act, 1921, established 'key' industries which were to be protected, a process consolidated in the Import Duties Act, 1932, which codified a fully protectionist regime.[102] Many of the early protectionist measures were justified on strategic grounds, as a response to supply weaknesses revealed by the war. However, infant industries, such as motor vehicles, also received protection, while in the 1930s 'agriculture became one of the most highly protected, heavily subsidised and organised of all British industries'.[103] Extraordinary subsidies were also paid, such as to the coal industry in 1925-6 to lessen industrial discontent and to aid readjustment to the changed market conditions compelled by the return to the gold standard. And finally, regional policies, which eventually developed financial assistance which was spatially differentiated, affected the market order and brought the state into closer contact with the company sector.

Were the whole range of goods markets to be surveyed there would no doubt emerge a very varied picture of state intervention, this in keeping with our earlier conclusion that governmental responses were pragmatic rather than part of some grand design. There was a strong sense of 'muddling through', with individual policy responses being dependent upon crisis management and the strength of sectional interests. This as maybe, there were nonetheless some important principles which guided action and which show a continuity with pre-war economic principles. In particular, it is clear that the Treasury was anxious to avoid policies which undermined the spontaneous forces of the market, the foundation of which they saw as entrepreneurial independence and initiative.[104] A further characteristic of interwar state intervention was a type of self-denying ordinance within the political class, a concern to preserve constitutional constraints (in particular those embodied in budgetary policies) which were seen as essential foundations of the free market order.

Conclusions

Economists have typically viewed government growth in terms of market failure; indeed, this underpins the whole Keynesian literature on the interwar period. However, market failure needs careful specification in order to distinguish between its two forms. On the one hand, there is technical economic failure, where markets performs inefficiently relative to government provision of goods and services. On the other hand, there is the case that even when markets operate efficiently in the technical economic sense, they may produce results − for example, income distributions and conditions of competition − which lack social acceptance and thus generate pressures for intervention.[105]

Keynes's case for increased state intervention between the wars derived from his analysis of technical economic failure in the labour market.[106] However, it was market failure in the sense of lack of social acceptance of market outcomes which proved the more influential in determining the course of events. The background to this was the 'adjustment to democracy' (Lowe's phrase) discussed earlier, while further supporting evidence is provided by the record of social expenditures. These were the most rapidly growing category of public expenditure, increasing in nominal terms by 47.1 per cent between 1924 and 1937, from 5.3 to 6.1 per cent of GDP.[107] Moreover, the temporal characteristics of this development are important, as social expenditures growth was much more rapid in the 1920s than the 1930s. The upward trend of real wage growth was slightly faster in 1924-29 than 1929-37;[108] nonetheless, it may have been that workers responded to economic depression by demanding a higher social wage, and that this process was all the stronger in the 1920s because of the frustrated hopes of the reconstruction period.

The issue of technical market failure is important in another sense, for it raises the question of the effectiveness of state intervention. The literature on the interwar British economy is greatly divided about the efficiency of the market mechanism in resource allocation and thus the justification for policy intervention. Adopting Broadberry's taxonomy,[109] there are the 'pessimists' (represented in the traditional Keynesian interpretation), who judge the market inefficient and thus as requiring state intervention; and the 'optimists' (represented by the new classical macroeconomics and others) who take the contrary view. We offer no conclusions about this here, save that there remains scope for a more systematic evaluation of interwar market operation and policy effectiveness.

Returning now to broader issues, our overall conclusion must be that in terms of government growth there was more continuity between the pre-war and interwar periods than has hitherto been acknowledged, thereby affirming the role of the Second World War in the development of the modern state. One important development, however, requires mention. As a consequence of political forces, and the evolution of government economic thinking, belief in the 'invisible hand' not so much evaporated as became politically irrelevant. Keynes's central message, that capitalist economies are not self-stabilizing,[110] was accepted in principle, although no government would countenance peacetime deficit-finance as the remedy for deficient demand.

One other observation about the interwar British state also seems appropriate in this context. It has been the general practice to view economic management during the First World War in the light of attempts to preserve *laissez-faire*. We might instead argue that deficiencies in the management of the war economy, in particular the reluctance to impose higher tax levels,[111] resulted in a huge debt burden which actually hastened the demise of the system that the authorities had sought to preserve. This has an echo in Keynes's complaint that 'capitalist leaders in the City and in Parliament are incapable of distinguishing novel measures for safeguarding capitalism from what they call Bolshevism.'[112]

Finally, in any analysis of the growth of government, there remains the problem of reference points. The interwar British state cannot be viewed in isolation from the experience of other advanced industrial countries. We need a comparative economic history, since, in Britain as elsewhere, government growth was as much conditioned by external developments as internal forces. Unfortunately, we do not yet have the raw material for such an exercise. The literature on government growth is largely national in orientation, and where it does have a European or international perspective it tends to focus on economic performance and macroeconomic policies.[113] Moreover, even this literature is very variable, with no comparable volume on the interwar period to that of Boltho's study of the postwar European economy.[114] The statistical basis for such an exercise, however, has greatly improved in recent years. We now have both Mitchell's collection and the fruits of the HIWED project (Historical Indicators of the Western European Democracies).[115] While there are some useful long-term studies of the European states in the Fontana economic history of Europe,[116] and the project begun by Milward on the origins of the European Community,[117] the full potential of comparative economic history has yet to be realized for the interwar period.

Notes

1. This paper is a preliminary report on work in progress, and is drawn from a larger project on economic management and the market order in twentieth-century Britain to be published by Edward Elgar in 1992; the section on public expenditure and taxation is based upon my earlier study, *Towards the Managed Economy: Keynes, the Treasury and the Fiscal Policy Debate of the 1930s* (London, 1985), chapters 3, 4. I should like to thank the British Academy and the University of Bristol research fund for financial assistance; and Alan Booth, Bernard Harris, Rodney Lowe and George Peden for their helpful comments on an early version of this paper. Any remaining errors of fact, analysis and interpretation are, of course, entirely my own.
2. Initial doubts about whether there was a Keynesian revolution in British economic policy were first raised by J. Tomlinson, 'Why was there never a "Keynesian Revolution" in Economic Policy?', *Economy and Society*, X (1981), 72-87, who was much influenced by the revisionist work of R.C.O. Matthews, 'Why has Britain had Full Employment since the War?', *Economic Journal*, LXXVIII (1968), 555-69. The debate now has an extensive literature; see A. Booth, 'The "Keynesian Revolution" in Economic Policy-making', *Economic History Review*, 2nd ser., XXXVI (1983), 103-23; *idem*, 'Defining a "Keynesian Revolution"', *Economic History Review*, 2nd ser., XXXVII (1984), 263-7; *idem*, 'The "Keynesian Revolution" and Economic Policy-making: A Reply', *Economic History*

Review, 2nd ser., XXXVIII (1985), 101-6; *idem*, 'Britain in the 1930s: A Managed Economy?', *Economic History Review*, 2nd ser., XL (1987), 499-522; Middleton, *Towards the Managed Economy*; *idem*, 'Britain in the 1930s: A Managed Economy? A Comment', *Economic History Review*, 2nd ser., XLII (1989); G.C. Peden, *Keynes, the Treasury and British Economic Policy* (London, 1988); N. Rollings, 'The "Keynesian Revolution" and Economic Policy-making: A Comment', *Economic History Review*, 2nd ser., XXXVIII (1985), 95-100; 'British Budgetary Policy 1945-54: A "Keynesian Revolution"', *Economic History Review*, 2nd ser., XLI (1988), 283-98; K. Schott, 'The Rise of Keynesian Economics: Britain 1940-64', *Economy and Society*, XI (1982), 292-316; and J. Tomlinson, 'A "Keynesian Revolution" in Economic Policy-making', *Economic History Review*, 2nd ser., XXXVII (1984), 258-62; *idem*, *British Macroeconomic Policy since 1940* (London, 1985); *idem*, *Employment Policy: The Crucial Years 1939-1955* (Oxford, 1987). At present the debate has made little progress, in part because we still do not have a generally accepted definition of the Keynesian revolution.

3. See the survey by P.D. Larkey, C. Stolp and M. Winer, 'Theorizing about the Growth of Government: A Research Assessment', *Journal of Public Policy*, I (1981), 157-220.

4. B.G. Peters and M.O. Heisler, 'Thinking about Public Sector Growth: Conceptual, Operational, Theoretical and Policy Considerations', in *Why Governments Grow: Measuring Public Sector Size* (ed. C.L. Taylor, London, 1983), p.178.

5. C.L. Taylor, 'Introduction: Multiple Approaches to Measurement and Explanation', in *Why Governments Grow*, p.14.

6. Peters and Heisler, 'Thinking about Public Sector Growth', pp.186, 191.

7. Royal Commission on the Private Manufacture of and Trading in Arms, *Report*, BPP 1935-6 (5292), vii, 483 (London, 1936); P. Noel-Baker, *The Private Manufacture of Armaments* (London, 1936), I; J.W. Grove, *Government and Industry in Britain* (London, 1962); R.C. Trebilcock, 'A "Special Relationship": Government, Rearmament and the Cordite Firms', *Economic History Review*, 2nd ser., XIX (1966), 364-79.

8. A.F. Lucas, *Industrial Reconstruction and the Control of Competition: The British Experiments* (London, 1937); L.P. Carpenter, 'Corporatism in Britain 1930-45', *Journal of Contemporary History*, XI (1976), 3-25; K. Middlemas, *Politics in Industrial Society: The Experience of the British System since 1911* (London, 1979); A. Booth, 'Corporatism, Capitalism and Depression in Twentieth-century Britain', *British Journal of Sociology*, XXXIII (1982), 200-23; L. Hannah, *The Rise of the Corporate Economy* (London, 2nd edition, 1983).

9. Figure 1, drawn from G. White and H. Chapman, 'Long-Term Trends in Public Expenditure', *Economic Trends*, no. 408 (1987), chart 2, details higher expenditure ratios for general government and its components than those presented later in this paper (which are drawn from C.H. Feinstein, *National Income, Expenditure and Output of the United Kingdom 1855-1965* (Cambridge, 1972), who provides data from which consolidated accounts can be calculated for 1900-65). Both the numerator and denominator are different, and a full reconciliation of the two series is precluded by the fact that White's and Chapman's table 2 is most inexact in its references to their main sources for pre-1948 data (A.T. Peacock and J. Wiseman, *The Growth of Public Expenditure in the United Kingdom* (London, 2nd edition, 1967); Feinstein, *National Income*). It should also be noted that White's and Chapman's series for spending on goods and services does not represent the public sector's command of total resources, which more properly should include public sector capital formation.

10. Peacock and Wiseman, *Growth of Public Expenditure*.

11. By 1920 nominal expenditure stood at over four times the 1913 level. While the intervening price inflation ensured that the real increase was much lower — at between 1.5 and 1.7 times, depending upon assumptions made about the price deflator — it was the nominal increase which nonetheless commanded public attention, strengthening the campaign for postwar retrenchment.

12. D.R. Cameron, 'The Expansion of the Public Economy: A Comparative Analysis', *American Political Science Review*, LXXII (1978), 1243-61; *Secular Trends of the Public Sector* (ed. H.C. Recktenwald, Paris, 1978), Proceedings of the 32nd Congress of the International Institute of Public Finance.

13. A. Wagner, 'Three Extracts on Public Finance', in *Classics in the Theory of Public Finance* (ed. R.A. Musgrave and A.T. Peacock, London, 1958), pp.1-15.

14. See K.A. Chrystal and J.E. Alt, 'Endogenous Government Behaviour: Wagner's Law or Gotterdammerung?', in *Current Issues in Fiscal Policy* (ed. S.T. Cook and P.M. Jackson, Oxford, 1979), pp.123-37; *idem*, 'Some Problems in Formulating and Testing a Politico-

Economic Model of the United Kingdom', *Economic Journal*, XCI (1981), 730-6; J.E. Alt and K.A. Chrystal, *Political Economics* (Brighton, 1983).

15. M. Friedman, *Theory of the Consumption Function* (Princeton, 1957); A. Wildavsky, *The Politics of the Budgetary Process* (Boston, 1964).
16. See Chrystal and Alt, 'Endogenous Government Behaviour', table 6.1.
17. *Ibid.*, p.132.
18. Thus much current empirical work cannot address many of the interesting questions about public expenditure growth which concern transfer payments and the political forces associated with them.
19. Data from appendix table 1.
20. OECD, *Public Expenditure Trends* (Paris, 1978), OECD Studies in Resource Allocation no. 5, p.12.
21. Middleton, *Towards the Managed Economy*, chapter 3.
22. J. Tomlinson, Review of Middleton, *Towards the Managed Economy*, *Economic History Review*, 2nd ser., XXXIX (1986), 306.
23. R.M. Titmuss, *Problems of Social Policy* (London, 1950); *idem*, 'War and Social Policy', reprinted in *Essays on 'the Welfare State'* (ed. R.M. Titmuss, London, 2nd edition, 1963), pp.75-87.
24. Mention should be made, however, of one sphere in which the general trend of an extension of the public sector did not operate to such a marked degree, that of employment (see M. Abramovitch and V.F. Eliasberg, *The Growth of Public Employment in Great Britain* (Princeton, 1957)). Public sector employment had expanded during the war, but as with expenditure, was curtailed in the immediate postwar period. Thereafter, public sector employment was only to rise marginally faster than total employment, increasing its share from 5.1 to 5.3% over 1924-37 (Feinstein, *National Income*, tables 57, 59, 60). There were, however, important compositional effects: employment in local government rose continuously, whereas employment in central government fell until the later 1920s and in the defence forces until the early 1930s. For data on the interwar experience of other European states, see R.C. Eichenberg, 'Problems in Using Public Employment Data', in *Why Governments Grow*, pp.136-53.
25. See OECD, *Historical Statistics 1960-1985* (Paris, 1987), table 6.5.
26. See Middleton, *Towards the Managed Economy*, figure 4.1.
27. B.E.V. Sabine, *A History of Income Tax* (London, 1966), p.154.
28. See B. Mallet and C.O. George, *British Budgets, Third Series, 1921-22 to 1932-33* (London, 1933); B.E.V. Sabine, *British Budgets in Peace and War 1932-1945* (London, 1970); Middleton, *Towards the Managed Economy*, chapter 4.
29. A. Johnston, *The Inland Revenue* (London, 1965), p.16.
30. Report of the Committee on National Debt and Taxation (Colwyn Committee), *Appendices* (London, 1927), p.128; *Eightieth Report of the Commissioners of His Majesty's Inland Revenue for the year ended 31st March 1937*, Cmd. 5574 (London, 1938), table 44.
31. Colwyn Committee, *Appendices*, p.98.
32. See Cameron, 'The Expansion of the Public Economy'; Taylor, 'Introduction', pp.11-21; Alt and Chrystal, *Political Economics*, chapter 8; P. Whiteley, *Political Control of the Macroeconomy: The Political Control of Public Policy Making* (London, 1986), chapter 2.
33. Middleton, 'The Constant Employment Budget Balance and British Budgetary Policy 1929-39', *Economic History Review*, 2nd ser., XXXIV (1981), 165-6.
34. R.C.O. Matthews, C.H. Feinstein and J.C. Odling-Smee, *British Economic Growth 1856-1973* (Oxford, 1982), table 10.7.
35. Philip (later Lord) Snowden: Labour MP; Chancellor of the Exchequer, 1924, 1929-31; Lord Privy Seal 1931-32. See R. Skidelsky, *Politicians and the Slump: The Labour Government of 1929-31* (London, 1967); R. McKibbin, 'The Economic Policy of the Second Labour Government 1929-1931', *Past and Present*, LXVIII (1975), 95-123.
36. Middleton, *Towards the Managed Economy*, pp.80-3.
37. Alt and Chrystal, *Political Economics*, p.194.
38. W.A. Niskanen, *Bureaucracy and Representative Government* (New York, 1971).
39. See E.W. Cohen, *The Growth of the British Civil Service 1780-1939* (London, 1941); H.E. Dale, *The Higher Civil Service of Great Britain* (Oxford, 1941); G.K. Fry, *Statesmen in Disguise: The Changing Role of the Administrative Class of the British Home Civil Service 1853-1966* (London, 1969); M. Beloff, 'The Whitehall Factor: The Role of the Higher Civil Service 1919-39', in *The Politics of Reappraisal 1919-1939* (ed. C. Cook and G. Peele,

London, 1975), pp.209-31; R. Davidson and R. Lowe, 'Bureaucracy and Innovation in British Welfare Policy 1870-1945', in *The Emergence of the Welfare State in Britain and Germany* (ed. W. Mommsen, London, 1981), pp.263-95; R. Lowe, 'Bureaucracy Triumphant or Denied? The Expansion of the British Civil Service 1919-39', *Public Administration*, LXII (1984), 291-310; and *idem, Adjusting to Democracy: The Role of the Ministry of Labour in British Politics 1916-1939* (Oxford, 1986).

40. See T.L. Heath, *The Treasury* (London, 1927); E.E. Bridges, *Treasury Control* (London, 1950); *idem, Portrait of a Profession: The Civil Service Tradition* (Cambridge, 1950); and *The Treasury* (London, 2nd edition, 1966); S.H. Beer, *Treasury Control: The Co-ordination of Financial and Economic Policy* (Oxford, 1956); H. Roseveare, *The Treasury: The Evolution of a British Institution* (London, 1969); G.C. Peden, *British Rearmament and the Treasury 1932-1939* (Edinburgh, 1979); *idem,* 'The Treasury as the Central Department of Government 1919-1939', *Public Administration*, LXI (1983), 371-85; Middleton, 'The Treasury in the 1930s: Political and Administrative Constraints to Acceptance of the "New" Economics', *Oxford Economic Papers*, new series, XXXIV (1982), 48-77; *idem,* 'The Treasury and Public Investment: A Perspective on Interwar Economic Management', *Public Administration*, LXI (1983), 351-70; and *idem, Towards the Managed Economy*.

41. Lowe, *Adjusting to Democracy*.

42. C. Webster, 'Healthy or Hungry Thirties?', *History Workshop Journal*, XIII (1982), 110-29; and *idem,* 'The Health of the School Child during the Depression', in *The Fitness of the Nation: Physical and Health Education in the Nineteenth and Twentieth Centuries* (ed. N. Parry and D. MacNair, Leicester, 1983), pp.70-85; M. Mayhew, 'The 1930s Nutrition Controversy', *Journal of Contemporary History*, XXIII (1988), 445-64.

43. P. Dunleavy and V. O'Leary, *Theories of the State: The Politics of Liberal Democracy* (London, 1987), pp.112-13.

44. Lowe, 'Bureaucracy Triumphant or Denied?', p.309.

45. Middleton, *Towards the Managed Economy*, p.40.

46. Committee on National Expenditure (May Committee), *Report*, BPP 1930-1 (3920), xvi, 1 (London, 1931), pp.12-13.

47. Middleton, *Towards the Managed Economy*, p.39. In addition, difficulties are also raised for any assessment of the impact of fiscal operations, a subject explored *ibid.*, chapter 7.

48. U.K. Hicks, *The Finance of British Government 1920-1936* (Oxford, 1938), pp.42-3.

49. Neville Chamberlain: Conservative MP; Minister of Health 1923, 1924-9, 1931; Chancellor of the Exchequer 1931-7; Prime Minister 1937-40; see Middleton, 'Fiscal Policy and Economic Management in the 1930s' (unpublished PhD dissertation, University of Cambridge, 1981), pp.131, 163-76.

50. W.D. Rubinstein, *Wealth and Inequality in Britain* (London, 1986), p.72.

51. T. Barna, *Redistribution of Incomes through Public Finance in 1937* (Oxford, 1945), p.236.

52. M. Olson, *The Rise and Decline of Nations: Economic Growth, Stagflation and Social Rigidities* (London, 1982).

53. Middleton, *Towards the Managed Economy*, p.88; see also *idem,* 'The Treasury in the 1930s'; Tomlinson, *Employment Policy*; Peden, *Keynes, the Treasury and British Economic Policy*.

54. However, F. Capie (*Depression and Protectionism: Britain between the Wars* (London, 1983)) does discuss the introduction of the general tariff with some reference to these concerns.

55. A. Booth, 'An Administrative Experiment in Unemployment Policy in the 'Thirties', *Public Administration*, LVI (1978), 140.

56. H. Hutchinson, *Tariff-Making and Industrial Reconstruction: An Account of the Work of the Import Duties Advisory Committee 1932-39* (London, 1965).

57. On monetary policy, see D.E. Moggridge, *British Monetary Policy 1924-1931: The Norman Conquest of $4.86* (Cambridge, 1972); S. Howson, *Domestic Monetary Management in Britain 1919-38* (Cambridge, 1975); *idem, Sterling's Managed Float: The Operations of the Exchange Equalisation Account 1932-9* (Princeton, 1980), Studies in International Finance no. 46; and I.M. Drummond, *The Floating Pound and the Sterling Area 1931-1939* (Cambridge, 1981); on fiscal policy, Middleton, 'The Constant Employment Budget Balance'; *idem,* 'The Measurement of Fiscal Influence in Britain in the 1930s', *Economic History Review*, 2nd ser., XXXVII (1984), 103-6; *idem, Towards the Managed Economy*; and S.N. Broadberry, *The British Economy between the Wars: A Macroeconomic Survey* (Oxford, 1986); and on regional policy, D.E. Pitfield, 'The

144

Quest for an Effective Regional Policy 1934-37', *Regional Studies*, XII (1978), 429-43; A. Booth, 'The Second World War and the Origins of Modern Regional Policy', *Economy and Society*, XI (1982), 1-21; C. Heim, 'Industrial Organization and Regional Development in Interwar Britain', *Journal of Economic History*, XLIII (1983), 931-52; idem, 'Interwar Responses to Regional Decline', in *The Decline of the British Economy* (ed. B. Elbaum and W. Lazonick, Oxford, 1986), pp.240-65; and Middleton, 'Unemployment in the North-east during the Interwar Period', in *Public Policy Studies: The North East of England* (ed. R.A. Chapman, Edinburgh, 1985), pp.20-43. There is, however, no modern work on industrial policy, although Elbaum and Lazonick's *Decline of the British Economy* and R. Roberts (The Administrative Origins of Industrial Diplomacy: An Aspect of Government-Industry Relations 1929-1935', in *Businessmen and Politics: Studies of Business Activity in British Politics 1900-1945* (ed. J. Turner, London, 1984), pp.93-104, and idem, 'The Board of Trade 1924-1939' (unpublished DPhil dissertation, University of Oxford, 1987) provide much of interest, while *British Industry between the Wars: Instability and Industrial Development 1919-1939* (ed. N.K. Buxton and D.H. Aldcroft, London, 1979) contains a detailed survey of individual industries; see also R. Lowe and R. Roberts, 'Sir Horace Wilson 1900-1935: The Making of a Mandarin', *Historical Journal*, XXX (1987), 641-62. For broader, macroeconomic policy surveys, see also D. Winch, *Economics and Policy: A Historical Study* (London, revised edition, 1972), and S. Howson and D. Winch, *The Economic Advisory Council 1930-1939: A Study in Economic Advice during Depression and Recovery* (Cambridge, 1977). There is currently no work which gives a broad survey of interwar microeconomic policies.

58. The main works are: A. Booth and S. Glynn, 'Unemployment in the Interwar Period: A Multiple Problem', *Journal of Contemporary History*, X (1975), 611-36; idem, 'Interwar Unemployment: Restatement and Comments', *Journal of Contemporary History*, XV (1980), 761-8; and idem, 'Interwar Unemployment: Two Views', *Journal of Contemporary History*, XVII (1982), 550-5; J. Tomlinson, 'Unemployment and Government Policy between the Wars: A Note', *Journal of Contemporary History*, XIII (1978), 65-75; idem, 'Interwar Unemployment: Two Views', *Journal of Contemporary History*, XVII (1982), 545-50; S. Glynn and P.G.A. Howells, 'Unemployment in the 1930s: The "Keynesian Solution" Reconsidered', *Australian Economic History Review*, XX (1980), 28-45; T. Thomas, 'Aggregate Demand in the United Kingdom 1918-45', in *The Economic History of Britain since 1700*, II, *1860 to the 1970s* (ed. R. Floud and D. McCloskey, Cambridge, 1981), pp.332-46; Middleton, 'The Treasury and Public Investment'; idem, *Towards the Managed Economy*; S. Glynn and A. Booth, 'Unemployment in Interwar Britain: A Case for Re-learning the Lessons of the 1930s', *Economic History Review*, 2nd ser., XXXVI (1983), 329-48; and 'Building Counterfactual Pyramids', *Economic History Review*, 2nd ser., XXXVIII (1985), 89-94; D.H. Aldcroft, *Full Employment: The Elusive Goal* (Brighton, 1984); S. Glynn, A. Booth and P.G.A. Howells, 'Neh, Neh, Neh and the "Keynesian Solution"', *Australian Economic History Review*, XXV (1985), 149-57; T.J. Hatton, 'Unemployment in the 1930s and the "Keynesian Solution": Some Notes of Dissent', *Australian Economic History Review*, XXV (1985), 129-45; idem, 'The Outlines of a Keynesian Solution', in *The Road to Full Employment* (ed. S. Glynn and A. Booth, London, 1987), pp.82-94; W.R. Garside and T.J. Hatton, 'Keynesian Policy and British Unemployment in the 1930s', *Economic History Review*, 2nd ser., XXXVIII (1985), 83-8; and Broadberry, *British Economy*.

59. The standard works of H.W. Richardson, *Economic Recovery in Britain 1932-39* (London, 1967) and D.H. Aldcroft, *The Inter-War Economy: Britain 1919-1939* (London, 1970) are now very dated; for modern surveys, see N.H. Dimsdale, 'British Monetary Policy and the Exchange Rate 1920-1938', *Oxford Economic Papers*, new series, Supplement, XXXIII (1981), 306-49; J.F. Wright, 'Britain's Inter-war Experience', *Oxford Economic Papers*, new series, Supplement, XXXIII (1981), 282-305; G.D.N. Worswick, 'The Recovery in Britain in the 1930s', in *The UK Economic Recovery in the 1930s* (Bank of England Panel of Academic Consultants, London, 1984), pp.5-28; Broadberry, *British Economy*; K.G.P. Matthews, *The Inter-War Economy: An Equilibrium Analysis* (Aldershot, 1986); and P.K. O'Brien, 'Britain's Economy between the Wars: A Survey of a Counter-revolution in Economic History', *Past and Present*, CXV (1987), 107-30.

60. E.M.H. Lloyd, *Experiments in State Control at the War Office and the Ministry of Food* (Oxford, 1924); S.J. Hurwitz, *State Intervention in Great Britain: A Study of Economic Control and Social Response 1914-1919* (New York, 1949).

61. R.H. Tawney, 'The Abolition of Economic Controls 1918-21', *Economic History Review*,

XII, 1-30; S. Howson, 'The Origins of Dear Money 1919-20', *Economic History Review*, 2nd ser., XXVII (1974), 88-107.

62. K.J. Hancock, 'The Reduction of Unemployment as a Problem of Public Policy 1920-29', *Economic History Review*, 2nd ser., XV (1962), 328-43.
63. Winch, *Economics and Policy*; Howson, *Domestic Monetary Management in Britain*; G.C. Peden, *British Economic and Social Policy: Lloyd George to Margaret Thatcher* (Oxford, 1985), pp.118-19.
64. G.R. Searle, *The Quest for National Efficiency: A Study in British Politics and Political Thought 1899-1914* (Oxford, 1971); H.V. Emy, *Liberals, Radicals and Social Politics 1892-1914* (Cambridge, 1973).
65. See also R. Pearson and G. Williams, *Political Thought and Public Policy in the Nineteenth Century: An Introduction* (London, 1984), chapter 5.
66. D. French, 'The Rise and Fall of "Business as Usual"', in *War and the State: The Transformation of British Government 1914-1919* (ed. K. Burk, London, 1982), pp.7-31; and *British Economic and Strategic Planning 1905-1915* (London, 1982).
67. P. Cline, 'Winding Down the War Economy: British Plans for Peacetime Recovery 1916-19', in *War and the State*, pp.157-81; Tawney, 'The Abolition of Economic Controls'.
68. Booth, 'Britain in the 1930s', p.500; Peden, *British Economic and Social Policy*; D.H. Aldcroft, *The British Economy*, I, *The years of turmoil 1920-1951* (Brighton, 1986).
69. For example, G.K. Fry, *The Growth of Government: The Development of Ideas about the Role of the State and the Machinery and Functions of Government in Britain since 1780* (London, 1979); S. Checkland, *British Public Policy 1776-1939: An Economic, Social and Political Perspective* (Cambridge, 1983).
70. French, *British Economic and Strategic Planning*, chapter 1.
71. C.W. Baker, *Government Control and Operation of Industry in Great Britain and the United States* (New York, 1921); Lloyd, *Experiments in State Control*; E.V. Morgan, *Studies in British Financial Policy 1914-25* (London, 1952); P. Abrams, 'The Failure of Social Reform 1918-20', *Past and Present*, XXIV (1963), 43-64; P.B. Johnson, *Land Fit for Heroes: The Planning of British Reconstruction 1916-19* (Chicago, 1968); S.M.H. Armitage, *The Politics of Decontrol of Industry: Britain and the United States* (London, 1969); R. Lowe, 'The Erosion of State Intervention in Britain 1917-24', *Economic History Review*, 2nd ser., XXVII (1974), 270-86; Howson, 'The Origins of Dear Money'; and *Domestic Monetary Management in Britain*; M. Swenarton, *Homes Fit for Heroes: The Politics and Architecture of Early State Housing in Britain* (London, 1981); and K. Burk, 'The Treasury: From Impotence to Power', in *War and the State*, pp.84-107.
72. Middleton, 'Britain in the 1930s'; G.C. Peden, 'Britain in the 1930s: A Managed Economy? A Comment', *Economic History Review*, 2nd ser., XLII (1989).
73. D.H. Aldcroft, 'The Development of the Managed Economy before 1939', *Journal of Contemporary History*, IV (1969), 117.
74. Booth, 'Britain in the 1930s', p.501.
75. J.B. Brebner, 'Laissez-Faire and State Intervention in Nineteenth-Century Britain', *Journal of Economic History*, Supplement, VIII (1948), 59-73.
76. Searle, *The Quest for National Efficiency*; J.F. Harris, *Unemployment and Politics 1886-1914* (Oxford, 1972); G. Sutherland, ed., *Studies in the Growth of Nineteenth-Century Government* (London, 1972); Emy, *Liberals, Radicals and Social Politics*; J.R. Hay, *The Origins of the Liberal Welfare Reforms 1906-1914* (London, 1975); A.J. Taylor, *Laissez-Faire and State Intervention in Nineteenth-Century Britain* (London, 1975); P. Clarke, *Liberals and Social Democrats* (Cambridge, 1978); M. Freeden, *The New Liberalism: An Ideology of Social Reform* (Oxford, 1978); S. Collini, *Liberalism and Sociology: L.T. Hobhouse and Political Argument in England 1880-1914* (Cambridge, 1979); Checkland, *British Public Policy*.
77. A rather better, though perhaps inelegant, term for the position in 1914 would be 'laissez collectives faire' (P. Sargant Florence, *Industry and the State* (London, 1957), p.9).
78. J. Tomlinson, *Problems of British Economic Policy 1870-1945* (London, 1981), chapter 1; Middleton, *Towards the Managed Economy*, pp.4-5, 32, 36-7.
79. Thus F.M. Miller ('The Unemployment Policy of the National Government 1931-1936', *Historical Journal*, XIX (1976), 454) rightly describes government unemployment policy in the 1930s 'as the "private enterprise" solution to the depression'; see also Lucas, *Industrial Reconstruction*; M.W. Kirby, *The British Coalmining Industry 1870-1946: A Political and Economic History* (London, 1977); C.E. Heim, 'Limits to Intervention: The Bank of England and Industrial Diversification in the Depressed Areas', *Economic*

History Review, 2nd ser., XXXVII (1984), 533-50; Roberts, 'The Administrative Origins of Industrial Diplomacy'; and *idem*, 'The Board of Trade'.

80. P.A. Hall, 'The State and Economic Decline', in *Decline of the British Economy*, p.275.

81. Sir Horace Wilson, Permanent Secretary, Ministry of Labour 1921-9; H.M. Government's Chief Industrial Adviser 1930-39; Permanent Secretary, Treasury and Head of Civil Service 1939-42.

82. Lowe and Roberts, 'Sir Horace Wilson', pp.657.

83. For broad surveys, see T. O'Brien, *British Experiments in Public Ownership and Control: A Study of the Central Electricity Board, British Broadcasting Corporation, London Passenger Transport Board* (London, 1937); *Public Enterprise: Developments in Social Ownership and Control in Great Britain* (ed. W.A. Robson, London, 1937); *idem*, ed., *Problems of Nationalized Industry* (London, 1952); L. Gordon, *The Public Corporation in Great Britain* (Oxford, 1938); E.E. Barry, *Nationalisation in British Politics: The Historical Background* (London, 1965).

84. E. Davies, 'The London Passenger Transport Board', in *Public Enterprise*.

85. R. Kelf-Cohen, *British Nationalisation 1945-1973* (London, 1973), p.7.

86. O'Brien, *British Experiments in Public Ownership and Control*, p.17.

87. Middleton, 'The Treasury and Public Investment'.

88. See, for example, the Macmillan Committee's report: 'Of our own nation pre-eminently it may be said that it has attained its great position not by the pursuit of any preconceived plan but by a process of almost haphazard evolution based on trial and error, and aided by the practical aptitudes and instincts of our race.... There has been little conscious direction of the national activities to definite ends' (Committee on Finance and Industry, *Report*, BPP 1930-1 (3897), xiii, 219 (London, 1931), p.4). More recently, B.B. Gilbert (*British Social Policy 1914-1939* (London, 1970), p.308) has noted: 'In Britain between 1919 and 1939, a public social policy did indeed evolve, but it was nearly unnoticed by Parliament, by the papers, or, in fact, by the men making the decisions ... This policy evolved, like the British empire, in a fit of absence of mind. But it was no less a policy.'

89. Harris, *Unemployment and Politics*.

90. D.K. Benjamin and L.A. Kochin, 'Searching for an Explanation of Unemployment in Interwar Britain', *Journal of Political Economy*, LXXXVII (1979), 441-78.

91. See M. Collins, 'Unemployment in Interwar Britain: Still Searching for an Explanation', *Journal of Political Economy*, XC (1982), 369-79; D. Metcalf, S.J. Nickell and N. Floros, 'Still Searching for an Explanation of Unemployment in Interwar Britain', *Journal of Political Economy*, XC (1982), 386-99; P.A. Ormerod and G.D.N. Worswick, 'Unemployment in Interwar Britain', *Journal of Political Economy*, XC (1982), 400-9; T.J. Hatton, 'Unemployment Benefits and the Macroeconomics of the Interwar Labour Market', *Oxford Economic Papers*, new series, XXXV (1983), 486-505; Broadberry, *British Economy*, chapter 10; see also Benjamin and Kochin's reply, 'Unemployment and Unemployment Benefits in Twentieth-Century Britain: A Reply to our Critics', *Journal of Political Economy*, XC (1982), 410-36.

92. E. Cannan, *An Economist's Protest* (London, 1927); H. Clay, *The Post-war Unemployment Problem* (London, 1929); W.H. Beveridge, *Unemployment: A Problem of Industry* (London, 2nd edition, 1930); J.R. Hicks, *The Theory of Wages* (London, 1932); A.C. Pigou, *Theory of Unemployment* (London, 1933); see also M. Casson, *Economics of Unemployment: A Historical Perspective* (Oxford, 1983).

93. For example, *Memoranda on Certain Proposals Relating to Unemployment*, BPP 1928-9 (3331), xvi, 873 (London, 1929), p.52.

94. Checkland, *British Public Policy*, p.343.

95. Middleton, *Towards the Managed Economy*, pp.117-20, 173-6.

96. A.T.K. Grant, *A Study of the Capital Market in Post-War Britain* (London, 1937); E. Nevin, *The Mechanism of Cheap Money: A Study of British Monetary Policy 1931-1939* (Cardiff, 1955); Howson, *Domestic Monetary Management in Britain*; R.S. Sayers, *The Bank of England 1891-1944* (3 vol., Cambridge, 1976); W.A. Thomas, *The Finance of British Industry 1918-1976* (London, 1978).

97. Moggridge, *British Monetary Policy*, chapter 2.

98. Middleton, *Towards the Managed Economy*, p.91.

99. Howson, *Sterling's Managed Float*.

100. H. Clay, *Lord Norman* (London, 1957), p.437.

101. Lucas, *Industrial Reconstruction*.

102. Capie, *Depression and Protectionism*.

103. Aldcroft, *The British Economy*, p.131; see also E.H. Whetham, *The Agrarian History of England and Wales*, VIII, *1914-39* (Oxford, 1978).
104. Middleton, 'Unemployment in the North-east', p.31.
105. F. Lehner and U. Widmaier, 'Market Failure and Growth of Government: A Sociological Explanation', in *Why Governments Grow*, pp.240-60.
106. J.M. Keynes, *The General Theory of Employment, Interest and Money* (London, 1936). Collected Writings of John Maynard Keynes, VII (1973).
107. Calculated from Feinstein, *National Income*, tables 3, 12, 33, 35.
108. Broadberry, *British Economy*, figure 2.5.
109. S.N. Broadberry, 'Unemployment in Interwar Britain: A Disequilibrium Approach' (unpublished DPhil dissertation, University of Oxford, 1982).
110. R. Middleton, 'Keynes's Legacy for Postwar Economic Management', in *Postwar British History* (ed. A. Gorst, L. Johnman and W. Scott Lucas, Leicester, 1989).
111. Between 1913/14 and 1918/19 the debt/GDP ratio rose from 0.26 to 1.24, with a consequent rise in the debt interest/GDP ratio from 0.01 to 0.05 (Middleton, 'The Treasury in the 1930s', p.54). The proportion of total expenditure that was tax-financed was only 36.2% between 1914/15 and 1919/20 as compared with approximately 50% between 1939 and 1945 (S. Pollard, *The Development of the British Economy 1914-1980* (London, 3rd edition, London, 1983), pp.32, 214).
112. J.M. Keynes, 'Am I a Liberal', in *Essays in Persuasion* (ed. J.M. Keynes, London, 1931). Collected Writings of John Maynard Keynes, IX (1972), p.299.
113. For example, H.V. Hodson, *Slump and Recovery 1929-1937: A Survey of World Economic Affairs* (London, 1938); H.W. Arndt, *The Economic Lessons of the Nineteen-Thirties* (London, 1944); C.P. Kindleberger, *The World in Depression 1929-1939* (London, 1973); Aldcroft, 'The Development of the Managed Economy'; *idem, From Versailles to Wall Street 1919-1929* (London, 1977); and *idem, The European Economy 1914-1970* (London, 1978).
114. A. Boltho, ed., *The European Economy: Growth and Crisis* (Oxford, 1982). There is, however, a recent international study of interwar unemployment; see *Interwar Unemployment in International Perspective* (ed. B. Eichengreen and T.J. Hatton, Dordrecht, 1988).
115. B.R. Mitchell, *European Historical Statistics 1750-1975* (London, 2nd edition, 1980); P. Flora, *et al.*, *State, Economy and Society in Western Europe 1815-1975*, I, *The Growth of Mass Democracies and Welfare States* (London, 1983).
116. *The Fontana Economic History of Europe*, V, *The Twentieth Century* (ed. C.M. Cipolla, Glasgow, 1976).
117. This is based at the Department of History and Civilization, European University Institute, Florence. Alan Milward's project, which is now directed by Richard Griffiths, is entitled 'Challenge and Response in Western Europe: The Origins of the European Community (1945-1950)'. It has produced a number of working papers; see also A.S. Milward, *The Reconstruction of Western Europe 1945-51* (London, 1985).

Appendix

Table 1
UK public sector accounts by economic classification as % of GDP at market prices 1900-39

	Public expenditure						Public sector receipts							
	Current goods and services	Gross capital formation	Subsidies and grants to private sector	Current grants paid abroad	Debt interest	Total	Taxes on income	Taxes on expenditure	Taxes on capital	National insurance contributions	Property income	Current grants from abroad	Total	Balance
1900	9.3	1.8	0.5	0.1	1.6	13.3	1.0	6.6	1.0	0.0	1.1	0.0	9.7	(3.6)
1901	10.0	2.0	0.5	0.2	1.6	14.4	1.5	6.7	0.9	0.0	1.1	0.0	10.3	(4.1)
1902	9.5	2.1	0.5	0.3	1.8	14.3	1.8	7.3	0.9	0.0	1.3	0.0	11.3	(3.0)
1903	8.5	1.9	0.4	0.2	2.0	12.9	1.9	7.3	0.9	0.0	1.4	0.0	11.5	(1.4)
1904	8.1	1.9	0.3	–	1.9	12.3	1.4	7.5	0.8	0.0	1.6	0.0	11.4	(0.9)
1905	7.9	1.6	0.3	–	1.9	11.8	1.5	7.4	0.8	0.0	1.6	0.0	11.3	(0.5)
1906	7.7	1.4	0.3	–	1.9	11.3	1.5	7.2	0.9	0.0	1.6	0.0	11.2	(0.1)
1907	7.6	1.3	0.3	–	1.8	10.9	1.5	7.2	0.9	0.0	1.7	0.0	11.2	0.3
1908	8.0	1.2	0.3	–	1.9	11.4	1.6	7.2	0.9	0.0	1.8	0.0	11.5	0.0
1909	8.1	1.1	0.7	–	1.9	11.8	1.5	7.0	1.0	0.0	1.8	0.0	11.4	(0.4)
1910	8.2	1.1	0.7	–	1.8	11.7	1.8	7.3	1.8	0.0	1.8	0.0	12.0	0.3
1911	8.1	1.0	0.7	–	1.8	11.6	1.8	7.2	1.1	0.0	1.8	0.0	11.9	0.3
1912	8.2	1.1	0.8	–	1.7	11.9	1.9	7.2	1.1	0.4	1.9	0.0	12.5	0.6
1913	8.1	1.2	0.9	–	1.7	11.9	1.8	7.0	1.1	0.8	1.8	0.0	12.4	0.4
1914	12.7	1.2	1.3	0.1	1.7	17.0	1.9	6.9	1.1	0.8	1.8	0.0	12.5	(4.5)
1915	33.3	0.5	1.1	0.2	2.3	37.4	2.6	6.8	1.0	0.7	1.7	0.0	12.8	(24.6)
1916	37.1	0.3	1.2	0.1	3.6	42.2	6.5	6.6	0.9	0.6	1.7	0.0	16.3	(25.9)
1917	37.1	0.1	1.6	0.2	4.1	43.2	9.5	4.9	0.7	0.5	1.8	0.7	18.1	(25.2)
1918	35.1	0.2	3.1	0.1	5.1	43.6	10.1	5.1	0.6	0.4	2.1	0.7	19.1	(24.5)
1919	16.7	0.6	5.1	0.1	5.9	28.5	11.3	7.1	0.7	0.4	1.4	0.3	21.1	(7.4)
1920	8.3	1.7	4.9	0.2	5.5	20.6	10.0	8.3	0.8	0.5	1.0	0.1	20.7	0.2
1920	8.2	1.7	4.7	0.2	5.7	20.5	10.2	8.3	0.8	0.5	1.1	0.1	20.9	0.4
1921	9.5	3.1	6.5	0.2	6.5	25.8	9.8	10.3	0.9	0.9	1.5	0.9	24.4	(1.4)
1922	9.5	2.6	5.9	0.2	7.4	25.6	9.4	11.2	1.3	1.3	2.1	0.3	25.6	0.0
1923	9.0	2.0	4.6	0.3	8.0	23.9	8.6	10.9	1.2	1.4	2.3	0.3	24.9	1.0
1924	9.0	2.2	4.3	0.2	7.9	23.6	7.9	10.0	1.4	1.4	2.3	0.2	23.3	(0.3)
1925	8.9	2.6	4.5	0.1	7.5	23.6	7.4	9.8	1.2	1.4	2.3	0.4	22.6	(1.0)
1926	9.6	3.1	5.2	0.1	8.3	26.3	7.0	10.8	1.5	1.7	2.6	0.5	24.0	(2.2)
1927	9.2	3.1	4.7	0.1	7.5	24.5	6.4	10.8	1.6	1.7	2.8	0.5	24.0	(0.5)
1928	9.1	2.7	4.7	0.1	7.7	24.3	6.1	11.0	1.8	1.8	3.0	0.5	24.2	(0.1)
1929	9.2	2.6	4.9	0.1	7.7	24.5	6.2	10.6	1.7	1.7	3.1	0.5	23.8	(0.7)
1930	9.5	2.8	5.6	0.1	7.6	25.5	6.5	10.3	1.7	1.7	3.3	0.6	24.1	(1.4)
1931	10.2	3.3	7.0	0.1	7.7	28.2	7.5	11.0	1.7	1.9	3.3	0.5	25.9	(2.2)
1932	10.1	2.8	7.2	0.1	7.8	27.9	6.2	12.0	1.7	2.1	3.3	0.0	27.4	(0.5)
1933	10.1	2.2	7.1	0.1	6.9	26.4	7.3	12.1	2.0	2.1	3.3	0.0	26.9	0.4
1934	9.9	2.1	6.7	0.1	6.1	25.0	6.4	12.0	1.7	2.1	3.2	0.0	25.4	0.5
1935	10.2	2.4	6.5	0.1	5.9	25.2	6.0	11.8	1.8	2.1	3.1	0.0	24.8	(0.4)
1936	10.9	2.9	6.1	0.1	5.6	25.5	5.9	12.0	1.8	2.1	3.0	0.0	24.8	(0.8)
1937	11.7	3.3	5.6	0.1	5.3	25.9	6.2	11.6	1.8	2.0	2.8	0.0	24.4	(1.5)
1938	13.4	3.6	5.7	0.1	5.1	28.0	6.9	11.3	1.4	2.0	2.8	0.0	24.3	(3.7)
1939	19.8	3.0	5.3	0.3	4.8	33.2	7.4	11.5	1.3	1.8	2.7	0.0	24.7	(8.4)

Sources: Feinstein, *National Income*, Tables 3, 12, 14, 34, 39; *Statistical Abstract for the United Kingdom 1835-1909*, BPP 1910 (5236), civ, 1 (London, 1910), p.9; *Statistical Abstract for the United Kingdom 1905-1919*, BPP 1921 (246), xl, 1 (London, 1921), pp.2-3; *Annual Abstract of Statistics 1935-46* (London, 1948), Table 251.

Notes:
For 1900-20 (first estimate) Southern Ireland is included; from 1920 (second estimate) onwards it is excluded. Feinstein, *National Income*, Table 39 does not provide data for 1920 (first estimate) and 1939. For 1920 the same figure as 1920 (second estimate) has been adopted (a lower bound estimate with a small margin of error); for 1939 a figure has been constructed by deflating the 1938 figure by the fall in GDPCP over 1938-9. Again this is likely to be a lower bound estimate, though with a higher margin of error.
Taxes on capital 1900-20 and 1933, Feinstein, *National Income*, Table 4.2, 34 only gives data for 1900, 1910 and 1920-38. The missing years are drawn from the statistical abstracts citated above, but these sources do not exactly correspond with the years in which Feinstein's data overlap, though the margins of error are small (£2m).

149

Table 2
General and central government expenditure as % of GDP

Year	Austria GG	Austria CG	Belgium GG	Belgium CG	Denmark GG	Denmark CG	Finland GG	Finland CG	France GG	France CG	Germany GG	Germany CG	Ireland GG	Ireland CG	Italy GG	Italy CG	Netherlands GG	Netherlands CG	Norway GG	Norway CG	Sweden GG	Sweden CG	Switzerland GG	Switzerland CG	UK GG	UK CG
1900	—	—	—	—	10.8	5.8	—	—	—	—	—	4.2	—	—	—	13.1	—	8.4	9.9	5.4	—	—	—	—	14.9	9.7
1901	—	—	—	—	10.5	5.6	—	—	—	—	14.2	4.9	—	—	—	13.7	—	6.0	—	—	—	—	—	—	—	—
1902	—	—	—	—	10.3	5.5	—	—	—	—	—	5.0	—	—	—	14.2	—	8.4	—	—	—	—	—	—	—	—
1903	—	—	—	—	10.9	5.4	—	—	—	—	—	4.7	—	—	—	12.8	—	8.2	—	—	—	—	—	—	—	—
1904	—	—	—	—	10.6	5.9	—	—	—	—	—	4.7	—	—	—	13.3	—	8.6	—	—	—	—	—	—	—	—
1905	—	—	—	—	10.0	5.4	—	—	—	—	—	4.7	—	—	—	17.0	—	8.3	—	—	—	—	—	—	12.4	6.1
1906	—	—	—	—	10.3	5.5	—	—	—	—	—	4.7	—	—	—	13.8	—	8.0	—	—	—	—	—	—	—	—
1907	—	—	—	—	10.6	5.4	—	—	—	—	15.1	5.3	—	—	—	12.8	—	8.1	—	—	—	—	—	—	—	—
1908	—	—	—	—	11.6	6.1	—	—	—	—	—	5.6	—	—	—	14.8	—	8.4	—	—	—	—	—	—	—	—
1909	—	—	—	—	12.7	7.0	—	—	—	—	—	5.5	—	—	—	13.9	—	8.3	—	—	—	—	—	—	—	—
1910	—	—	—	—	12.3	6.6	—	—	—	—	—	5.3	—	—	—	15.1	—	8.3	9.3	4.7	—	—	—	2.1	12.7	6.6
1911	—	—	—	—	12.0	6.1	—	—	—	—	—	5.1	—	—	—	14.6	—	8.1	—	—	—	—	—	—	—	—
1912	—	—	—	—	10.9	5.6	—	—	—	—	—	5.0	—	—	—	15.4	—	8.2	—	—	—	—	—	—	—	—
1913	—	—	—	—	10.4	5.4	—	—	—	—	17.0	6.0	—	—	—	14.4	—	8.3	—	—	10.4	5.4	14.0	3.1	12.7	7.0
1914	—	—	—	—	11.5	6.6	—	—	—	—	—	—	—	—	—	27.5	—	8.3	—	—	11.2	5.7	—	—	—	—
1915	—	—	—	—	—	—	—	—	—	—	—	—	—	—	—	47.6	—	13.0	—	—	—	—	—	—	32.7	28.2
1916	—	—	—	—	—	—	—	—	—	—	—	—	—	—	—	56.9	—	15.7	—	—	10.4	6.0	—	—	—	—
1917	—	—	—	—	—	—	—	—	—	—	—	—	—	—	—	51.2	—	14.7	—	—	—	—	—	—	35.7	32.8
1918	—	—	—	—	—	—	—	—	—	—	—	—	—	—	—	48.0	—	19.2	—	—	14.3	9.6	—	—	48.4	45.7
1919	—	—	—	—	—	—	—	—	—	—	—	—	—	—	—	36.2	—	26.2	—	—	—	—	—	—	—	—
1920	—	—	—	—	—	—	—	—	34.2	28.9	—	—	—	—	—	36.1	—	15.4	12.8	7.2	10.3	5.6	—	—	27.4	21.9
1921	—	—	—	—	15.3	8.8	—	—	—	23.7	—	—	—	—	—	34.9	—	14.9	—	—	—	—	—	—	28.7	20.7
1922	—	—	—	—	15.1	8.4	—	—	—	30.4	—	—	—	—	—	21.2	—	17.9	—	—	17.5	9.3	—	—	26.6	18.3
1923	—	—	—	—	13.4	7.0	—	—	29.3	24.6	—	—	—	—	—	20.1	—	20.9	—	—	—	—	—	—	24.1	16.6
1924	12.7	—	—	—	12.6	6.8	—	—	—	21.1	—	—	—	—	—	17.5	—	15.2	—	—	14.9	7.3	17.0	4.6	23.8	16.0
1925	9.7	—	—	—	13.4	7.1	—	11.9	—	18.0	22.4	10.2	—	—	—	14.7	—	12.2	—	—	—	—	—	—	23.6	15.4
1926	11.5	—	—	—	14.2	7.4	—	12.1	21.9	16.9	24.3	11.2	—	—	—	14.8	—	11.8	—	—	14.1	7.1	—	—	25.6	16.3
1927	11.4	—	—	—	13.7	6.9	—	12.2	—	17.7	24.5	11.4	21.5	15.2	—	20.4	—	10.8	—	—	—	—	—	—	24.3	15.2
1928	11.5	—	—	—	13.5	6.8	—	12.8	22.1	16.1	26.3	13.2	21.3	14.7	—	14.3	—	11.0	—	—	14.0	6.8	—	3.8	23.8	15.1
1929	10.8	—	—	—	13.1	6.5	—	14.7	—	16.1	27.3	14.0	20.9	14.8	—	14.3	—	11.2	—	—	—	—	—	4.9	23.6	15.0
1930	13.8	—	—	—	13.5	6.6	—	15.9	—	19.0	29.4	15.8	20.8	14.6	—	19.8	—	11.8	17.4	8.4	14.0	6.7	17.4	—	24.7	15.6
1931	15.7	—	—	—	14.3	7.0	—	16.2	—	19.3	30.5	16.1	21.7	15.1	—	21.3	—	15.8	20.1	9.7	—	—	—	4.4	27.3	17.3
1932	13.4	—	—	—	15.5	7.4	—	16.6	31.4	23.1	30.7	15.1	23.2	16.1	—	19.8	—	17.9	19.4	9.3	18.5	9.0	22.1	5.3	26.3	17.4
1933	16.6	—	—	—	17.3	9.1	—	18.3	—	23.7	31.1	16.0	25.9	17.6	—	26.1	—	20.8	18.9	9.1	—	—	—	5.5	25.0	15.3
1934	17.5	—	—	23.1	16.6	8.2	—	17.5	—	23.6	32.7	19.5	27.3	18.7	—	20.3	—	19.6	18.3	8.9	17.1	8.5	23.7	6.1	23.5	14.6
1935	15.9	—	—	22.0	17.5	7.9	—	19.2	35.4	24.8	29.8	18.9	27.8	19.0	—	54.9	—	21.1	18.1	9.0	—	—	—	6.3	23.7	14.6
1936	15.2	—	—	20.2	15.5	7.5	—	18.4	—	24.6	28.9	19.4	27.4	18.7	—	36.3	—	19.5	17.8	9.0	16.5	8.5	24.1	6.5	24.0	14.7
1937	14.3	—	—	19.8	16.6	8.4	—	18.8	—	22.5	29.4	19.4	27.8	19.1	—	26.1	—	17.7	17.2	8.6	—	—	—	6.1	24.6	15.2
1938	—	—	—	23.4	16.7	8.1	—	16.7	29.2	22.2	29.4	21.1	32.9	23.4	—	25.5	—	19.4	18.1	9.0	17.7	9.5	23.9	7.0	28.6	19.0
1939	—	—	—	—	19.2	10.7	—	25.5	—	—	36.9	29.1	28.6	19.6	—	37.5	—	20.6	19.1	10.0	—	—	—	10.7	33.4	24.0

Source: Flora, *et al.*, *State, Economy and Society*, pp. 355, 360, 362-3, 363, 376-7, 383-4, 400-1, 408, 414, 426, 433-4, 440-1.

Notes:

1. GG = general government, defined as all levels of government; CG = central government. Social insurance expenditures are included in the data for Denmark, France (general government), Germany, Ireland, Norway, Sweden, Switzerland and UK.

2. With the exception of Belgium, central government expenditure is from the aggregate series; for Belgium, where no such data are available, the total expenditure from the series for expenditure by functional [...] which [...] due to its more comprehensive definition of central government, overstates expenditure relative to the other series).

Table 3
General and central government taxes as % of GDP

	Austria		Belgium		Denmark		Finland		France		Germany		Ireland		Italy		Netherlands		Norway		Sweden		Switzerland		UK	
	GG	CG	GG	CG	GG	CG	GG	CG	GG	CG	GG	CG	GG	CG	GG	CG	GG	CG	GG	CG	GG	CG	GG	CG	GG	CG
1900	–	–	–	–	–	4.9	–	–	–	–	–	–	–	–	20.1	10.8	–	6.7	7.5	4.8	8.2	5.3	–	–	7.9	5.5
1901	–	–	–	–	–	4.8	–	–	–	–	–	2.5	–	–	–	10.6	–	6.4	–	4.9	–	5.0	–	–	–	6.0
1902	–	–	–	–	–	4.9	–	–	–	–	4.3	2.6	–	–	–	11.4	8.0	6.6	–	4.8	–	4.9	–	–	–	6.6
1903	–	–	–	–	–	4.9	–	–	–	–	4.7	2.6	–	–	–	10.3	–	6.6	–	4.8	–	5.4	–	–	–	7.1
1904	–	–	–	–	–	6.0	–	–	–	–	4.1	2.4	–	–	–	10.7	–	6.5	–	4.6	–	5.7	–	–	–	6.5
1905	–	–	–	–	7.4	4.9	–	–	–	–	–	2.3	–	–	–	11.0	–	6.4	8.3	4.9	–	5.8	–	–	9.6	6.4
1906	–	–	–	–	8.2	5.7	–	–	–	–	–	2.5	–	–	–	10.4	–	6.4	–	4.8	–	5.1	–	–	–	6.1
1907	–	–	–	–	–	5.0	–	–	–	–	4.0	2.3	–	–	–	9.1	7.8	6.3	–	4.9	–	5.3	–	–	–	6.0
1908	–	–	–	–	–	5.0	–	–	–	–	–	2.5	–	–	–	9.9	–	6.1	–	5.9	–	5.0	–	–	–	6.5
1909	–	–	–	–	–	4.2	–	–	–	–	4.3	2.7	–	–	–	9.4	–	6.2	–	5.0	–	5.4	–	–	–	6.0
1910	–	–	–	–	–	4.4	–	–	–	–	4.3	2.9	–	–	–	10.3	–	6.2	7.9	4.8	9.1	5.4	5.7	2.1	8.8	5.5
1911	–	–	–	–	–	4.5	–	–	–	–	–	3.0	–	–	–	9.4	–	6.3	–	4.8	–	5.4	–	–	–	7.8
1912	–	–	–	–	–	4.7	–	–	–	–	–	3.2	–	–	16.2	9.6	7.7	6.0	–	4.6	–	5.3	–	–	–	6.7
1913	–	–	–	–	7.3	4.9	–	–	–	–	4.3	2.9	–	–	–	9.3	–	6.0	–	4.6	8.2	5.1	7.3	2.4	–	6.6
1914	–	–	–	–	–	4.3	–	–	–	–	–	2.9	–	–	–	8.9	–	6.3	–	5.4	–	4.9	–	–	–	6.9
1915	–	–	–	–	–	–	–	–	–	–	–	–	–	–	–	9.1	–	6.0	7.1	4.6	–	6.0	–	–	10.6	7.8
1916	–	–	–	–	–	–	–	–	–	–	–	–	–	–	–	8.7	–	7.4	–	5.5	–	5.5	–	–	–	8.7
1917	–	–	–	–	–	–	–	–	–	–	–	–	–	–	–	8.2	16.2	13.7	–	10.8	11.7	7.6	–	–	–	12.5
1918	–	–	–	–	–	–	–	–	–	–	–	–	–	–	–	8.3	–	12.3	–	9.9	–	8.2	–	–	–	13.3
1919	–	–	–	–	–	–	–	–	–	–	–	–	–	–	–	8.7	–	11.1	–	9.2	–	7.8	–	–	–	16.9
1920	–	–	–	–	–	9.3	–	–	13.7	12.5	–	–	–	–	–	10.2	–	11.8	7.5	3.8	–	6.4	–	–	20.1	18.1
1921	–	–	–	–	–	8.0	–	–	–	14.5	–	–	–	–	13.5	11.5	–	11.5	–	8.2	–	7.0	–	–	–	20.5
1922	–	–	–	–	–	7.2	–	–	–	14.0	–	–	–	–	–	11.2	14.8	11.5	–	6.8	–	7.0	–	–	–	18.0
1923	–	–	–	–	10.8	6.5	–	–	–	14.4	–	–	–	–	–	12.0	–	11.0	–	6.5	12.2	6.5	–	–	–	17.5
1924	14.9	10.3	–	10.8	–	7.1	–	–	–	15.4	–	–	–	–	–	12.0	–	10.0	–	6.5	–	6.4	–	3.6	–	15.4
1925	16.1	10.4	–	–	–	7.4	–	9.5	16.6	15.8	14.8	9.8	–	–	12.4	10.3	–	9.1	12.6	6.7	–	6.0	–	–	18.4	14.9
1926	15.5	11.3	–	–	12.7	7.9	–	9.8	–	16.0	–	9.1	17.1	13.7	–	10.1	–	9.4	–	7.8	–	6.2	–	–	–	15.6
1927	15.6	11.0	–	16.4	–	7.3	–	10.6	–	17.4	16.6	10.3	16.1	12.9	–	11.0	13.5	9.7	–	8.8	–	6.3	–	–	–	14.4
1928	–	11.1	–	–	–	7.4	–	10.5	–	17.1	–	11.7	16.2	13.1	–	11.0	–	9.0	–	7.9	10.5	6.3	–	–	–	15.0
1929	–	11.5	–	–	11.9	7.7	15.7	11.5	–	20.5	–	11.7	16.0	12.8	–	11.6	–	8.4	–	7.9	–	6.2	13.0	4.3	–	14.6
1930	–	11.9	–	12.2	–	8.1	–	10.7	17.8	16.8	17.5	12.1	16.6	13.3	–	13.4	13.4	9.3	15.0	8.2	–	6.1	–	5.9	18.3	14.5
1931	–	13.1	–	–	–	8.6	–	10.6	–	16.7	–	12.5	16.6	13.1	17.4	14.2	–	9.1	–	9.3	–	6.9	–	4.8	–	16.3
1932	–	13.6	–	–	13.5	8.4	–	10.9	–	15.0	18.9	12.4	17.4	14.2	–	13.8	–	9.4	–	8.8	–	7.5	–	5.2	–	17.2
1933	–	13.3	–	–	–	8.5	–	10.9	–	18.0	–	12.4	19.2	16.3	–	14.0	–	–	–	9.0	13.0	7.7	–	4.7	–	16.3
1934	–	13.8	–	–	–	8.2	–	11.4	–	18.2	–	13.5	20.1	16.8	–	16.3	13.5	10.7	–	9.0	–	8.0	–	5.4	–	15.6
1935	–	14.0	18.0	18.2	–	8.1	–	11.3	17.7	17.1	20.8	14.5	19.5	16.0	17.7	14.3	–	10.4	16.4	9.8	–	8.4	–	5.1	18.7	15.0
1936	–	14.9	–	15.8	–	8.9	–	10.8	–	14.5	–	15.9	20.3	16.8	–	14.4	–	10.4	–	10.2	–	8.7	–	4.8	–	14.9
1937	–	13.9	–	14.9	–	8.8	–	10.9	–	15.2	22.7	17.6	19.8	16.3	17.7	14.5	–	11.0	–	10.4	–	8.7	12.0	4.8	–	14.8
1938	–	–	16.3	14.6	13.3	9.0	14.9	10.9	–	15.9	–	–	19.9	16.0	–	14.8	–	11.1	–	11.3	13.9	9.6	–	5.3	–	15.1
1939	–	–	–	14.8	–	–	–	10.7	–	–	–	20.6	–	15.7	17.6	14.9	–	11.2	–	11.1	–	10.8	–	5.8	–	15.3

Source: Flora, et.al., State, Economy and Society, pp. 263, 264, 266, 268.

Note:
1. GG = general government, defined as all levels of government; CG = central government.

10

'Free Traders' in a Protectionist World: The Foreign Economic Policy of the Netherlands 1930-1950 (with particular reference to Europe)

Richard Griffiths

'The seas are open, trade will revive', were the words with which Van Hogendorp ushered in the era of peace after the end of the Napoleonic Wars. Although in the short term history was to prove him wrong, as a slogan it could be said to have characterized Dutch foreign economic policy assumptions up to the present day. The need for a wide variety of imports, reflecting the Netherlands' relatively high level of incomes and the weight of processing industries in its economic structure, coupled with the necessity to find foreign outlets for its export niches, left the country with no other optimal policy alternative. Whilst such conditions prevailed it seemed to produce a felicitous combination of visible results and minimal policy effort. When they collapsed, however, the resulting trauma and feelings of impotence were considerable. It is the reaction of Dutch policy-makers in such circumstances with which this article is primarily concerned.

What it seeks to do in the process is to explain the reduction in the focus of Dutch aspirations from more global multilateral settlements to an arrangement encompassing a small number of Continental European countries. This shift in ambitions in the area of foreign trade coincided with the emergence of what is usually described by political scientists and historians as 'the movement towards European integration'. There is no space here to describe the debate which is just beginning to develop on the nature of and explanation for this phenomenon in the late 1940s and early 1950s. Suffice it to say that there are three, not necessarily mutually exclusive, lines of approach. The first emphasizes the role of ideas, particularly federalist ideals; the second focuses on leading political personalities and their negotiating methods, whilst the third concentrates on the driving force of economic imperatives. In the case of the Netherlands the case for this last approach is in danger of being lost by default. Part of the intention of this article, therefore, is to redress the balance and to contribute to the enrichment of the discussion.

At the high point of Dutch prosperity in the interwar years (1925-9, when the economy was expanding in real terms at a rate of 4.4 per cent per annum[1] and industry at 5.0 per cent[2]) virtually 55 per cent of GDP was earned from foreign transactions. Of this figure, merchandise exports amounted to 35 per cent, earnings derived from the provision of services to 9 per cent and income transfers from the ownership of foreign assets to 11 per cent. A decade later, as the economy was struggling to pull itself out of the depression, this picture had experienced a profound change. The contribution of foreign earnings to GDP had fallen to 34 per cent with most of the decline concentrated in merchandise exports which, in 1935-39, contributed only 18 per cent to GDP. The service sector had recovered somewhat better from the depths of the recession with an 8 per cent contribution to GDP, and had also overtaken foreign income transfers which also amounted to 8 per cent.[3] What this implied in practice for the development of exports in relation to the development of real GDP is shown in Table 1.[4]

Table 1
Indices of real GDP and export volume 1929-1939
(1929 = 100)

	GDP	Exports
1929	100.0	100.0
1930	98.9	91.2
1931	94.5	80.9
1932	85.0	62.8
1933	88.5	60.0
1934	87.5	60.2
1935	89.9	60.3
1936	94.7	63.2
1937	100.1	72.1
1938	96.9	66.1
1939	104.4	59.9

Source: Calculated from CBS, *Macro-economische ontwikkelingen 1921-1939*

All the signs pointed to the fact that the Dutch were experiencing something of an export-led recession. It was not only the volume of trade, however, which had contracted in the course of the 1930s: its geographical composition also underwent a marked transformation. The data for this is shown in Table 2 which covers all Dutch trading partners absorbing more than 5 per cent of exports in 1929. The striking feature is the marked decline in the importance of the German market after the introduction of the *Neue Plan* in 1934 and the fall from peaks in the early 1930s in the role of both France and Belgium. Also interesting is the recovery of the Dutch East Indian market after the slump until 1933/4 and, aside from a drop immediately after the sterling devaluation, the relatively steady share of the United Kingdom.

Table 2
Share of major markets in Dutch exports
(per cent)

	Germany	U.K.	Belgium & Luxembourg	Dutch East Indies	France
1929	22.5	20.2	10.3	9.3	5.8
1930	20.8	22.0	11.3	8.3	7.9
1931	19.2	24.1	13.2	7.1	8.8
1932	21.1	18.8	13.9	7.8	10.1
1933	21.4	17.0	14.1	4.2	9.9
1934	24.5	18.6	11.7	4.2	8.2
1935	18.4	20.8	11.3	8.4	7.0
1936	14.9	21.4	12.7	5.5	7.4
1937	14.9	21.0	11.8	8.0	6.6
1938	14.6	22.1	10.6	9.5	5.9
1939	13.8	22.9	9.7	10.1	5.4

Source: Calculated from CBS, *Tachtig jaren statistiek in tijdreeksen, 1899-1979* (The Hague, 1979), pp.112-18.

This forms part of a more general picture in which the share of the rest of Europe also held up fairly well, and the share to the rest of the world increased from around 14 per cent to closer to 20 per cent by the end of the decade.[5] The product composition of Dutch exports also showed a marked shift, away from food, drink and tobacco, and towards manufactures and semi-manufactures. From peaks of virtually 50 per cent in the early 1920s, the share of food etc. had fallen to near 40 per cent by the end of the 1920s and declined further still to 32-3 per cent by the end of the 1930s. This picture was virtually mirrored by manufactures and semi-manufactures, whose share in exports increased from 32 per cent in the early 1920s to 38 per cent at the end of the 1920s and to just under 48 per cent by the outbreak of the war.[6] This partly reflected the surge in industrialization which occurred in the 1920s but it also demonstrates the increasing competition which the Dutch faced in agricultural markets at the end of the 1920s, the deteriorating terms of agricultural trade and, after 1930, the rising walls of agricultural protectionism.

If we turn towards analysing the decline in Dutch export performance in the 1930s it is necessary to distinguish between two sets of factors at work. On the one hand the decline could simply be attributable to a fall in demand in the markets of the major trading partners, either as a result of falling levels of consumption and investment or as a result of their autarkic recovery policies (i.e. Dutch exports fell because their partners bought less). On the other hand it is possible to pose the hypothesis that the Dutch failed to keep their market shares (i.e. that they were disproportionately penalized by the decline in demand and failed to participate fully in whatever recovery did occur). In order to test these two possibilities we can construct an index of the Dutch share of trade in its major export markets.[7] The countries were weighted according to their share of Dutch exports in 1929 and include all countries accounting for 1 per cent or more of Dutch exports in that year.[8]

Table 3
Weighted index of the Dutch share of the markets of its major trading partners 1929-1939 (1929 = 100)

1929	100	1935	87.7
1930	105.7	1936	85.3
1931	110.0	1937	83.7
1932	101.8	1938	87.5
1933	93.9	(1947)	(60.3)
1934	93.8		

Source: Calculated from League of Nations, *International Trade Statistics* (Geneva, various years) and for 1947 United Nations, *Yearbook of International Trade Statistics.*

The results of this exercise, shown in Table 3, suggest that the Dutch actually increased their import penetration in their major markets substantially in 1930 and 1931, and that even in 1932 exports performed better than they had done in 1929 (though not in relation to 1928 or 1925-6). Thus the period of major trade collapse, in which the real value of Dutch exports had fallen by virtually 40 per cent, was statistically entirely a function of declining import demand. Thereafter, however, the failure of exports to revive can be ascribed primarily to an almost continuous erosion of Dutch market shares.

This still leaves us with the task of explaining the relatively poor export performance after 1933. An obvious culprit lies in the fact that the Netherlands remained loyal to the gold standard, and an unchanged parity of the guilder, long after its major competitors had abandoned it and allowed their currencies to depreciate on international markets. What was to become the sterling area had left the gold standard in September 1931 and the dollar had followed suit in March 1933. By the beginning of 1934 these two key world currencies had fallen to about 60 per cent of their previous levels after which a stabilization became apparent. The Dutch, if they were to compete in foreign markets, would have to match this depreciation by reducing nominal export prices, though not necessarily to the same degree since competitors often used the currency depreciation to restore profitability rather than to reduce prices. Although the recent debate has concentrated on the gold standard question,[9] there are grounds for questioning whether an earlier devaluation would have had much effect in promoting exports, although there are many other areas in which it would have alleviated the situation not the least of which was the savagely deflationary and ultimately self-defeating domestic policy of the Colijn cabinets.[10] The reason for doubting the effectiveness of an earlier devaluation on export performance lies in the fact that its theoretical benefits presuppose a market functioning on the basis of supply and demand principles in which demand would be responsive to changes in relative prices. But such conditions could hardly have been said to have existed in the 1930s. Virtually everywhere the composition of imports was predetermined by autonomous controls and by networks of bilateral trading agreements, a fact which was appreciated by Colijn and used in his rationalization of remaining loyal to the gold standard and which was also conceded by the main proponent of devaluation within the cabinet, the Economics Minister M.P.L. Steenberghe.[11] To some extent this view is also partly confirmed by the failure of Dutch market shares to show any significant improvement following the 20 per cent depreciation of the guilder in September 1936.

The initial foreign policy response of the government was to maintain its faith in multilateral conferences aimed at bringing down the mounting wall of protectionism. In July 1927 an agreement had been reached in Geneva to abolish all quantitative trade restrictions, subject to ratification by eighteen states. When this number was not reached, the Netherlands had joined six other states, none of which actually had such restrictions, in unilaterally abandoning the right to introduce them until July 1931.[12] In February 1930 the Dutch were again to be found among the ranks of the eighteen states agreeing to a tariff truce, an initiative which collapsed when, three months later, the United States introduced the Hawley-Smoot tariff, unleashing a round of retaliatory increases throughout much of Europe.[13]

Alongside a commitment to multilateral solutions, there developed a first interest in more limited regional forms of accommodation. This found its expression in a vague and vacuous agreement with Sweden, Denmark and Norway known as the Oslo Convention which, in fact, did little more than bind the signatories to prior notification of tariff increases to allow time for representation by the injured parties. It promised little and achieved even less, collapsing in January 1932 when, in the middle of negotiations, the Dutch imposed quotas on veal and beef imports directed primarily at Denmark.[14] The new standard bearer for the policy of regional co-operation became the Ouchy Convention, concluded in June 1932 with Belgium and Luxembourg. Under the agreement, the parties undertook to impose no new quotas on each other's exports and to lower tariffs on intra-area trade by 10 per cent per annum over the next five years. Since the old tariffs were to be maintained against non-contracting parties, the success of the agreement depended on other countries waiving their rights to equality of treatment. When, in November 1932, the United Kingdom refused, the Convention collapsed.[15] The final internationalist effort and perhaps the most resounding failure was the World Economic Conference held in London in July 1933. Colijn, recently appointed as Prime Minister, had chaired the economic committee. However, the refusal of the United States to commit itself to a level at which it would stabilize the dollar robbed the discussions of any basis for future planning and the conference disbanded without result.

Colijn's premiership was accompanied by a marked change in the direction and sense of purpose in foreign economic policy starting in the one area where the Netherlands had some control: its own colonial markets.[16] In presenting his policy programme to cabinet, Colijn recounted how the other delegates at the London conference had smiled at his innocence when he had explained that the Netherlands and its colonies still treated each other as separate nations.[17] The government now took powers to impose quotas on colonial imports which, where appropriate, would actively discriminate in favour of trade with the home country. The result was a slow recovery in the Dutch share of the East Indian market from a low point of 12.4 per cent in 1933 to 16.7 per cent in 1936 and 22.2 per cent in 1938. The extent to which this had been facilitated by the new policy is reflected in the calculation that between 1933 and 1936, the value of Dutch trade in quota-covered categories had risen by 96 per cent against a rise of only 2 per cent in categories not protected in this way.[18]

In dealing with its two major trading partners — Germany and the United Kingdom, which in 1929, absorbed 22.3 and 21.8 per cent of Dutch exports respectively — the government had much less room for manoeuvre. In the case of Germany the 'frozen debt' situation which had resulted from the imposition of exchange controls in 1931 had made it necessary to deal with Germany first. In February 1932 the government had already concluded a curiously one-sided initiative known as the *Sonderkonto* agreement. Under this arrangement German importers with permission to import but without a foreign currency allowance could deposit an equivalent sum in marks with the *Nederlandsche Bank*, the sums to be made available, at slightly discounted rates, for the payment of Dutch imports. However Dutch importers were not obliged to use this facility and when, in 1934 under the *Neue Plan*, the Germans cut the foreign exchange allowances, unspent mark balances began to accumulate and in August 1934 the Dutch decided to call a halt. In December, after one false start, a new clearing agreement was concluded which embraced both commercial and financial transactions and which was binding on all parties in the Netherlands. One fundamental problem remained — if the Dutch were to avoid a further accumulation of blocked mark balances, they either had to step up imports from Germany or curtail Dutch exports. Thus the government, which was at the same time striving to protect industry and agriculture, found itself involved (via preferential quotas and manipulated exchange rates) in an import drive from Germany and when, in 1935, that began not to work out, it began to curtail exports. Now, this decision was not simply a reflection of the overall clearing imbalance, it also reflected the priority between financial and commercial claims. Whereas the allocations for paying off the *Sonderkonto* and meeting the interest payments on frozen debt were guaranteed, the amounts available for Dutch exporters were what was left. In effect the banks and financial interests had made themselves preferential claimants on Germany.[19] Of the 433 million guilders deposited with the Dutch Clearing Institute in 1935 and 1936, no less than 144 million was earmarked for the satisfaction of financial claims.[20] Had this amount been used instead for German purchases of Dutch goods, it could have raised the total levels of exports in those two years by 10 per cent, but for that to have occurred would have meant that the government would *de facto* have had to abandon all existing claims arising from Germany's default — a not very plausible situation. As a result of these developments the Dutch share in the German market had slipped from 5.9 per cent in 1934 to 4.0 per cent in 1936. At this point the product composition and geographical orientation of German imports became increasingly subjected to the dictates of the rearmament programme, and Germany's commitment towards exports also began to wane. Moreover, since subsequent clearing agreements allowed Germany to use the system for its payments for services and for Dutch colonial imports, the room for Dutch merchandise exports, short of allowing the mark balances to pile up, remained restricted.

The preoccupation with Germany forms an important element in the explanation for the failure to achieve a more satisfactory accommodation with the United Kingdom. The UK had followed the sterling devaluation by constructing a network of bilateral trading agreements with its colonies and dominions, the so-called 'Commonwealth Preferences'. After that, the negotiators turned their attention to the countries of Europe with whom, more often than not, the UK had a balance of trade deficit. The negotiating strategy adopted was that if these countries agreed to divert their sources of imports so as to reduce this deficit, they would be rewarded by preferential access to the British market. The products which the UK was interested in promoting were textiles and coal, but in these areas the Dutch had little to offer – in textiles they were themselves a net exporter whilst their ability to offer concessions on coal was hamstrung by an agreement placing Germany in a position of privileged supplier. Similarly the 'import drive' from Germany made it difficult to countenance the promotion of British imports of semi-manufactures and machinery. Thus the trade agreement concluded in July 1935 amounted, in effect, to guaranteeing existing shares in each other's markets. This was, in itself, no small achievement but the chance of expanding mutual trade was irrevocably lost.[21] The share of the Netherlands in the UK market stabilized at around 3 per cent, which was considerably lower than the levels close to or above 4 per cent recorded in the 1920s.

The relations with Belgium and France, which were the third and fifth foreign outlets respectively, can be dealt with relatively quickly. Both countries had maintained their existing exchange rates after the sterling and dollar devaluations which left them, as indeed they left the Netherlands, as relatively high-cost islands. A combination of slow domestic growth and increasing resort to protectionist measures muted their demand for imports and, after the failure of the Ouchy Convention and despite warm words of mutual encouragement as they formed the so-called 'Gold Bloc' in the aftermath of the collapse of the London Conference, they showed little inclination to give practical expression to mutual trade preferences. The devaluation of the Belgian franc, fifteen months before the guilder followed the same path, provided a further blow to Dutch export ambitions in that direction. From peaks in the early 1930s, the Dutch share of both markets slipped rapidly to below levels recorded at any time in the interwar years.

Immediately after the war the damage inflicted on the productive capacity of the economy combined with the demands of domestic reconstruction limited the surplus available for export. In 1946 the share of GNP available for export amounted to 8.7 per cent and although the figure had doubled to 16.9 per cent the following year, it still remained below the pre-war level. In 1947 exports of services contributed 3.2 per cent to GNP whilst income from capital transfer from abroad was less than 1 per cent.[22] Since the economy was at the same time sucking in imports, this left a balance of payments problem of considerable dimensions which, despite the provision of loans and credits from abroad, soon drove the available gold and dollar reserves down towards a dangerously low threshold. It was at this point that exports began to respond. In 1948 they reached 22 per cent of GNP, in 1949 27 per cent, in 1950 they regained the late 1920s level of 35 per cent and in 1951 and 1952 they surged to 41 and 42 per cent respectively.[23] The data in Table 4, however, suggest a slightly different story. Although the Table reflects the general surge of the economy, the real value of exports did not exceed the 1938 level until 1949, and did not return to the peak of 1929 until as late as 1952. Part of the discrepancy is due to the fact that the post-war national income data need to be revised upwards by 7-10 per cent, in line with recent CBS re-calculations; part is due to different methods of calculation, and part is undoubtedly due to shifts in the terms of trade and the effects of the 1949 devaluation.

Table 4
Indices of real GDP and export volume 1946-1952

	GNP	Exports
(1938)	72.8	66.3
1946	n.a.	12.4
1947	n.a.	27.0
1948	88.0	39.3
1949	94.6	58.4
1950	96.7	80.9
1951	96.7	93.2
1952	100	100

Source: GNP: P. Fortuyn, Kerncijfers 1945-1953 van de sociaal-economische ontwikkeling in Nederland (Deventer, 1983); Exports: CBS, Statistische en econometrische onderzoekingen, 1951 no. 2, 1957 no. 1.

It reflected, in part, the general surge in import demand throughout Europe in these years, but also the Dutch success in capturing a greater share of those markets. In order to measure this second effect, the procedure described for Table 3 was repeated, using on this occasion those countries accounting for more than 1 per cent of Dutch exports in 1959.[24] Since this period witnessed the virtual eclipse of Indonesia as an export market from a post-war peak of just over 10 per cent in 1949, a second set of calculations was made in which it has been included. To facilitate the measurement of change, the index in Table 5 has been constructed using 1952 as the basis for comparison.

Table 5
Weighted index of the Dutch share of the markets of its major trading partners 1947-1952
(1952 = 100)

	Excluding Indonesia	Including Indonesia
(1938)	72.7	80.3
1947	53.4	51.1
1948	66.0	62.6
1949	79.4	76.1
1950	104.7	103.6
1951	89.5	89.3
1952	100	100

Source: Calculated from League of Nations, International Trade Statistics (Geneva, various years); and for 1947, United Nations, Yearbook of International Trade Statistics.

Although it is difficult to compare the pre- and post-war periods,[25] the Dutch share in its partners' imports was probably only two-thirds of the immediate pre-war level in 1947; and 1946 was in all likelihood even worse.[26] It is also worth bearing in mind that 1938 itself was fairly abysmal, and that it was only in 1949 that this level was regained. The following year, however, saw a further surge, albeit aided by special factors which will be examined later, which took the levels of import penetration above and beyond even the relatively halcyon days of the late 1920s and, although it fell back immediately afterwards, it still remained in that order of magnitude.

Part of the reason for this poor showing in the 1940s was the fact that most of the traditional Dutch outlets were drawing an increasing share of their imports from the United States: if one country's share increases dramatically, everyone else's automatically decreases. However this was only part of the problem. The increased share of European imports from the United States was not matched by any equivalent increase in export earnings, which resulted in an acute dollar deficit on most countries' balance of payments. Now in a perfect world, the solution to this would have been to sell some other currency to buy the necessary dollars, but such was the demand for dollars that any currency countenancing such a move would have risked being drained of its dollar reserves, as the ill-fated experiment in sterling convertibility demonstrated in July/August 1947. The result was that countries which would anyway have been inclined to restrict the levels and product composition of trade, to match the dictates of their individual reconstruction policies, were forced to implement a second layer of controls in order to protect their currency reserves. When Germany had done this in 1931, it had sent shock-waves reverberating through world financial markets; in the aftermath of World War II import quotas, tariffs and inconvertible currencies were part of the everyday vocabulary of European commercial and financial transactions. We have already seen how the German situation had complicated Dutch foreign economic policy in the 1930s; similar considerations applied to relations with virtually every trading partner in the post-war world. It is against this background which the shifts in trading patterns shown in Table 6 need to be seen.

Table 6
Structure of Dutch exports and imports by major trading partners and the USA (per cent)

	Germany	U.K.	Belgium & Luxembourg	Dutch East Indies	France	USA
EXPORTS						
1938	14.6	22.1	10.6	9.6	5.9	4.3
1946	6.4	10.9	20.8	3.3	7.0	7.2
1947	3.1	12.8	15.6	7.1	7.3	3.2
1948	5.9	14.5	15.6	7.4	8.1	3.1
1949	10.7	16.3	13.3	10.2	7.1	3.4
1950	20.6	14.7	13.5	5.9	4.5	5.0
1951	13.9	15.9	14.8	5.8	4.5	6.1
1952	13.9	12.5	15.6	5.9	4.4	6.7
IMPORTS						
1938	21.3	8.7	11.7	7.0	4.7	10.5
1946	2.5	16.9	13.7	0.9	4.4	24.3
1947	2.3	9.9	12.2	4.6	4.7	28.0
1948	5.4	8.8	14.7	6.7	4.9	17.4
1949	6.8	11.6	14.3	7.6	6.7	16.5
1950	12.3	10.5	18.4	6.5	4.7	11.5
1951	12.4	8.7	18.3	7.9	4.1	11.0
1952	14.0	9.3	17.2	6.5	3.4	12.8

Source: Calculated from CBS, *Tachtig jaren statistiek in tijdreeksen, 1899-1979* (The Hague, 1979), pp.112-18.

The most immediate source of concern for Dutch policy-makers was indeed the dollar problem, the dimensions of which are illustrated by the data for the United States shown in Table 6. However, the United States was only part, albeit the most important part, of the dollar area. If one takes the area as a whole, it supplied 19 per cent of Dutch import requirements in 1937/38 as compared with 35 per cent in 1946 and 33 per cent in 1947. The figures for exports for those three periods were 9, 10 and 6 per cent respectively.[27] The financing of these deficits had created a difficult but not insurmountable problem in the first eighteen months after the war, but towards the end of 1946 alarm bells began to ring in The Hague. In September the Central Planning Bureau had drafted a dollar purchasing programme for 1947 envisaging civil expenditure alone of $730 million (fl. 1936 million) which was more than twice as high as the level which dollar imports turned out to be in 1946 (fl. 819 million). These were to be distributed between industry, with $582 million (fl. 1544 million), and agriculture, with $148 million (fl. 393 million).[28] Even before the question reached cabinet, the obvious unwillingness of the Ministry of Finance to contemplate a programme of this scale had forced a radical reassessment.

By November 1946 the programme had been considerably reduced and the cabinet found itself considering two proposals – one for $544 million and one for $400 million. The cuts in the $544 million programme had been achieved entirely at the expense of industry (whose allocation fell by 35 per cent), whilst food had been preserved in real terms; the $400 million programme required deep cuts in both.[29] After a fierce debate, and against the advice of the Finance Minister and the president of the Central Bank, it was decided by cabinet to adopt the $544 million programme.[30] This was by no means the end of the matter. In February 1947 Lieftinck reopened the issue by pointing out that $165 million worth of orders had already been placed in 1946, with payments due in 1947. He demanded, and obtained, cabinet approval for including these in the 1947 totals.[31] In May the government received a series of reports recommending even further cutbacks. As far as civil purchasing was concerned, it recommended limiting purchases to $455 million, with industry to receive $280 million and agriculture $175 million. If the sums were lowered any further, it was agreed, it would 'be impossible to avoid calamities'.[32] The cabinet met no less than five times to consider these reports and managed to massage the figure upwards to $486 million (fl. 1289 million), but this was still 11 per cent lower than the figure agreed in November 1946, and 33 per cent less than the original figure suggested in September, with most of the force of the cuts falling on industry.[33] In October 1947 the industrial allocation was further reduced in order to cover an extra $45 million arising from the increased cost of food imports.[34]

The dollar crisis continued to make itself felt in the planning for 1948. Marshall Aid was coming on tap slower than might have been wished, the liquidation of foreign assets was yielding less than had been anticipated, and the outlook was that reserves would rapidly dwindle to below a level which the Central Bank considered prudent. As a result the cabinet in November 1947 agreed a dollar purchasing programme of $320 million for the first half of 1948.[35] It was almost immediately forced to slice that figure back to $75 million for the first quarter of the year,[36] whilst the second quarter allocation was first fixed at $90 million[37] before being raised to $120 million.[38]

It is impossible to read through the Dutch cabinet minutes without gaining the impression that the dollar problem dominated the perspective for economic reconstruction, and it is difficult to sympathize with the revisionism which seeks to diminish the impact of Marshall Aid for the economy. Indeed, in his study of the period, A.S.

Milward specifically exempts the Netherlands from his generally revisionist standpoint, arguing that whatever the counter-factual model adopted the country could not have financed the capital goods imports required for reconstruction without the injection of dollar aid which the Marshall Plan provided.[39] On the other hand, P. van der Eng attempts to demonstrate the relative marginality of Marshall Aid for the Netherlands by suggesting that in macro-economic terms it contributed only a relatively small impulse to growth rates, and that the impact of the immediate dollar crisis could have been averted by spending reserves.[40] But this misses the point that it is not a question of juggling with macro-economic variables, but one of meeting highly specific import needs which had to be paid for in a currency which the Dutch quite simply could not earn in sufficient quantities. Moreover, the suggestion that a country could simply run its reserves down to nothing is plausible in theory, but rather a-historic in practice. It is possible that part of the dollar cutbacks were offset by purchases in other markets and currency zones, but until the extent of that is demonstrated we are left with a conclusion that the 'perceived problem' had a 'real' dimension, and that there was a direct link between foreign exchange availability and the slackening in industrial recovery visible throughout 1947. It was Marshall Aid which released the Dutch economy from its immediate foreign exchange constraints and allowed the reconstruction boom to rip. In the slightly longer perspective the pressures were reduced by shifting import sources (with US-funded European payments schemes carrying part of the deficits), and ultimately by increasing exports to the USA (notably after the 30 per cent devaluation of 1949).

Within Europe the greatest cause for concern was Germany which, as Table 6 clearly demonstrates, had virtually disappeared as a trading partner in the immediate post-war years. Nothing which the war had done could erase the fact that Germany was indispensable for the long-term recovery of the Dutch economy. There were two ways in which this could happen – either a larger part of Germany, preferably without Germans, could be allowed to recover as part of a 'Greater Holland' or, if this were not possible, Germany could be allowed to recover under some form of international supervision. When, mercifully, the Allies stamped on the wilder annexationist dreams, Dutch policy goals could be expressed in the following way: the Netherlands would consider no form of international co-operation which would exclude its largest trading partner.

Table 7
Dutch annexation claims 1945-1948

Date of claim	Area (km²)	Inhabitants	Decision
September 1945	10,500	1,500,000	Rejected
May 1946	4,438	403,000	Rejected
	3,586	298,000	Accepted
November 1946	1,750	119,000	Accepted
July 1948	692	39,000	Accepted
September 1948	69	9,200	Granted by Allies

Source: R.T. Griffiths, *Economic Reconstruction Policy in the Netherlands and its International Consequences, May 1945-March 1951*, European University Institute Working Paper no. 76 (Florence, 1984).

The Dutch claims for German territory, as is shown in Table 7, gradually withered under the twin realizations that the Allies would not countenance any transfer of territory on the scale which the cabinet apparently envisaged, and that any territorial adjustments would indeed be accompanied by the sitting inhabitants, which would cause an assimilation problem of considerable magnitude.[41] But if the Dutch could not get their hands on German territory, they were unsympathetic to any plans for the large-scale dismantling of German productive capacity, though making sure at the same time that they received what they considered their rightful share of any spare capacity. The reason was that German markets, and therefore the recovery of purchasing power, were considered more important than the acquisition of plant and equipment which would be difficult to integrate into the economic structure. Within the *Conseil tripartite* they resolutely refused to become identified with French plans which would limit the degree of German industrial recovery.[42]

Whilst grand designs for the future of German were really outside the scope of Dutch policy influence, more alarming was the fact that so too was the availability of Germany as a trading partner. Before the war, Germany had been the major supplier of fuel, fertilizer, manufactured goods and semi-manufactures, and the largest market for Dutch surpluses of agricultural produce, particularly of fresh vegetables. In addition the earnings from transport services had been a vital element in covering the trading deficits not only with Germany but also with the rest of the world.[43] Early in 1946 it became apparent that not only would the Netherlands not be able to use the Mark balances they had accumulated during the war for trading and commercial purposes, but that the Americans and British were going to insist on the settlement of any deficits in dollars. It was equally clear that German imports would be cut to the bone, which would reduce the chances of closing any deficits with traditional agricultural exports. Finally, it seemed likely that the Allies would try to minimize the foreign exchange costs of shipping by deflecting trade from Rotterdam to North German ports.[44] As the head of the Dutch negotiating team put it, 'We are confronted with practically a Chinese Wall on our eastern frontier'.[45] After an abortive attempt to get the Americans to float the German economy on a rotating credit of $160 million paid into a Dutch-fronted trading trust,[46] attention turned to trying to breach the Chinese Wall. What the government wanted was an agreement from the Joint Import-Export Agency (JIEA), the body liaising with the British and American zones, to buy fixed quotas of goods and services from the Netherlands. What they had to be content with for 1947 was a far from satisfactory payments agreement. This separated mutual trade into 'essentials' and 'non-essentials'. All payments for 'essentials' would be transacted in dollars, all 'non-essentials' would be paid for in credits which could only be used for non-essential purchases. The problem for the Dutch was that virtually everything they might conceivably want was on the 'essentials' list, whilst most of their traditional exports, and their potential surpluses on shipping and transit services, were treated as non-essentials.[47] In 1948 the Dutch managed to extract a somewhat better agreement, on paper at least, whereby the JIEA 'committed' itself to purchasing and supplying goods at a far higher level than in 1947/48, promising a reduction in the Dutch deficit. The distinction between 'essentials' and 'non-essentials', however, still remained.[48] In practice the results were disappointing: import licences were often subject to long delays or, inexplicably, were refused altogether, and the transit services, instead of being a surplus, actually ended up in deficit.[49]

It was thus with no great optimism that the new negotiations were reopened for a trade agreement in August/September 1949, but the Dutch had not reckoned with the change-over in Allied control over Germany. Midway through the negotiations, the JIEA representatives took their German counterparts into a separate room and they emerged with a proposal which exceeded the wildest Dutch expectations. 'With

162

one stroke all the obstacles which until the most recent past had continuously aroused our concern and vexation have been removed', wrote the jubilant delegation leader, pointing out that the Dutch retained complete freedom over their own import controls and had only to concede that they would restrict certain exports.[50] 'For this new agreement with the Western zones we have chiefly to thank the JIEA which, in the process of dying, had still accomplished this one good deed ... it was not to be expected that we would have achieved such a generous agreement had we to deal with the Germans alone'.[51] He had every reason to be pleased. As Table 6 shows, the share of Dutch exports going to Germany doubled in 1949 compared with 1948 and doubled again the following year. In 1950 the Netherlands accounted for 11 per cent of all German imports, higher than in any other year in the 1950s, and this explains virtually the entire surge in the import penetration observable in Table 5. It was not to last. In the course of 1950 the German balance of payments swung into deficit and the Germans reimposed quantitative import controls. At the same time they began to restructure the mechanisms of agricultural protection so as to exempt them from international trade liberalization measures within the OEEC. But the Dutch had glimpsed the promised land – it was a vision they were not to forget.

The problem of trading with Germany provides at least part of the explanation for the Dutch commitment, albeit often reserved, towards Benelux – though it is not intended here to recover in detail the excellent secondary literature on the subject.[52] Highly industrialized Belgium could be expected to fill some of the vacuum for fuel and raw materials left by the virtual disappearance of Germany as a trading partner, but whereas the Dutch had been able to pay for these imports from Germany by agricultural exports and by service earnings, Belgium had no inclination to buy Dutch food surpluses to the same degree, and had no need for their shipping services. The result was that the payments deficits, which were envisaged as inherent in the immediate reconstruction period, assumed a structural dimension throughout the early post-war period. Indeed, the Dutch-Belgian payments deficit was the largest in all of western Europe right up to 1951,[53] and so special monetary arrangements became inextricably intertwined with trade considerations throughout the various early stages of Benelux's creation. The Dutch, in fact, showed precious little inclination to implement the customs union agreed in 1944 once a national government had been reinstalled, and were tipped into acceptance when, early in 1946, they had exhausted their credits under the 1943 monetary agreement. Against a backdrop of dwindling iron and steel imports,[54] the Prime Minister drew the less than enthusiastic conclusion, 'We cannot, without complications, avoid a customs union. The Belgians must be given the feeling that we are treating the matter in a *bona fide* way'.[55] In April 1946 the agreement was signed to implement the union within a year, although technical difficulties delayed the event until January 1948. In return the Dutch obtained a doubling of their credit margins under the monetary agreement. In May 1947 the Dutch further liberalized their imports from Belgium, in return for an agricultural protocol making them preferential suppliers of agricultural products (though Belgium had the right unilaterally to close the frontiers if its internal price levels were threatened) and a further increase in credits.

Given that there were already such unresolved problems and irresolute positions, why was it, at a ministerial meeting at Château d'Ardenne in June 1948, that a declaration was made that a full economic union would be achieved by January 1950? The answer can be summed up as follows. By early 1948, as far as the Dutch were concerned, Belgium had become part of the dollar area. It was also becoming clear that the only way Belgium seemed likely to avoid granting new credits (virtually giving away its exports) was if someone else were willing to do so. But whilst America had the dollars, it was unlikely to part with them unless something happened which would strengthen its political vision of increased regional co-operation in Europe. That something was what the Château d'Ardenne declaration was supposed to provide. As stated in cabinet, 'Up to now Benelux has been more a façade than a reality. Nonetheless it has delivered important results in the international field. However, it is no longer possible to use Benelux as an advertising object; it must now be given real content.'[56]

That was easier said than done! What the Belgians wanted, and what the Union implied, was a considerable liberalization of the Dutch economy both internally and externally which, if the reconstruction boom were not to be punctured, would entail a further worsening of the balance of payments. A less ambitious programme was needed, a pre-union period, coupled with a further line of credit.[57] The Prime Minister was even in favour of abandoning the scheme altogether were it not that 'agreements have been made and dates named'.[58] What was to save the day was the prospect that the differential devaluations of September 1949 would reduce the size of the deficit, and a Belgian agreement to waive gold-cover under certain conditions.

Whilst the Benelux relationships at least contributed to a mutual intensification of trade, the same could not be said of Dutch trade with the United Kingdom. Once again it was the export side which gave the most cause for grievance. In the first place it was felt that the British abused their monopsonistic powers on world markets when it came to settling the price for agricultural imports. Moreover, they had taken advantage of Dutch structural surpluses of market garden produce (because of the low level of German trade) to make purchases in these categories contingent upon increased meat and dairy exports at the same artificial prices.[59] A further concern was that although the UK market was increasing in importance, it was virtually entirely because of agriculture. Dutch export of industrial goods was hampered by the often unexplained refusal to grant import licences, and by the fact that the imposition of purchase tax made it difficult to compete with so-called 'utility goods'.[60] In 1949 there was a further complication that Dutch trade with the sterling area had swung into surplus, and it was felt that the Netherlands was accumulating non-convertible assets at a rate likely to exceed its spending capacity. The sudden opening of the German market was seen, therefore, as a way of escaping the stranglehold which the UK held over the Dutch economy and of solving the sterling problem.[61] With the same intensity as the Dutch had sought long-term agricultural purchasing contracts previously, they now sought to disentangle themselves from any such commitment,[62] and when, at this point, the British virtually invited the Dutch to join the sterling area with no qualms whatsoever.[63]

Germany also played a major role in influencing Dutch reaction to the various attempted embraces by the French in these years. It was not the only influence – others were a distrust of French political intentions and stability, and a fear of the implications of French protectionism. Moreover, whilst the French were offering the potential spoils of market integration, the simple fact was that Dutch import penetration of the French market remained firmly below the level of the interwar period right through to 1954. Thus when, early in 1946, in the middle of the conflict on implementing the Benelux customs union, the French suggested that the union be expanded to include themselves, the offer was politely but firmly refused. One of the arguments used was that the Dutch could not consider joining any such club until the position of Germany had been clarified – though they probably would have used any argument if they thought it would have helped. Again in 1947 and in early 1948 the offer of a customs union with France was rebuffed.[64] By late 1949, however, after the signing of the Dutch-German trade agreement, a distinct change in policy is discernible. In the middle of a series of negotiations to establish a set of monetary arrangements between Benelux, France and Italy, known as Fritalux, it was the Dutch turn to introduce demands for a customs union — but one which embraced West Germany. This proved to be too much for the French to swallow and the negotiations collapsed.[65] But when in May 1950, Robert Schuman proposed including Germany on an equal footing in a Franco-German coal and steel pool, participation in which was open to other European states, the Dutch were fully conscious of the political implications. Despite deep reservations on the institutional form, they agreed to participate in the negotiations.[66] That Dutch policy goals were not at that time focused upon the 'six' is demonstrated by the even deeper reluctance with which the Dutch agreed to take part in the discussions on the Pleven Plan, launched later in 1950, for the creation of a European Army.[67]

By the end of 1949 there were other developments afoot which promised a breakout from the strangling bilateralism which had gripped Dutch economic diplomacy for nearly two decades, and which appeared to offer the chance of normalcy once more in western Europe. When Marshall Aid was announced, the Americans had made clear that its disposition was to be a European matter. A direct consequence of this was the creation by sixteen European states of the Organization for European Economic Co-operation (OEEC), which was initially responsible for the distribution of aid among its members. This development had been welcomed by the Dutch because they felt that within such a multilateral body they had a better chance of representing their position than the grim results to date had suggested they could achieve bilaterally.[68] In late 1949, again under American pressure, the OEEC extended its interests towards achieving an intra-European multilateral payments settlement and towards 'trade liberalization'. The former was of obvious interest to the Dutch since it offered the prospect of resolving part of its balance of payments problems, including that with Belgium, within a European Payments Union funded by American dollars, although it contained the danger that, as the Dutch exhausted their credit quota, they would increasingly have to settle in hard currency or gold.[69] The 'trade liberalization' programme, ironically perhaps, was a greater source of concern: the Dutch, who already had balance of payments problems, would have to sacrifice (part of) one line of defence. The OEEC plan was directed solely at quantitative restrictions and thus left tariffs untouched. It left 'state trade', which covered predominantly agricultural trade, totally outside the scope of the operation, and the rules covering private trade were such as to allow the remaining quotas to be concentrated on agricultural discrimination. Finally, the measures were reversible.

The Dutch response was to launch a series of initiatives on a number of fronts. In June 1950 the Stikker Plan, aimed at sector integration, was presented in the OEEC but it was a scheme so riddled with inconsistencies that it was soon consigned to the scrap-heap. In December 1950 the government began a long and ultimately fruitless campaign to promote intra-European tariff reductions within GATT and finally, in 1951, it tried to link the Mansholt Plan for a freeing of agricultural markets to a European conference of agricultural ministers, also without success.[70] The frailty of the OEEC programme was demonstrated in 1950 when Germany was forced to reverse its trading concessions, with direct knock-on effect on the Netherlands.

It was against this background that the Dutch discovered their commitment to the two elements which dominated their policy for the next five years — a customs union which would produce irreversible intra-European trade concessions, and the forum of the 'six' for obtaining it, the trade-off being in the form of securing German inclusion in any arrangements against the possible upward drift of external protection. The purity of the 'free trade' logic had made way for a more practical expediency which satisfied the country's main economic priority. Within a smaller negotiating framework the Dutch attempted to gain the negotiating leverage which they all too patently lacked either in larger multilateral forums or in bilateral deals. As a tactic it was eventually to succeed, when the Beyen/Spaak memorandum was incorporated in the Messina resolution of June 1955 which eventually led to the Treaty of Rome. However, in realizing this goal the Netherlands had in fact sacrificed larger free-trading ambitions, since the matter of mutual trading concessions, by which remaining barriers outside the community could be reduced, had thereby ceased to be a question of exclusive national policy.

Notes

1. Centraal Bureau voor de Statistiek (CBS), *Macro-economische ontwikkelingen, 1921-1939 en 1969-1985. Een vergelijking op basis van herziene gegevens voor het interbellum* (The Hague, 1967).
2. J.J. Seegers, 'Produktie en concurrentievermogen van de Nederlandse industrie in het interbellum', *Economisch- en Sociaal-Historisch Jaarboek* (1987), 194.
3. CBS, *Macro-economische ontwikkelingen 1921-1939*, pp.55-6, 63-4.
4. It is impossible to give the data for the real value of service exports or income transfers from abroad since the CBS has not published those data, nor the price deflator which would allow them to be calculated.
5. This is, of course, partly a statistical illusion. If trading links with one important partner implode, the relative importance of all the others automatically increases.
6. CBS, *Tachtig jaren statistiek in tijdreeksen, 1899-1979* (The Hague, 1979), p.114.
7. J.L. van Zanden, 'Nederland in het interbellum', *Economisch-Statistische Berichten*, 3644 (1988), 172-8, 186.
8. In addition to the countries in Table 1 this includes the USA, Denmark, Sweden, India, Argentina, Italy, Norway, Switzerland and Canada. Spain was omitted because of difficulties involved in its trade statistics after the Civil War. Together these countries absorbed 87.6 per cent of Dutch exports in 1929.
9. See CBS, *Macro-economische ontwikkelingen*, and Van Zanden, 'Nederland in het interbellum'.
10. J.L. van Zanden, *De dans om de Gouden Standaard* (Amsterdam, 1988).
11. R.T. Griffiths, *The Netherlands and the Gold Standard 1931-1936* (Amsterdam/Dordrecht, 1987).
12. League of Nations, *Quantitative Trade Controls* (Geneva, 1943).
13. League of Nations, *Commercial Policy in the Interwar Period* (Geneva, 1942).
14. P.A. Blaisse, *De Nederlandse handelspolitiek* (Utrecht/Brussels, 1948), pp.126-7.
15. Blaisse, *De Nederlandse handelspolitiek*, pp.212-16.
16. It was demonstrated even more resolutely by the recognition of the need to protect the domestic market, wherever possible, for domestic production. See, for example, A. van Schaik, *Crisis en protectie onder Colijn. Over economische doelmatigheid en maatschappelijke aanvaardbaarheid van de Nederlandse handelspolitiek in de jaren dertig* (Alblasserdam, 1986).
17. Algemene Rijksarchief (ARA), Ministerraad (MR), Kabinet 1933/35d, *Nota van de voorzitter over onze economische politiek*, 8.8.1933.
18. Blaisse, *De Nederlandse handelspolitiek*, pp.293-7.
19. *Ibid.*, pp.234-59.
20. F.A.G. Keesing, *De conjuncturele ontwikkeling van Nederland*, p.217.
21. Blaisse, *De Nederlandse handelspolitiek*, pp.293-7.
22. The national income figures for these calculations are derived from CBS, *Statistische en econometrische onderzoekingen*, VII, no. 3 (1953), 96; the merchandise export figures

from CBS, *Tachtig jaren statistiek*, pp.104-8; and the services and income transfer data from the *Nota inzake de deviezen positie*.

23. The national income and trade figures for these calculations are derived from CBS, *Tachtig jaren statistiek*, respectively, pp.144-6 and 112-18.
24. The year was chosen because it marked the general achievement of trade liberalization and *de jure* convertibility in Europe. The calculations are not that sensitive to changes in weights and we could equally have chosen any year between 1955 and 1959. The composition of countries has changed: Indonesia, Argentina, India and Canada have dropped out to be replaced by Austria, Australia, South Africa and Brazil. Those countries accounted for 79.4 per cent of Dutch exports in that year.
25. The fact is that the Dutch share in the new West German market, shorn of its eastern territories and eastward trading links, was probably 'naturally' higher than in the pre-war boundaries. This, however, serves if anything to flatter the comparison.
26. This picture is confirmed by the forward projection made in Table 1.
27. *Tweede nota inzake de deviezenpositie*, March 1948. *Bijlagen Handelingen Tweede Kamer* (1947/48), 772, p.11.
28. Ministerie van Economische Zaken (MEZ), Directoraat-Generaal van Handel en Nijverheid (DGH & N), 2164/1; Centraal Planbureau (CPB), *Centraal Economisch Plan. Eerste Nota (Globaal Plan)*, September 1946.
29. Ministerie van Algemene Zaken (MAZ), Kabinet 351.88(7): 33, *Nota inzake dollarinkoopprogramma 1947*, 16.11.1946.
30. Algemeen Rijksarchief (ARA), Ministerraad (MR), 570, Minutes of the economic committee of cabinet, 29.11.1946.
31. *Ibid.*, 19.2.1947.
32. MAZ, Kabinet, 332.45, *Eindverslag Deviezenprioriteitencommissie*, 17.5.1947, and *Prioriteitencommissie: subcommissie voor de goederensector, Nota 1*, 18.4.1947.
33. ARA, MR, 570, Minutes of the economic committee of cabinet, 19.1.1947, 23.5.1947, 22.5.1947, 4.6.1947, 11.6.1947.
34. *Ibid.*, 22.10.1947, 29.10.1947.
35. *Ibid.*, 26.11.1947.
36. *Ibid.*, 10.12.1947.
37. ARA, MR, 571, Minutes of the economic committee of cabinet, 24.3.1948.
38. *Ibid.*, 30.4.1948.
39. A.S. Milward, *The Reconstruction of Western Europe, 1945-1951* (London, 1984), pp.104-7.
40. P. van der Eng, *De Marshall hulp. Een perspectief voor Nederland, 1947-1953* (Houten, 1987), p.168.
41. See, for example, the discussion in ARA, MR, 388, 9.9.1946, 16.9.1946.
42. R.T. Griffiths and F.M.B. Lynch, 'L'échec de la "Petite Europe"', le Conseil tripartite 1944-1948', in *Guerres mondiales et conflits contemporains*, no. 252 (1988).
43. MAZ, Kabinet, 351.88 (43): 33, *Memorandum betreffende de economische verhouding tussen Nederland en Duitsland*, 5.2.1946. This was already well known, but it obviously did no harm to remind oneself now and then.
44. *Ibid.*, *Het economische verkeer met Duitsland*, 28.3.1946.
45. *Ibid.*, Letter Teppema to Huijsmans, 22.8.1946.
46. *Ibid.*, *The Netherlands' General Attitude to Trade with Germany*, 13.9.1946; *Proposal for a Central Body for Trade with Germany*, 16.9.1946; *Onderhandelingen met OMGUS*, 23.9.1946.
47. *Ibid.*, *Verslag der besprekingen met de Britsch-Amerikaansche zones van Duitsland*, 1.2.1947; *Verslag van een reis naar Berlijn ter bespreking van de Nederlandsch-Duitsche economische betrekkingen van 25 Februari-1 Maart 1947*, 10.3.1947.
48. *Ibid.*, note Teppema to Van den Brink, 5.8.1948.
49. *Ibid.*, *Besprekingen over het handels- en betalingsverkeer met de Westelijke zones van Duitsland*, 5.4.1949.
50. *Ibid.*, *Handels- en betalingsverkeer met West Duitsland*, 7.9.1949.
51. *Ibid.*, *Nadere besprekingen in Frankfurt inzake de uitvoering van het nieuwe handelsaccoord met West-Duitsland van 22 t/m 24 Sept. 1949*, 26.9.1949.
52. See, for example, J.E. Meade, *Negotiations for Benelux: An Annotated Chronicle, 1943-1956* (Princeton, 1957). See also A.J. Boekestein, 'The Formation of Dutch Benelux Policy', and T.E. Mommens, 'Agricultural Integration in Benelux', both in *The Netherlands and the Integration of Europe, 1945-1957* (ed. R.T. Griffiths, Amsterdam, 1990).
53. Milward, *The Reconstruction of Western Europe* (London, 1984), p.223.

54. ARA, MR, 570, Minutes of the economic committee of cabinet, 26.3.1946.
55. *Ibid.*, 21.1.1946.
56. ARA, MR, 571, Minutes of the economic committee of cabinet, 2.6.1948.
57. *Ibid.*, 25.8.1948.
58. *Ibid.*, 23.2.1949.
59. ARA, MR, 570, Minutes of the economic committee of cabinet, 12.2.1947, 26.2.1947.
60. MAZ, Kabinet, 351.88 (42): 33, *Handelsverkeer met het Verenigd Koninkrijk*, 21.10.1948.
61. *Ibid.*, *De komende financiële- en handelsbesprekingen met het Verenigd Koninkrijk*, 5.12.1949.
62. ARA, MR, 583, Documents of the economic committee of cabinet, 4.1.1950.
63. MAZ, Kabinet, 351.88 (42): 33, *Financiële besprekingen tussen het Ministerie van Financiën en UK Treasury van 9 en 10 december 1949*, 24.12.1949. ARA, MR, 571, Minutes of economic committee of cabinet, 27.12.1949.
64. Griffiths and Lynch, 'L'échec de la "Petite Europe"'.
65. R.T. Griffiths and F.M.B. Lynch, 'L'échec de la Petite Europe: Les négociations Fritalux/Finebel, 1949-1950', *Revue historique*, no. 274 (1985), 159-93.
66. A.E. Kersten, 'A Welcome Surprise, The Netherlands and the Schuman Plan Negotiations', in *Die Anfänge des Schuman-Planes 1950/51* (ed. K. Schwabe, Baden-Baden, 1982).
67. J. van der Harst, 'European Union and Atlantic Partnership: Political, Military and Economic Aspects of Dutch Defence, 1948-1954 and the Impact of the European Defence Community' (PhD thesis, European University Institute, Florence, 1988).
68. J. Schram, 'Nederland en het Marshallplan', in *Nederland in de wereld 1870-1950: opstellen over buitenlandse en koloniale politiek* (ed. P. Luykx and A. Manning, Nijmegen, 1988).
69. Milward, *Reconstruction*, pp.264, 277.
70. R.T. Griffiths, 'De eerste fase van de Westeuropese eenwording', in *Big is Beautiful? Schaalproblemen in de overheid en samenleving* (ed. T.P.W.M. van der Krogt, *et al.*, The Hague, 1987); and R.T. Griffiths, 'The Abortive Dutch Assault on European Tariffs 1950-1952', in *Modern Dutch Studies. Essays in Honour of Professor Peter King on the Occasion of his Retirement* (ed. M.J. Wintle, London, 1988).

Index

116, 117
- War of 1899-1902, 97, 98, 105, 116
Boers, 10, 97, 98, 111, 121
Bolshevism, 141
Boltho, A., 141
Boogman, J.C., 48
Book of Orders/Book of Dearth of 1586, 35
Books of Rates, 38
Booth, A., 135, 136
Borneo, 10, 107, 108, 110, 111, 114, 117, 118, 121
Bosse, P.P. van, 109
Boxer Rebellion of 1900-1, 115
Brabant, 14, 76, 112
Brazil, 9, 69, 70, 72, 102, 106, 167
Brebner, J.B., 136
Breskens, 15
Breslau, 67, 70
Brielle, 14, 21, 27
British Broadcasting Corporation, 137, 147
British Straits Settlements, 110
Broadberry, S.N., 140
Brooke, James, 107
Brouwershaven, 14
Brugmans, I.J., 81
Bruijn, J.R., 61
Brussels, 111
- Convention of 1903, 114
Burgundy, House of, 21

C
Cadiz, 55
Cairo, 95, 96
Calais, staple of, 31
Campo Major, 70
Campomanes, P.R., 74, 75, 87
Canada, 10, 97, 100, 106, 166, 167
- Confederation of 1867, 100, 101
Canary Islands, 53
Canning, George, 85
Cape, the, see also Africa, South and Boer republics, 95, 98
Caribbean Region, 52-4, 58, 120
Castile, 54
Castillon, Guy van, 15
Catalonia, 62, 63, 66
Catholics, Roman, 32, 37
Cecil, William, Lord Burghley, 28-30, 37, 38
Celebes, 112, 114, 122
Central Electricity Board, English, 137, 147
Central Planning Bureau, Dutch, 160
Centralization in the Netherlands, see also

Unitarism, 76-78
Ceram, 122
Chamber of Notables, Egyptian, 96
Chamber of Commerce, Amsterdam, 82, 88
Chamberlain, Joseph, 98, 104
Chamberlain, Neville, 133, 144
Channel, English, 36, 58, 59
Chapman, H., 142
Charles the Bold, Duke of Burgundy, 21
Charles II, King of England, 54, 57, 59
Charles V, German Emperor, 12, 21, 22, 25, 27, 33
Charles VI, German Emperor, 62
Charles III, King of Spain, 74, 87
Charles IV, King of Spain, 74
Charles XII, King of Sweden, 9, 69, 70, 72
Château d'Ardenne declaration of 1948, 163, 164
Checkland, S., 138
Child, Josiah, 8, 47, 52, 55, 56, 57, 61
China, 10, 99, 100, 102, 105, 108, 113, 115, 116, 118, 121
Chinese Wall, 162
Christall, K.A., 127
Civil War, English, 52, 59
Civil War, Spanish, 166
Clarendon, Edward Hyde, Earl of, 60
Clearing Institute, Dutch, 156
Clerical Parties, Dutch, 111, 113-5, 118
Cline, P., 135
Cloth Act of 1552, 34
Cockayne Project, 50
Colbert, Jean-Baptiste, 50
Colijn, H., 118, 155, 156, 166
Colonialism, 90-106, 107-124
Committee on Finance and Industry, 147
Commonwealth Preferences, 157
Compagnie van Assurantie, 60
Congo, 111
Congo river, 108
Conseil Tripartite, 162
Conservatives, 95, 108, 109, 112, 130, 131, 134
Constantinople, 100
Constitutions, Dutch, 76, 87
Cormantine, 58
Corn Law, Dutch, of 1835, 85
Cornwall, 66
Council of State, English, 53
Council for Trade, English, 53, 56
Council, Privy, English, 28-32, 34, 35, 37, 38
Courland, 69
Court, Pieter de la, 55, 61, 79

Court, Tudor, 29
Cremer, J.T., 112-5, 118, 122
Cromwell, Oliver, 60, 61
Cromwell, Thomas, 28, 29, 38
Cultivation System, Dutch, 108, 120
Cumbria, 35
Curaçao, 108, 110, 115, 120, 121
Customs Union of 1944, 163

D
Dalagoa line, 111
Danzig, 60, 66, 70
Davis, L.E., 103
Davis, Ralph, 52
Dayak, 123
Decentralization in the Netherlands, see
    also Frederalism, 76, 77
Defoe, Daniel, 59
Delfland, 16, 26
Delft, 13, 19, 26
Deli, 108-10, 115, 121
    - Company, Dutch, 108, 112, 118, 121
    - Planters Union, 118
    - Railway Company, 118
Denmark, 14, 52, 59, 123, 155, 166
Departmental Law of 1807, 77
Depression of the 1930s, 10, 125-151,
    152-168
Dilke, Charles, 104
Dillen, J.G. van, 43
Djambi, 113-5, 122
Djeddah, 116
Dordrecht, 12, 14-6, 19, 21, 23, 25, 26
Dover, 57
Downing, George, 54, 57, 60
Dreischor, 15
Drenthe, 76
Dresden, 67, 70
Dunkirk, 51, 60
Durgerdam, 25
Dutch-German Trade Agreement of 1949,
    165
Dutch-Japanese Commercial Treaty of
    1858, 108
Dutch-Spanish Peace of 1648, 59
Dyestuffs Act of 1920, 139

E
East India Company, Dutch, 59, 68, 69,
    75, 107
East India Company, English, 51, 65, 68,
    69, 94
East Indian Tariff Acts, 109, 110, 112
East Indies, see also India and Indonesia,
    10, 34, 50, 51, 56, 59, 63-5, 67, 69, 70,
    107-24, 153, 156, 159
Edelstein, Michael, 93
Edward VI, King of England, 28
Edward VII, King of England, 92, 93, 103
Egypt, 10, 94-7, 102, 104, 110, 111, 121
Eindhoven, 67, 70
Ekelund Jr., R.B., 39
Elgar, Edward, 141
Elizabeth I, Queen of England, 28-30, 35,
    37, 38
Elmina, 107-9
Emy, H.V., 135
Eng, P. van der, 161
Enlightenment, 9
Entente of 1904, 100
Estonia, 69, 70
Estremadura, 70
Etherington, N., 116
Ethical Policy, Dutch, 113, 114, 116, 118
Europe, 51, 53, 63-7, 90, 91, 94, 95, 99,
    107, 109, 111, 115-7, 119, 121, 129,
    141, 152, 153, 155, 157-9, 161, 163,
    165, 167, 168
European Army, 165
    - Community, 11, 141
    - Concert, 1813-1831, 85
    - Defence Community, 168
    - Integration, 152
    - Payments Union, 165
Executive Government in the Batavian
    Republic, 77

F
Federalism, 76
Fieldhouse, D.K., 90
Flanders, see also Southern Netherlands, 9,
    14, 34, 51, 52, 62, 63, 65, 67, 69, 70
Flores, 112, 122
France, 30, 34, 50, 51, 54, 55, 57-9, 63-8,
    70, 71, 76, 84-6, 89, 94, 97, 100,105,
    108, 112, 118, 129, 153, 157, 159, 162,
    164, 165
Franco-German Coal and Steel Pool, 165
Frankfurt, 167
Fransen van de Putte, I.D., 108-10, 121
Fraustadt, 67, 70
Free ship, free goods, 59
Free Standing Company, 104
French, D., 135
Friedman, M., 127
Friesland, Lord of, 24
Friesland, province of, 24, 25
Fritalux, 165

112, 118
Neue Plan of 1934, 153, 156
Neufville, Jan Isaäc de, 48
New England, 59, 64
New Guinea, 111, 114, 117, 118
New Holland, 111
New Netherland, 54, 59
New Zealand, 100, 101, 106
Newcastle, 36
Newfoundland, 64
Niedorp, 14, 18
Nieuw-Lekkerland, 16
Niger Company, Royal, 94
Nine Years' War, 62, 68, 70
Nisero incident, 110
Niskanen, W.A., 131
Noord-Holland Canal, 83
Norfolk, 32, 35, 38, 56
Norman, Lord, 139, 147
North Borneo Company, British, 110
North Sea, 58, 60
Norway, 60, 155, 166
Norwich, 55

O
O'Brien, P., 103
Obdam, 18
Oeconomische Tak/Economic Section, 74
Olson, M., 134
Ommelanden, 16
Opmeer, 18
Orange Free State, see also Africa, South
and Boer republics, 97
Orangists, Dutch, 75
Organization for European Economic
Co-operation, 163, 165
Osdorp, 21, 25
Oslo Convention, 155
Ottoman Empire, see Turkey
Ouchy Convention of 1932, 155, 157
Oude Tonge, 14
Outer Regions, East Indies, 114, 115, 118,
119, 122, 123

P
Pacific, 109
Packet Company, Royal, Dutch, 112, 117,
118, 122
Paris, 75, 95, 100
Parliament, British, 32, 51, 53, 85, 99,
132, 141
Parliament, Dutch, see States General
Patriots, Dutch, 9, 45, 49, 74, 87
Peacock, A.T., 127, 128
Peden, G.C., 135

Peking, 99, 100
Pellegrini, Carlos, 106
Persia, 105
Persian Gulf, 59
Pestel, F.W., 75
Peter the Great, Czar of Russia, 9, 69, 70,
72
Peters, B.G., 125
Petroleum Company, Royal Dutch, 114,
118, 119
Petty, William, 74
Philip the Good, Duke of Burgundy, 21
Pinto, Isaac de, 79
Pleven Plan of 1950, 165
Poland, 72
Ponko, V., 35
Poor Law of 1536, 28
Porto Franco, 74, 85, 87
Portugal, see also Iberian Peninsula, 51,
59, 62, 69-72, 110-2, 115, 117, 123
Protectionism, 79, 83-5, 88, 152-168
Prussia, 65, 85
Puglia, 53
Pulorun, 58
Pultava, 70
Puritans, 37

R
Radicals, English, 146
Rehnskjiold, Charles Gustavus, 70
Reid, A., 121
Restraining Orders of 1712, 70
Revolt, Dutch, 18
Rhine, 85
Rhodes, Cecil, 97, 98, 105
Ricardo, David, 40, 44, 80, 81, 84
Riga, 66, 69
Rijnland, 16, 24, 26
Rijsoord, 14
Robinson, Henry, 8, 52, 55-7
Robinson, R.E., 10, 90, 91, 93-5, 97, 98,
101, 102
Roe, Thomas, 51
Roëll, J., 116
Roëll, W.F., 84, 88
Roermond, 23
Rothschild, bankers, 98, 102, 105
Rotterdam, 16, 19, 22, 24-6, 108-12, 124,
162
Rotterdamse Lloyd, Steamship Company,
109
Rousseau, J.-J., 76
Royalists, English, 52
Russia, 34, 52, 55, 69, 72
Russo-Japanese War of 1904-5, 115